The Making of Martyrdom in Modern Twelver Shīʿism

The Making of Martyrdom in Modern Twelver Shīʿīsm

From Protestors and Revolutionaries to Shrine Defenders

Adel Hashemi

I.B.TAURIS
LONDON • NEW YORK • OXFORD • NEW DELHI • SYDNEY

I.B. TAURIS
Bloomsbury Publishing Plc
50 Bedford Square, London, WC1B 3DP, UK
1385 Broadway, New York, NY 10018, USA
29 Earlsfort Terrace, Dublin 2, Ireland

BLOOMSBURY, I.B. TAURIS and the I.B. Tauris logo are trademarks
of Bloomsbury Publishing Plc

First published in Great Britain 2022
This paperback edition published 2023

Series design by Adriana Brioso
Cover image: Night of General Qasem Soleimani's burial, in Tehran, Iran, June 2019.
(© Hamid Vakili/NurPhoto/Getty Images)

A catalogue record for this book is available from the British Library.

A catalog record for this book is available from the Library of Congress.

ISBN: HB: 978-0-7556-3395-1
PB: 978-0-7556-4715-6
ePDF: 978-0-7556-3396-8
eBook: 978-0-7556-3397-5

Typeset by RefineCatch Limited, Bungay, Suffolk

In loving memory of my father,
Mohammad Hossein Hashemi

Contents

List of Figures viii
Preface ix

Introduction 1

1 The Emergence of the Shīʿī Form of Martyrdom 15
2 Martyrdom Revival in Twelver Shīʿīsm 41
3 Revolution, War, and Martyrdom 73
4 Civic Martyrdom 89
5 Martyrdom Reimagined 97
6 Shrine Defenders: A New Beginning 113
7 From Karbalā to Damascus 129

Appendix: Martyrdom in Classical Islam 137
Notes 153
Bibliography 195
Index 209

Figures

3.1 War zones propaganda 80
6.1 Mohsen Hojaji being escorted moments before decapitation by ISIS fighters 117
6.2 The adaptation of Hojaji's capture painted by Hassan Rouholamin 118
6.3 Mourners attend the funeral procession of Hojaji in Tehran 119
6.4 A portrait of Qasem Soleimani on the main road to the airport in Beirut 120
6.5 Coffins of Qasem Soleimani and others killed by a U.S. drone strike surrounded by mourners during a funeral procession in Tehran 121
6.6 We are the nation of martyrdom 123
6.7 Artworks showing doctors during the Covid-19 pandemic like soldiers of the Iran-Iraq war 125
6.8 Celebration of Nowruz with Qasem Soleimani depicted as an element of the *Haft-Sīn* table 126

Preface

This is a study of martyrdom within the context of Islam. However, the focus of this work will be on martyrdom in Twelver Shīʿīsm. I will particularly discuss the understanding and practice of martyrdom in modern Iran, especially since the 1979 Islamic revolution. The foundation of this book comes from my Ph.D. research. So, its development goes back to when I started my dissertation research on the subject of martyrdom at McMaster University's Department of Religious Studies. A lot has changed in the politics of the Muslim world since I started this study. The most notable development has been the outbreak of the Syrian civil war that turned into a full-fledged sectarian conflict and significantly disrupted the social and political landscape of the Middle East. This book will address how the ongoing conflicts affected the understanding of martyrdom among the Shīʿītes in the region, with particular attention to Iran and the role of the Islamic Republic in channeling the zeal for martyrdom as it became directly involved in the proxy war in Syria.

Completing this work required support from various individuals, and I am deeply indebted to many people whose support, assistance, and encouragement brought this book to fruition. I would like to express the deepest appreciation to my Ph.D. director, Professor Liyakat Takim. He gave me much needed direction and focus throughout my research for this project. I would also like to acknowledge my appreciation to the rest of my dissertation readers and members of the Department of Religious Studies at McMaster University for their helpful and insightful comments and suggestions: Dr. Travis Kroeker, Dr. Dana Hollander, Dr. Celia E. Rothenberg, and Dr. Eileen Schuller. I am also grateful to Dr. Paul Middleton from the University of Chester and Dr. David Cook from Rice University, who took the time to read parts of the initial drafts of this research and gave me invaluable feedback.

Moreover, I owe a particular debt of gratitude to Professor James Piscatori for all the inspiration and encouragement he gave me during my graduate studies at the Australian National University. I feel this work would have turned out weaker and differently had I not been exposed to his expertise on political Islam. My brief experience of studying with him was one of the most precious things in my academic life.

I am grateful to Sophie Rudland, Senior Commissioning Editor, and Yasmin Garcha, Assistant Editor, at Bloomsbury. They have been particularly supportive and cooperative from the start. I am also very thankful to Ben Harris for copyediting the final version of the book with admirable editing precision and care.

Of course, completing this book would not have been possible without the support of many friends and family. Special thanks and gratitude to my mother, Fatemah Sabbaghian, whose love and good wishes have always been with me; forever, I will be grateful for her being my hero and a wonderful and loving mother. Moreover, I am grateful for having my wonderful siblings, Samira, Hamed, and Vahid, whose unconditional love and support have been my source of inspiration. I would also like to thank my cousin, Dr. Nader Hashemi, Director of the Center for Middle East Studies at Denver University, who has always been supportive both intellectually and financially. Finally, my most important supporter throughout my graduate studies and writing this book has been my wife and the love of my life, Naeimeh Jafari. Her patience, unlimited love and support, and her positive attitude in all these years that we have been together mean the world to me. She gave me the energy I needed to stay focused on this book over the years. She has been much more than I deserve, a thoughtful wife, a loving mother, a great friend, and a successful scientist. I have to finish by thanking God for giving us a lovely and kind daughter, Noora. In the past six years, Noora has been the constant inspiration and joy of my life.

Introduction

What is Martyrdom?

Death is not something one would desire under normal circumstances by any means. Yet, it can be seen as a way (probably the last resort) to escape from the harsh and unbearable realities of life. Those unbearable pressures, due to severe stress, anxiety, public scandal, poverty, illness, and so on, would lead a person struggling with them to end his or her life and all miseries by committing suicide. This inclination toward death comes out of despair and would be out of the question for anyone living a happy or bearable life. Choosing to die can provoke a heroic response when a compelling political, humanitarian, social, ethical, or national related cause becomes the motive for taking one's life, actively or passively. These noble motives provide a meaning to the act of ending one's life by virtue of making it relatable to a sympathetic audience; hence, we may call them virtuous suicides. These deaths occur to prove a point or to make a difference in the world of the living.

There remains a relatively new kind of death, called martyrdom, which evolved with the development of the Abrahamic traditions, the idea of the existence of one supreme God, and the concept of the afterlife. In other words, while acts of heroism in war (noble death), and courageously being killed for one's people, soil, and country had long been known and recognized among people of ancient times, attributing a celestial value for the violent death proved to be a new and important development in the history of Israelite religion just before the turn of the Common Era. Although in the idea of noble death among the Greco-Roman pagans we see traces of dying for gods in the form of the practice of *devotio*, as Jan Willem Van Henten observed, the fallen heroes actually did not expect anything in return from the gods other than the victory of their people through transferring the wrath of the gods to their enemy.[1] What martyrdom added to the topic was the otherworldly expectations arising from a virtuous suicide when the primary motive for taking one's life had to do with God, or more specifically, with Christ in the case of Christian martyrdom. So, it is fair to claim that the idea of martyrdom, as we understand it today, is a relatively new concept compared to the long history of religion on earth. It begins in a certain period roughly around the end of the Second Temple era.

The most common and simple definition of martyrdom could be "dying for God." The modern concept of martyrdom, or the journalistic way of understanding this issue, however, makes martyrdom synonymous with "the act of dying for a religious commitment."[2] In other words, martyrdom in today's popular understanding, particularly in the case of martyrdom in the Muslim world, has to do with the willingness to kill and the intention to be killed for a religious conviction. The expression of martyrdom in terms of religious commitments puts martyrdom in the same category as all other (virtuous) suicides, which does not help us understand this phenomenon accurately. As Paul Middleton has stated, unlike suicide in any of its forms, martyrdom, in its original sense, is not anything close to "unfortunate necessity" or "an act of self destruction," but rather, for martyrs, choosing death actually means "rushing towards life."[3] Therefore, martyrdom, in this sense, is almost completely different from the simple act of suicide.

Scholars of martyrdom have tried to define the concept of martyrdom with special attention to its Greek origin ("being a witness") so as to differentiate martyrdom from other forms of suicide. The definitions, however, vary based on scholars' views on the origin of the concept of martyrdom and whether martyrdom can be traced to the pre-Christian era as well. Jan Willem van Henten and Friedrich Avemarie, for example, argue for the existence of martyrdom before the Jewish and Christian terminologies of martyrdom appeared, and define it almost without direct reference to God and a particular religious tradition to expand the notion of martyrdom. For them, a martyr in an "extremely hostile situation prefers a violent death to compliance with a demand of the (usually pagan) authorities."[4] Arthur Droge and James Tabor also put together five criteria for any act to be counted as martyrdom. Firstly, there should be situations of persecution. Secondly, the necessity of martyrs' noble and heroic choice of death. Thirdly, martyrs' eagerness to die, even to the point of killing themselves. Fourthly, the act of martyrdom resulting in vicarious benefits. Finally, and the most important factor in their view, the expectation of after-death reward and vindication.[5]

Brad Gregory, in *Salvation at Stake*, comes with some prerequisites for any act to be considered significant religious martyrdom, emphasizing the need for survivors who believe in the virtue of the person who has been violently killed as a martyr. In other words, martyrdom is not an objective issue; it should be witnessed and believed by others. Gregory also argues that "the notion of martyrdom" needs to be cultivated in society. Moreover, there must be people willing to punish what they regard as heterodoxy by death, and, on the other hand, there "must be people willing to die for their religious convictions."[6] David Cook takes a similar stance and sees martyrdom as a result of a clash between two opposing belief systems. For him, this clash is "constructed in the minds of the martyr, the enemy, the audience and the writer of the historical-hagiographical narrative."[7]

Other scholars have tried to connect the origin and definition of martyrdom to either Judaism or Christianity. The argument for the role of the Jewish tradition in martyrdom is that, although martyrdom became widespread and relevant in the Christian world during the first couple of centuries through "persecution, suffering and death" of the early Christians, the roots of the concept go back to the Jewish proto-martyrs described in the books of Daniel and Maccabees.[8] In other words, scholars like William Frend have argued that Christian martyrdom was actually inspired by Jewish traditions a couple of centuries before the Common Era.[9] On the contrary, Glen Bowersock, in his *Martyrdom and Rome*, argues that Christian writings on martyrdom introduced the idea in Judaism as the stories of slain Jews were written after the accounts of (Droge & Tabor, 1992, p. 237) Christian martyrs.[10] Basically, Bowersock's thesis is that Christian martyrdom was something entirely new and had no antecedents. Daniel Boyarin takes the middle ground, arguing that one cannot make a case for whether martyrdom originated in Christianity or Judaism as the Christian and Jewish traditions in the first two centuries were not "two separate entities" to make us think of "one (and not the other-either-one) as the point of origin of a given practice."[11] He then proposes his definition and considers martyrdom "as a 'discourse,' as a practice of dying for God and of talking about it, a discourse that changes and develops over time and undergoes particularly interesting transformations among rabbinic Jews and other Jews, including Christians, between the second and the fourth centuries."[12]

Putting aside the Christian versus Jewish debate on the origin of martyrdom, some scholars root for the Greco-Roman tradition of the noble death, which made death "fashionable,"[13] as the basis for the development of martyrdom in Abrahamic religions.[14] Finally, Judith Perkins postulates a different view. She neither pays attention to the comparison of the martyrdom-like examples in different traditions nor seeks the roots of martyrdom in persecutions, sense of heroism (in noble death), or keeping the law (in the Jewish cases like the

Maccabees), but values the cultural and social significance of suffering, particularly among Christians, that created the phenomenon of martyrdom.[15]

To sum up, as Paul Middleton argues in *Radical Martyrdom and Cosmic Conflict in Early Christianity*, none of the positions mentioned above draw a perfect picture of the nature and origin of martyrdom.[16] There are many factors essential in the formation of the concept of martyrdom. Or, we might say that martyrdom is an umbrella term for a recurring concept in history with different forms and factors.

Martyrdom from Bible to the Qur'an

"Even if for the present I would avoid the punishment of mortals," Eleazar confidently declares, "yet whether I live or die I shall not escape the hands of the Almighty. Therefore, by bravely giving up my life now, I will show myself worthy of my old age; and leave to the young a noble example of how to die a good death willingly and nobly for the revered and holy laws."[17] A couple of centuries later, Rabbi Akiva also proudly makes this clear to his disciples just before his last breath: "Throughout my life I have been troubled about this verse, [*And thou shalt love the Lord with all thy soul* . . .] and with all thy soul which means: Even if he take thy life. For said I, 'When will it be in my power to fulfil it?' But now that the opportunity is mine, shall I not fulfil it?"[18] Also, just a few years later his contemporary, Polycarp, fearlessly faces burning in fire and replies to his executioner: "Eighty and six years have I served him [Christ], and he has done me no wrong. How then can I now blaspheme my King and my Saviour?"[19] Next, fast-forward to 680, and it is Ḥusayn who stands tall and raises his voice against a hostile army, saying, "Do you not see how right is not acted upon and falsehood is not prevented? Then let the believer desire the meeting with God, for I see death as being nothing other than happiness while life with the oppressors as the most undesirable."[20] Facing death to avoid the transgression of God's law, hoping for the otherworldly reward, loving God to the end, imitating "the Lord" in his suffering, or fulfilling God's command to glorify his name all acted in one way or another as motivations for these exemplary believers and their like-minded contemporaries to shed their blood. By doing so, they set the bar for generations to come in their respective traditions when the opportunity comes to give up their lives for God and to embrace martyrdom.

What did lead the early faithful adherents of Abrahamic traditions to come up with the idea of giving up life, their most precious possession, for a God-related cause? What in the second century found its own term (martyrdom) did not appear out of the blue; rather, it developed slowly, beginning several centuries earlier, and various factors influenced its formation along the way. Dealing with the history and formation of martyrdom is out of the scope of the current study. In a nutshell, the development of the concept of martyrdom had probably something to do with the troubled relationship between God and his people: sin and disobedience to his covenants, which (allegedly) resulted in the Hebrews' punishment by exile and death and destruction at the hands of foreign nations. The calamities which they faced through exile and later persecutions were understood by the Hebrews to be the direct result of their sin; hence, for the Israelites, submission to violent death and destruction seemed the necessary price they had to pay in order to achieve atonement and win back God's trust and support.

Besides the issue of sin, fear of God or avoiding his wrath and punishment was another rationale, elaborated in the late Jewish scriptures, for sticking to God's law even to the point of death. In that sense, the faithful would endure any worldly pain, torture, and punishment by the hands of pagans in order not to violate God's covenant and thereby face his incomparable and unbearable otherworldly punishment. There was also the issue of the promised God's eschatological rewards, which compelled believers like the pious Jews mentioned in the book of Maccabees to choose death over negating God's law in the face of tyrannical rule. Similarly, we see many references to the virtue of dying for God which revolved around the biblical commandment to love the Lord unconditionally. It seems that, for Jews and Christians in the early Common Era, the love of God provided a stronger motivation and rationale for martyrdom than the fear of God. In other words, martyrdom could be best described by the martyr's absolute devotion to God and his/her commitment to love him. Hence, Clement famously considered martyrdom "the perfect work of love."[21] Derived from the love of God's commandment, we can discern the impact of the Christian duality of God vs. Satan or the cosmic battle between the forces of good and evil on the formation of the concept of martyrdom. In other words, martyrs in this sense were soldiers of God, and eager to shed their blood as one step toward the promised kingdom of God. Christian martyrdom in its fully developed understanding, more than anything else, had to do with the combination of extreme love of God and the commitment to participate in the cosmic battle between good and bad and the eventual victory of God over Satan. So, by the time Islam emerged in the late seventh century, the concept of martyrdom had been already well understood among the Jews and Christians of the time, especially in terms of the love of God and its eschatological and cosmic ramifications. Islam then borrowed the terminology of martyrdom from those traditions.

In my understanding of the issue, a difference between the concept of martyrdom in Islam and that of Judaism and Christianity is that in Islam, unlike its predecessors, martyrdom emerged during the lifetime of its founder (Prophet Muhammad), and was first articulated by him as part of the process of state-building.[22] The crucifixion of Jesus was crucial in shaping Christian theology, therefore imitating Jesus through suffering persecution and being killed for the sake of Christ were viewed as great virtues and created the foundation of martyrdom in the Christian tradition. Within Islam, by contrast, it was Muhammad's life and his efforts to build a social order in this world, and not his death or his status after death, that shaped Muslim identity and behavior. Therefore, for Muslims, the very death of Muhammad itself has had minimal impact on Islamic theology in general, and the concept of martyrdom in particular. The Qur'an, in fact, separated the fate of the Prophet from the essence of Islam. In early Islam, martyrdom was developed because of Muhammad's efforts to establish a faith-based society; his direct collision with the Meccan pagans needed sacrifices by his followers on a regular basis. While in early Christianity, when martyrdom emerged among Christians, the focus was mostly on otherworldly salvation through faith in Christ, his crucifixion, the second coming, and the final cosmic battle between God and Satan, from the beginning Muslims fought to create a just social order in the form of an Islamic state. In other words, martyrdom in Islam started with an objective purpose to facilitate the establishment of God's law. The emphasis on jihad in the path of God was, in fact, a major theme in the Qur'an, with several verses addressing the issue; hence, jihad gained significant value in the eyes of early Muslims.[23] In this sense, for the early Muslims, martyrdom or dying while struggling in the path of God was the pinnacle of jihad and it had to be regulated. So, among the first criteria that were developed for the act of martyrdom to be considered a righteous act, the martyr's intention before death was seen as the essential factor in martyrdom. In other words, as David Cook and Asma Afsaruddin have touched on the issue, in Islam, personal intention was key to the moral worth of the act of martyrdom.[24]

The appendix provides an in-depth discussion of the Islamic definitions of martyrdom and its criteria. Here, I begin with a brief lexical study of martyrdom in the Qur'an. The Arabic word for martyrdom is *itishhādah* (استشهاد), and martyr is *shahīd* (شهيد), meaning "witness." The Qur'an did not coin the term used for the concept of martyrdom; it appears that Islam probably borrowed it from

Christianity. Arthur Jeffrey in *the Foreign Vocabulary of the Qur'an* observes that the word *shahīd* "itself is genuine Arabic, but its sense was influenced by the usage of the Christian communities of the time."[25] In the Qur'an, the words from the root *sh-h-d* (ش ه د) and its variant forms appear around 160 times in various contexts. Of all those terms from the root *sh-h-d*, the word *shahīd*, which is at the center of our discussion, is generally understood according to its lexical meaning of "legal witness," or simply "witness."[26] In some verses, God calls himself *shahīd*, in the sense that he witnesses everything in the world and does not miss anything.[27] Yet, in a few cases, *shahīd* in its plural form (*shuhadā*) sits ambiguously beside terms like "the Prophets," "the truthful" (those who bear witness to the truth), and "the righteous."[28] According to the Qur'an, those groups all join together as recipients of God's mercy and blessings on the day of judgment. In one of the verses, the Qur'an actually defines *shuhadā* as "those who believe in God and his messengers."[29] The Prophet Muhammad himself is specifically mentioned in the Qur'an as a witness (*shahīd*) to his people, above all other witnesses of the community.[30] In a couple of verses, believers are quoted praying to God to be included with those who bear witness (*shāhidīn*).[31] Finally, the Qur'an speaks about God's knowing and having power over both the "seen" (*shahādah*) and "unseen" (*ghayb*) worlds.[32]

It is safe to argue that the term *shahīd* and its siblings in the Qur'an have little in common with the meaning of martyr as one being killed for God's sake. Although the concept of martyrdom is present in the Qur'an, its terminology did not make it in the book. There are some verses that, without mentioning the term *shahīd*, speak about jihad in the path of God and promise to those who will be killed in this way the greatest rewards in the afterlife, including a guaranteed place in paradise and the forgiving of their sins. Perhaps this is why gradually it became a common belief among Muslims that there are actually exclusive rewards, as mentioned, for martyrs. Verses 9:111 and 3:169–70 are important and among the most cited verses by Muslim scholars when it comes to the otherworldly rewards of martyrs.[33] However, even in these verses, the emphasis on the martyr's rewards is to contrast them with the ill fate of unbelievers and hypocrites. In the case of the latter, for example, verse 3:168 talks about those who argue that the slain Muslims were losers who could have done better with their lives instead of dying on the battlefield.[34] In this context, the counterargument in verses 3:169–70 emphasizes and visualizes the very happy ending of martyrs, counting them as true winners. So, it is not really about the privilege of martyred believers over their non-martyred counterparts, rather, it seems to be more of a showcase to demonstrate the binary of believers versus non-believers and their eternal happiness vs. misery, respectively.

In fact, what can be implied from the Qur'an as a whole is that not only slain "martyrs," but also, as a general rule, those who sincerely believe in God, his messengers, and the day of judgment, and perform good deeds will end up in paradise with their sins being forgiven by then;[35] and this was, of course, a well-established fact among Muslims from the beginning.[36] It can be said, though, that not everyone is at the same level, so those who dare to sacrifice their greatest possession, their lives, for God's sake must get the greatest rewards. While this might be reasonable and is found in the *ḥadīth* literature, the Qur'an did not distinguish between the rewards of martyrs and those of other believers. In verses 4:69–70, being an obedient believer is counted as equal to those chosen servants of God including *shuhadā*:

> Whoever obeys God and the Messenger will be among those he has blessed: the messengers, the truthful, those who bear witness to the truth [*shuhadā*], and the righteous—what excellent companions these are! That is God's favour. No one knows better than him.

Most exegetes interpret *shuhadā* in the verse as "martyrs,"[37] though some stick to its literal meaning and read *shuhadā* primarily as bearing witnesses to truth (God) and people's deeds.[38] Reading *shuhadā* in this verse (and other similar verses) as "martyrs" even reveals that martyrdom and being killed in the path of God does not provide membership to an exclusive club of elites. Martyrs share this position with other sincere believers who simply happen to miss martyrdom despite otherwise being at the same level of faith of, or even above, those who actually die violently as martyrs. The Qur'an, in fact, uses this indiscriminate approach in praising all true believers regardless of their fate in this world: "There are men among the believers who honoured their pledge to God: some of them have fulfilled it by death, and some are still waiting. They have not changed in the least" (33:23). However, a kind of counterargument would say that the category of martyrs (if we interpret *shuhadā* as referring to martyrs) is exemplified and praised in the Qur'an, and this in effect is a privilege for them that others have to wish to be honored by accompanying the martyrs in heaven.

Speaking about exclusive rewards reserved for martyrs is more in tune with post-Qur'anic traditions than with the explicit text of the Qur'an itself. As discussed, no such privilege exists in the Qur'an. Perhaps this was due to the fact that during the lifetime of the Prophet, inspired by his presence and charisma, Muslims had more zeal and willingness to die for the sake of the newly emerged monotheistic religion. Hence, there was no serious need for the Qur'an to overemphasize the merit of martyrdom in the form of exclusive and extraordinary otherworldly rewards for the martyrs. However, this is not to say that everyone willingly rushed to jihad and martyrdom under the Prophet's rule; judging by the Qur'an itself, despite his charisma, even Muhammad himself on some occasions had a hard time convincing his followers to take up arms and fight for Islam without reservation and fear of destruction. We know this from a couple of verses where the Qur'an seems frustrated with some Muslims' reluctance toward jihad in the path of God.[39]

The full-blown concept of martyrdom in Islam as we understand it today was theorized after the Prophet in *ḥadīth* and theological works. I speculate that traditions that highlight the unmatched merits of martyrdom came to light after the Prophet due to an urgent need to encourage the rather reluctant Muslims tired of military campaigns to take serious risks and willingly give up their lives in cases of necessity (particularly due to the constant threat of the Byzantine Empire since the start of the conquests in the early seventh century).[40]

The Qur'an's lack of emphasis on martyrdom is clear in the absence of explicit historical reference to past martyrs. Interestingly enough, other than the general verses that praise those slain in the path of God, there is no account of martyrdom in the Qur'an. Many biblical figures and martyrs, such as John the Baptist,[41] are mentioned by the Qur'an, but in most cases the focus is on the story of their lives, actions, and missions, and not on their martyrdom. Above all, Jesus in the Qur'an is not crucified, a position that challenges the entire martyrdom paradigm in Christianity.[42] There are a few exceptions, such as the Pharaoh's sorcerers; yet in their case, the Qur'an does not clarify whether the Pharaoh actually kills them for their belief in Moses or whether somehow they manage to escape death.[43] So, what matters most in the Qur'an is the story of their conversion and faith and not their eventual fate. Another Qur'anic story with the theme of martyrdom is again related to Moses, where a closeted believer among the Pharaoh's family reveals his belief in God and asks the Pharaoh to spare Moses's life.[44] Again, the believer's fate is not clear as it has nothing to do with the moral of the story. On one occasion, however, we see the Qur'an's partial focus on a death narrative in the story of the unknown Companions of the Pit (*Aṣḥāb al-ukhdūd*), in which a group of believers are burned to death in a huge fire.[45] The narration, however, is so mysterious and ambiguous that exegetes cannot agree on whether the Companions of the Pit are the victims or the killers (the most likely scenario).[46]

Moreover, the Qur'an does not even explicitly celebrate the martyrdom of high-profile early Muslim martyrs, most prominently among them Ḥamzah, the Prophet's younger uncle, who was killed at the battle of Uḥud in 625.[47] This was despite the fact that he was seen as the champion of Islam and crucial in the early success and development of the religion, and his martyrdom was a severe blow to the young Muslim community of Medina;[48] hence, the Prophet posthumously called him *sayyid al-shuhadā* ("the lord of the martyrs"),[49] a title which later was used for Ḥusayn, the third Shīʿī Imām.[50]

Previous Studies on Martyrdom in Islam

The concept of martyrdom has often been examined in the form of case studies, and in Twelver Shīʿīsm it is the martyrdom of Ḥusayn, the third Imam, that dominates the discussion of martyrdom. Most of the studies on martyrdom in Shīʿīsm discuss the redemptive effects of Ḥusayn's martyrdom and its social and political consequences.[51] Other works were conducted in an anthropological and specifically ethnographic context focusing on symbols and rituals related to commemorating Ḥusayn and the other Imams' martyrdom.[52] There are also general works that broadly compare and contrast the classical and modern understanding of martyrdom in Islam by looking at both Sunni and Shīʿī traditions.[53] Yet, several other works mostly focus on jihad and martyrdom in the modern period, particularly suicide bombings inspired by jihadist ideologies. They specifically deal with political and/or legal issues related to jihad and suicide bombing, particularly in the Sunni world.[54] There are also some encyclopedia entries on martyrdom, which provide a good overview of the meaning of martyrdom in the Qur'an and *ḥadīth* literature.[55]

Of all the works mentioned above, David Cook's book, *Martyrdom in Islam*, is the most comprehensive study of martyrdom in general which covers materials from Sunni, Sufi, and Shīʿīte Islam with a very short introductory comparative review of the phenomenon of martyrdom in the world religions. His argument, with which I agree, is that martyrdom in the formative period of Islam was not an essential theme, rather it was primarily a by-product of jihad in the path of Allāh against the enemies of Islam. I will discuss this concept in more detail in Chapter 2. Cook then goes on to distinguish different categories of martyrdom and (general and specific) rewards associated with it as delineated in the post-Qur'anic *ḥadīth* literature; these include active martyrdom on the battlefield as well as different sorts of passive or non-violent martyrdoms, or even the case of martyrs of love (a sincere lover who dies while chasing their love). Cook, moreover, speaks about sectarian martyrdom and how Shīʿīsm developed its own understanding of martyrdom around the idea of persecution at the hands of dominant Sunnis, particularly in the first three centuries, quite similar to early

Christian martyrdom. He wraps up his discussion by turning to martyrdom in the contemporary context in which he pays attention to new jihadist ideologies that emerged in the twentieth century and their use of martyrdom for their purpose, particularly in the form of suicide attacks.

Meir Hatina's book, *Martyrdom in Modern Islam*, can be seen as a sequel and an updated version of Cook's *Martyrdom in Islam*. Hatina also begins his book with a short comparative study of martyrdom in the three Abrahamic religions before turning to contemporary Islam. His discussion of martyrdom in the modern period as a result of the rise of political Islam benefited from his careful and meticulous analysis of the classic martyrdom literature. This was similar to what Cook did in his book. Hatina's main argument is that martyrdom cannot be summarized in the mere act of sacrifice for a religiously motivated cause; rather, it is a discursive phenomenon coming from a mixture of cultural, political, and historical narratives. In his words, "the martyr has no existence without memorialization, commemoration, and narration."[56] In his last two chapters, as is common in the studies of martyrdom in the contemporary period, Hatina deals with martyrdom in the form of suicide attacks by providing a comprehensive literature review of the subject among Muslim scholars. Hatina also observes the importance of Ayatollah Khomeini's pan-Islamism and his emphasis on sacrifice for Islam as a driving force behind the rise of suicide attacks by the Shīʿītes in Lebanon in early 1980s; a practice which eventually "penetrated the Sunni discourse," and made active martyrdom an essential part of Sunni extremists, such as al-Qaeda and Hamas in Palestine.[57]

Finally, since many studies on martyrdom are connected to the issue of jihad, I finish this brief literature review with Asma Afsaruddin's excellent work, *Striving in the Path of God*, which, like Cook and Hatina's books, as well as this book, tends to provide a holistic history of ideas related to jihad and martyrdom (though mostly the former). Her approach is to juxtapose the two ends of the concept of jihad, which she summarizes in two key words: *qitāl* ("fighting"), associated with military jihad and martyrdom, and *ṣabr* ("patience") which reflects the idea of non-violent jihad. Her main argument is that the growth of the militant aspect of jihad and martyrdom is a product of later developments in Islam.

Thesis and Plan

The central thesis of this study is that martyrdom in Shīʿīsm has been developed to differentiate itself from the classic understanding of martyrdom. As a minority sect for most of its formative history, Shīʿīsm embraced and internalized martyrdom and redefined it with added theological significance inherited from the paradigm-shifting martyrdom of Imam Ḥusayn in 680. Ḥusayn's martyrdom became the blood running through the veins of all other Shīʿī movements and revolts until today. As the martyrs of Karbalā went down like a moth around a candle to sacrifice themselves before Ḥusayn, martyrdom in Twelver Shīʿīsm evolved to be seen as dying for the sake of the Imams. This came from the tenet of Twelver Shīʿīsm that holds the Prophet and the Imams as the gates of God and the only means to achieve salvation. However, a paradoxical dilemma of Twelver Shīʿīsm was that it grew out of the blood of its martyred saints but, since the tragedy of Karbalā and in particular after the period of the historical Imams at the beginning of the tenth century, adopted a doctrinally quietist appearance. This awkward situation ultimately was destined for change in the modern period in favor of political activism and the revival of martyrdom seeking to champion the cause of the Imams. As the Islamic revolution of 1979 gave birth to an increasingly powerful Twelver Shīʿī government, martyrdom was glorified unprecedentedly and tied to the state's domestic and regional hegemonic aspirations as a stride toward global Shīʿī dominance and the long-awaited messianic ideals. This was best demonstrated during the recent Syrian crisis and the Iran-led coalition of Shīʿī fighters to defeat the rise of Salafī jihadis in the region.

This book consists of seven chapters and an appendix in addition to this introduction. Chapter 1 discusses the formation of sectarian martyrdom during the formative stage of Shīʿīsm. It goes on to review historical events, most importantly the martyrdom of Ḥusayn and later Shīʿī-branded revolts in response to the tragedy of Karbalā. The chapter ends with a short discussion of martyrdom according to Twelver Shīʿī traditions. Chapter 2 tracks the development and revival of ideas and practices of martyrdom among Sunni Islamists, particularly since the abolition of the Caliphate in 1924. The chapter also discusses the parting point between the discourses of martyrdom in modern Sunnism and modern Twelver Shīʿīsm. The chapter ends with examining the rise of political activism and martyrdom-seeking in Iran prior to the 1979 Islamic revolution.

Chapter 3 continues the discussion of the development and revival of martyrdom in contemporary Twelver Shīʿīsm by evaluating the impact of the Islamic revolution and the eight-year war between Iran and Iraq from 1980 to 1988 on the revived attention to the concept of martyrdom by the leaders of the Islamic Republic. Chapter 4 discusses the concept of civic martyrdom in Iran following the war and the formative stage of the Islamic Republic. It examines the various forms of state-sanctioned martyrdom and shows the depth of martyrdom-seeking culture beyond war zones. It ends with a quick discussion of the appropriation of the concept of martyrdom by opposition movements.

Chapters 5 and 6 track the most recent developments in the concept of martyrdom in Twelver Shīʿīsm. They discuss how the sectarian tensions in the past two decades produced a new zeal for martyrdom-seeking among the Shīʿa. The chapters focus on the phenomenon of shrine defenders that emerged during the Syrian civil war and was popularized particularly with the rise and fall of the Islamic State (ISIS) in Iraq and Syria. Chapter 7 tries to make sense of the development of martyrdom in Twelver Shīʿīsm by connecting the current state to the martyrdom of Ḥusayn and the long-overdue messianic hopes of the return of al_Mahdi, the foretold redeemer of humanity.

Finally, the appendix surveys the classical understanding of martyrdom according to Sunni *ḥadīth* literature and Qur'anic exegesis (*tafsīr*). It serves as a reference for the classic definitions, criteria, and rewards of martyrdom that, in the most part, are shared with the Shīʿī tradition.

1

The Emergence of the Shīʿī Form of Martyrdom

Martyrs of the Community: Sectarian Factor

Historically speaking, in Islam, martyrdom in the form of violent death for one's belief in God (and his Prophet) at the hands of unbelievers (as it was the case in early Christianity) was limited to a relatively short period before the migration of Muslims from Mecca to Medina in 622. During that time, those who had accepted Muhammad as the Prophet were persecuted by the pagans of Mecca. Most of the poor and unprotected Muslims were targeted by the Meccans. They were usually tortured to the point of death unless they renounced their faith. However, we can name just a handful of Muslim martyrs who were killed because of their faith in the Prophet.[1] Perhaps the most famous Muslim tortured in that period was Bilāl, one of the Prophet's most trusted and loyal companions. Bilāl was a slave of a Meccan merchant, and after conversion to Islam, he was severely tortured by his master, Abū Jahl. When he was on the verge of martyrdom, Abū Bakr, probably by the order of Muhammad, negotiated with Bilāl's master and finally freed him.[2] Although Bilāl was not martyred, he has been remembered as a paradigmatic martyr-like hero in early Islam.

Not all fellow Muslims who were tortured were as fortunate as Bilāl, as Sumayyah and her husband Yāsir (two elderly and lower-class followers of Muhammad) did not survive the harsh treatment of the Meccan pagans; they have been regarded as the first martyrs in Islam.[3] However, at the center of attention was their young son, ʿAmmār, not due to martyrdom but because he, like Bilāl, escaped martyrdom. ʿAmmār was among the first converts and remained a very loyal friend and companion of the Prophet; yet he recanted his faith to survive torture whereas his parents did not. It is reported that Muhammad received ʿAmmār warmly after the incident and endorsed his tactical and non-genuine betrayal.[4] Reportedly, a verse of the Qur'an (16:106)[5] was revealed regarding that incident to vindicate ʿAmmār.[6] The verse also cleared the way for adopting the practice of *taqīya* (cautionary dissimulation of religious belief and practice in the face of persecution), especially by the Shīʿa as a minority sect. Nevertheless, ʿAmmār himself was martyred on the battlefield years later in his old age in 657 as he fought for ʿAlī ibn Abī Ṭālib, the first Shīʿa Imām.[7] Al-Balādhurī states that at the time of his martyrdom, Muslims knew a *ḥadīth* from the Prophet stating that: "ʿAmmār is always with the truth and he would be killed by a group of rebels."[8] ʿAlī also allegedly paid tribute to ʿAmmār, acknowledging that no one had the slightest doubt that ʿAmmār was destined to heaven and his murderer would go to hell.[9] Hence, when he was martyred in the battle of Ṣiffīn (fought between ʿAlī, the then-Caliph, and Muʿāwīyah ibn Abī Sufyān, the governor of Syria and future Umayyad Caliph), the followers of ʿAlī used the incident as proof of the righteousness of their leader, on the one hand, and of the hypocrisy of Muʿāwīyah and his followers, on the other. In response, Muʿāwīyah claimed that the real killer of ʿAmmār was the one who brought him to the battle in the first place (that is, ʿAlī).[10]

In Shīʿī sectarian literature, other than the *Ghadīr* tradition in which Muhammad allegedly appointed ʿAlī as his successor and pointed to his *wilāyah* over all Muslims, we see Muhammad's individual recommendations to his close companions regarding ʿAlī. According to a tradition, Muhammad revealed to ʿAmmār the turbulent future of Islam after his death and demanded him to follow ʿAlī and fight on his side; he then told ʿAmmār, "obeying ʿAlī is like obeying me (Muhammad), and obeying me is like obeying Allāh."[11] It was in the light of this tradition that the Shīʿa interpreted the martyrdom of ʿAmmār. In retrospect, what made the martyrdom of ʿAmmār so special for the later Shīʿa was that it served in a way to defend the Caliphate/Imamate of ʿAlī. ʿAmmār was a sage for the community, and a towering figure in early Shīʿīsm; hence, both in his forced betrayal as a young follower of the Prophet and in his controversial martyrdom as a respected disciple of ʿAlī, ʿAmmār was influential in how the later Shīʿa approached and formulated martyrdom as the last resort for the defense of faith and a tribute to the truth that (for them) lies on the side of the proper authority of the time (the Prophet and the Imams). It is important here to note again that this is a retrospective reading of history as, at the time, until the middle of the second Islamic century, there was no completely distinguishable Shīʿa identity with its own specific coherent theology. However, we can argue that history makes faith, in the sense that every aspect of an established belief system can be traced back in recorded history and the collective knowledge and traditions of the people adhering to the faith. Hence, the martyrdom of ʿAmmār and other early followers of the Prophet's family should have had profound effects on shaping the concept of martyrdom in Shīʿīsm as we know it today.

In the early period of Muhammad's tenure in Mecca, martyrdom, or being killed for one's faith, was not something that Muslims were seeking, though it was honorable for those who could not escape it. The blood of Muslims was needed to flow through their veins rather than on the ground when the Muslim community was small and vulnerable. Hence, the Prophet asked those Muslims in danger to secretly migrate to the Aksumite Empire of Ethiopia to escape persecution and possible martyrdom; ʿAmmār was one of them.[12] The situation, however, changed dramatically in Medina where the Prophet received the much-needed allegiance of the city's two major tribes, the Aws and Khazraj. He established a local Muslim state and engaged in a series of battles with the Meccan pagans until their eventual victory over Mecca and subsequently the rest of Arabia. There we see an unprecedented emphasis on martyrdom and fighting martyrs, though apparently the martyrdom terminology (*shahīd* being "martyr") had not been popularized then. So, the Qur'anic jihad verses[13] were revealed highlighting rewards for those slain in the path of God to encourage Muslims to accompany Muhammad by taking part in the battles against the enemies of Islam without the fear of their possible death in the process. Therefore, it was Ḥamzah, the chief commander of the young Muslim community (and, of course, a member of the de facto sacred family of the Prophet) who was named *sayyid al-shuhadā'* ("master of the martyrs") rather than the very first defenseless martyrs in the Meccan period such as Sumayyah and Yāsir.

In all probability, highlighting the act of (active military) martyrdom was not due to its inherent importance (as we do not see such attention to martyrdom in Mecca), but simply a means to motivate Muslims to defend their faith and the community at any cost once Muslims had established themselves as a new viable force in Arabia. Al-Ṭabarī, for example, reports that before Muhammad's first battle with Meccan pagans (the battle of Badr) began, he distanced himself from his troops and started praying to God and asked him to grant the Muslim army victory; he then continued: "[I]f this group be defeated no one will remain to worship you."[14] Ṭabarī narrates that Muhammad tried to encourage his followers to risk their lives for defending the young Muslim community: "[S]wear to God that the life of Muhammad is on his hand whoever is patient in the fight for God and does not turn his back and is killed on the battlefield God will grant him to paradise."[15] After hearing this from the Prophet, a Muslim named ʿAmīr ibn Hāmām who had some dates on his hand and was eating them replied: "Amazing! For going to heaven they just have to kill me!" Then he dropped the dates and picked his sword and went to fight and was eventually killed.[16] Muhammad needed brave followers like ibn Hāmām, who were not afraid of anything; hence, he reminded them what rewards would be waiting for Muslims once they died; nothing was special about martyrdom, except being a martyr was just one assured way to heaven, and a fallen Muslim was recognized as a war hero. We even see the tradition of asking forgiveness from God for martyrs. It is said that the Prophet asked God to forgive the martyrs of Uḥud, just as he did for other deceased Muslims.[17] Recognizing this sort of tradition probably means that the idea of immediate forgiveness of all sins of the martyr appeared later in Islamic history.

In early Islam, when it was rapidly developing as a new religion in the neighboring regions, participation in battles against pagans and non-Muslims was necessary for the survival of the Prophet's mission, so military martyrdom was theorized and praised by Muhammad. In the context of the constant state of conflict between Muslims and non-Muslims, the Qur'an and prophetic traditions were concerned with fighting and being killed for God (*qitāl fī sabīl-i allāh*). After the Prophet's death, during the Muslim conquests under the leadership of the soon-to-be-called Sunni Caliphs, Muslims continued to celebrate the martyrdom of their fellow believers slain on the battlefield by non-Muslims.[18] However, for the majority of Muslims in the central parts of the Islamic territories and particularly after the conquests, the opportunity to die a martyr in the original sense (of dying in a fight against unbelievers) greatly diminished. Therefore, the definition of martyrdom was expanded to focus mostly on other types of dying for God that had nothing to do with dying on the battlefield where Muslims and non-Muslims fought with each other.[19]

The martyrdom paradigm soon changed in early Islamic history through the lines of sectarian divisions, as each sect had its own revered martyrs and did not recognize the other party's martyrs. The phenomenon of sectarian martyrs comes from the fact that every group tends to proclaim that its belief system is authentic, while that of the rivals is considered an unacceptable deviation from the truth. In this light, polemic works of the Shīʿa consider the Shīʿītes as true Muslims, and even trace back the very beginning of Shīʿīsm to the time of the Prophet.[20] Apparently, the first scholar who claimed this was a tenth-century Isma'īlī Shīʿa, Abū-Ḥātam al-Rāzī: "Verily, the first title appeared in Islam during the lifetime of the Messenger of Allāh was Shīʿa and that was the title of four of the [Prophet's] disciples; they were Abū-Dhar, Salmān al-Fārsī, Miqdād ibn al-Aswad, and ʿAmmār ibn Yāsir."[21] Those early followers of ʿAlī, and other like-minded Shīʿa figures, such as Mālik al-Ashtar, Ḥujr ibn ʿAdī, and Mītham al-Tammār, shed their blood in support of ʿAlī in one way or another.[22] With their death, they inspired later generations of Shīʿas to continue their struggle in keeping alive what they believed was the proper, yet mostly forgotten path in Islam, that is sticking with the *wilāyah* of ʿAlī and his successors (the other Imams) and respecting the Prophet's family (*ahlul bayt*) as he mentioned on some occasions, such as the event of Ghadīr.[23]

The initial dilemma, however, with the very phenomenon of sectarian martyrdom was that, since non-Muslims normally caused martyrdom, if a Muslim were to be killed by another Muslim that would create an uneasy situation. The problem was where to put martyrdom in the equation when both sides of the conflict were followers of the Prophet. This was the case in the battle of Jamal in 656 and other early conflicts after Muhammad. This awkward situation was justified when Muslims were clearly divided into Shīʿa and Sunni roughly from the latter half of the first Islamic century, particularly after the tragedy of Karbalā that the followers of the Prophet's family found themselves at odds with the soon-to-be-called Sunni Caliphate system of beliefs. One of Ḥusayn's disciples at Karbalā, al-Zuhayr ibn al-Qayn, in his efforts to persuade the Kūfan army not to fight with the family of the Prophet, was among the first who pointed to the creation of two separate religious groups within Islam:

> O people of Kūfa! A warning for you of the punishment of God, a warning that a Muslim is obligated to give as advice to his fellow Muslim. Until now, we are brothers and partisans of a single religion and part of a single religious community, given that the sword has not come between us, and you are deserving of sincere advice. But should the sword be drawn, the safeguard (*ʿiṣmah*) will be broken; we will be an *ummah* and you will be an *ummah*. Verily God has tried us through the offspring of his Prophet Muhammad (s.), to see what you and we will do. Verily we call you to support of them (*nasrihim*) and to the abandonment (*khidhlan*) of the tyrant, ʿUbayd Allāh b. Zīyād.[24]

The massacre at Karbalā was, in effect, a decisive moment for the future of Shīʿa believers to brand themselves as saved and the enemies of the Prophet's family as cursed.[25] Therefore, it became easy to see those sympathetic to the Shīʿī cause who died in sectarian conflicts as real martyrs. We can understand this from devotional and liturgical texts. In a famous and much-recited Shīʿī prayer, *zīyārat ʿāshūrā*, reportedly composed by the fifth Imām (Muhammad al-Bāqir) sometime after the tragedy of Karbalā during the reign of the Umayyads, this duality of the martyrs of Karbalā versus the cursed enemies of the Imams (*Ahlul-Bayt*) is evident and made its way to the core belief of the Shīʿa. In this *zīyārah*, we read:

> May the curse be upon those people who laid down the foundations for the oppression and wrongs done upon you, the family of the Prophet [*Ahlul-Bayt*]. May Allāh curse those people who denied you your position (O' *Ahlul-Bayt*) and removed you from your rank which Allāh himself had granted you. May the curse of Allāh be upon those people who killed you and may the curse of Allāh be upon those people who made it easy for them by preparing the grounds of your killing. I turn to Allāh and I turn towards you and turn away from them and their adherents, followers and friends . . . And may the curse of Allāh be upon the nation that carried out, saw and were silent at your killing.[26]

In later sections of the *zīyārat ʿāshūrā*, the faithful further denounce those responsible for the killing of Ḥusayn, and ask for God's forgiveness and wish to have the same kind of death as that of the Prophet's family, that is martyrdom:

> I disassociate myself from them through Allāh and through all of you and I seek nearness to Allāh and then to you through love for you and your friends and disassociation with your enemies and from those who want to fight against you and disassociation from their adherents and followers. O' Allāh! Make me at this moment, one who receives from you prayers, mercy and forgiveness. O' Allāh! Make me live the life of Muhammad and the family of Muhammad and permit me to die the death of Muhammad and the family of Muhammad.[27]

This implies that, for the newly emerging distinct Shīʿī system of thought, the casualties from Ḥusayn's camp were true martyrs, not different from those martyrs who fought non-Muslims alongside the Prophet. For the Shīʿa, Āshūrā was a revival and the embodiment of the concept of martyrdom as violent death of the oppressed and helpless believers at the hands of the enemies of God. So, similar to the Meccan period and most of the Judeo-Christian martyrdom tradition, sectarian martyrs, in the Shīʿī sense, were not understood primarily as fallen military heroes, but rather as "exemplary believers" who gave up their lives in the face of injustice or unbelief without losing their faith.[28] In other words, sectarian martyrs, as still understood today, were champions of the way of truth (*shuhadāʾ al-ḥaqq*). Particularly for the minority Shīʿa, they were often remembered and celebrated as those who had the discernment and courage to seek and stick to the truth at the times of trial (*fitnah*) when most people went astray and relinquished their faith.

In retrospect, the Twelver Shīʿī concept of martyrdom in its sectarian understanding is defined by and linked to the sufferings of *Ahlul-Bayt* following the death of the Prophet. According to the mainstream Shīʿa, ʿAlī and his designated successors (supposedly divinely appointed Imams) were oppressed and deprived of their right to succeed the Prophet and were killed by sword or poison. Hence, one can argue that, in the Shīʿī sense, the family of the Prophet were the genuine and ultimate martyrs, and others were called martyrs because of them. In other words, much like the idea of martyrdom in Christianity and its dependence on the crucifixion and resurrection of Christ, the Shīʿa martyrs bore witness to the sufferings of the Prophet's family, which started with the dramatic death of Fāṭimat al-Zahrā, the daughter of Muhammad.

The significance of Fāṭimah in Twelver Shīʿīsm, and in the Shīʿī approach to martyrdom, cannot be overlooked. She is revered as the mother of the Imams (*umm al-ʿaʾimmah*), and even in a tradition Muhammad called Fāṭimah the 'mother of his father' (*umm-i ʿabīhā*).[29] Muhammad also reportedly described his daughter as the mistress of all the women in the world (*sayyidat nisāʾ al-ʿālamīn*).[30] She is known among the Shīʿa as the first martyr of the Imamate and is called the truthful martyr (*al-siddīqat al-shahīdah*). In popular Shīʿa piety, no tragedy apart from Ḥusayn's martyrdom rivals the sorrowful fate of her untimely death (martyrdom) which occurred less than a hundred days after the Prophet. According to Shīʿī sources, Fāṭimah inundated herself with sorrow and weeping for the loss of her father partly as a protest against the usurpation of what she thought was the right of her husband ʿAlī as the rightful successor to the Prophet. She embraced alleged vicious physical attacks carried by ʿUmar ibn al-Khattab (the eventual second Caliph). The tale of storming into Fāṭimah's home—reportedly a few days after the death of the Prophet in order to get the allegiance of ʿAlī for Abū Bakr—and burning the front door along the way which caused her fatal chest injury, has become known as the first tragedy after the Prophet, a sorrowful event that opened up the way for more injustice toward the Imams and the family of the Prophet (*Ahlul-Bayt*), culminating in the tragedy of Āshūrā.[31]

In Shīʿī myths, the figure of Fāṭimah plays an important role after her martyrdom. Through Muhammad, God revealed to her all tragic events that would happen to her children, especially the martyrdom of Ḥusayn. Traditions tell us that from heaven she witnessed her children's sufferings and mourned for them. She will remain in a state of mourning, waiting for vengeance, until the day of judgment.[32] In Shīʿī folktale, Fāṭimah with her wounded chest and a sorrowful appearance frequently appears in dreams to the pious. In such dreams, Fāṭimah often makes the person lament for Ḥusayn or thank them for their practice of weeping for Ḥusayn.[33] It is reported that, on the day of judgment, Fāṭimah appears in a grand manner that astounds all the Prophets, the truthful, and the martyrs, and they all close their eyes while she passes to reach God's throne. Fāṭimah then asks God to fulfill his pledge and exact vengeance from those who wronged her and martyred her children. Assuring her of punishing all who oppressed her and her family, God gives Fāṭimah the power to intercede for her followers and the Shīʿa of her children (the Imams).[34] These tales and traditions show the great status of Fāṭimah, both in Shīʿa theology and in popular piety, which is at the same level as Muhammad and ʿAlī. Fāṭimah being the de facto mother of the Shīʿa, and the connecting bond between the Prophethood and the Imamate, has a prominent position in the formation of the myth of martyrdom in Shīʿism. In other words, it is fair to argue that Shīʿa martyrs by shedding their blood in the path of Imamate and *wilāyah* in fact tend to please Fāṭimah.

The life and martyrdom of ʿAlī after the death of the Prophet also represent a significant tragedy in Shīʿism. For the Shīʿa, the tragedy began when most Muslims failed to acknowledge the will of Muhammad to entrust ʿAlī with the leadership right after the Prophet's death. It took some twenty-five long years before ʿAlī was given a chance to lead the community, only to be martyred less than five years later after facing continuous opposition and betrayal and engaging in three battles (Jamal, Ṣiffīn, and Nahrawān). ʿAlī died of a poisonous sword wound at the hands of one of the Kharijites.[35] ʿAlī's fatal wound occurred on the morning of the nineteenth day of Ramadan and he died less than two days later on the night of the twenty-first day on one of the holiest nights of the year, known as the *Laylat al-qadr* ("the night of decree"), the night in which it is believed that the whole Qur'an was revealed to the Prophet. Moreover, the *Laylat al-qadr* is the night of blessing and forgiveness; and on that night every year, the angels reportedly descend from heaven to the Imām of the age to configure the fate of all human beings for the next year. Being martyred on such a night added to the significance of the martyrdom of ʿAlī for the Shīʿa. Furthermore, ʿAlī's martyrdom and the *Laylat al-qadr* have been intertwined: mourning for his martyrdom is now part of the rituals of the night.

The martyrdom of ʿAlī and the injustice toward him during his life after Muhammad had such a profound impact on shaping Twelver Shīʿism that ʿAlī is called "the first wronged person in the world," based on the following tradition from the tenth Imām, al-Hādī, a title which has remained popular among the Shīʿa. We might, however, interpret this as the first wronged person in terms of rank and importance since obviously the literal meaning of the phrase is not correct:

> Peace be upon you, O' *walī* of Allāh, I bear witness that you are the first wronged person in the world, and the first person that his rights were violated. You,

> nevertheless, acted patiently, seeking the reward of Allāh, until death came upon you. I bear witness that you met Allāh and you are martyr. May Allāh punish your killer with different torments.[36]

Putting the theological Shīʿī interpretations of ʿAlī's status and that of his eleven descendants (as martyred infallible Imams) aside, a short review of the historical accounts of the Shīʿī revolts and their relations to the Imams' cause gives us a better understanding of martyrdom in Twelver Shīʿism. ʿAlī's prominence and authority were indisputable among the early Shīʿa, yet after ʿAlī's martyrdom there was no charismatic leader who could unite the community. As Maria Massi Dakake put it, "[I]f the historical sources indicate that the Shīʿite camp united fiercely behind ʿAlī toward the end of his life, expressing their absolute devotion, or [*wilāyah*], toward him and *ʿadāwah* or *barāʿah* [enmity] toward all of his many enemies, they also detail the gradual disintegration of this unity in the ideological and leadership confusion that followed his death."[37]

Ḥasan, ʿAlī's older son and the second Imām in the Twelver tradition, briefly replaced his father as Caliph but struggled to attract the same level of loyalty among his father's former companions.[38] Having failed to secure enough support, Ḥasan was forced to surrender power to Muʿāwīyah through a controversial peace treaty.[39] This caused resentment among some of his key companions who, based on their oath of allegiance to ʿAlī's cause, were unwilling to accept Muʿāwīyah as a legitimate Muslim ruler. Ḥasan survived an assassination attempt by a group of his soldiers and received angry reactions from his Shīʿa allies for his seemingly tactical deal with Muʿāwīyah. Reportedly, Ḥujr ibn ʿAdī, a prominent Shīʿa of ʿAlī, was deeply disappointed with the treaty and called Ḥasan *yā mudhil al-muʿminīn* (o' the believers' humiliator).[40] Ḥasan's retreat to Medina and his eventual death by poison (reportedly planned by Muʿāwīyah) gave Muʿāwīyah the opportunity to strengthen his rule over all Muslims.

As part of his effort to solidify his position as Caliph, Muʿāwīyah, particularly after the death of Ḥasan, was eager to wipe out all favorable memories of ʿAlī by forcing all mosques to curse him before every Friday prayer, even in the city of Kūfa where ʿAlī had based his government and most of his followers lived.[41] This caused resentment among some of the most loyal former disciples of ʿAlī, again notably Ḥujr ibn ʿAdī, who was publicly outspoken about Muʿāwīyah's decree and vehemently refused to curse ʿAlī. Ḥujr's refusal to denounce ʿAlī resulted in his imprisonment, and subsequently he was beheaded by Muʿāwīyah's order in the year 53 of the Islamic calendar.[42] Al-Masʿūdī, a tenth-century historian, believed that Ḥujr was the first martyr since the Meccan period who was killed in captivity.[43] Ḥujr's status as a great martyr has been preserved among the Shīʿa; his shrine near Damascus in Syria had been a place of pilgrimage before it was destroyed by a Salafī jihadi group on May 2, 2013, during the recent Syrian civil war.[44]

The martyrdom of Ḥujr, in fact, was one of a few cases of sectarian martyrdom in early Shīʿīsm. The deprivation and alienation of the Prophet's family and their supporters from political power after the assassination of ʿAlī left much desire for vengeance and the need to protect ʿAlī's legacy by returning the Caliphate to the Prophet's family. However, serious acts of resistance and martyrdom for a purely Shīʿī cause rarely happened before the rise of Ḥusayn almost twenty years after ʿAlī's death. This lack of collective attempt by the Shīʿa in part can be linked to the inability of the Shīʿa to settle around an unquestionable authority of ʿAlī's caliber. Ḥasan's forced reconciliation with Muʿāwīyah, a peace treaty that even after Ḥasan's death his younger brother (Ḥusayn) kept intact for nearly ten years until the death of Muʿāwīyah, more than anything else showed how little the broad followers of ʿAlī were willing to sacrifice their lives for the sake of the Prophet's family in the post-ʿAlī era. Similar to the martyrdom of Ḥujr, Ḥasan's death (or martyrdom due to poison, according to later Shīʿī traditions) hardly caused an uproar among the Shīʿa.[45] Even the tragedy of Karbalā and Ḥusayn's martyrdom could have been prevented had he managed to earn the same authority, and had the same charisma, as his father (ʿAlī), and had he been able to effectively mobilize the Shīʿa (of Kūfa) against the Umayyads.[46]

Before the martyrdom of Ḥusayn, the Shīʿī version of martyrdom, that is dying for the cause of the Prophet's family, was not a trend among those sympathetic to the cause. Things changed forever with the tragedy of Karbalā. To better grasp the magnitude of Ḥusayn's martyrdom, we need to review the related historical events. With Muʿāwīyah's death, Yazīd, his reportedly impious son, succeeded him. The succession caused the resentment of the community of the Shīʿa, particularly in Kūfa. Immediately after taking power, Yazīd asked his governor of Medina to forcefully take the oath of allegiance from influential citizens of the city, most importantly Ḥusayn ibn ʿAlī and ʿAbdullāh ibn Zubayr (son of a famous Prophet's disciple, Zubayr ibn Al-Awwām, who later opposed ʿAlī and was responsible for the battle of Jamal). They both refused to endorse Yazīd's rule and fled from Medina to Mecca, which was a safer place for them due to its sanctity. ʿAbdullāh remained in Mecca and later succeeded in capturing the city from the Umayyads for a few years before finally being defeated and killed in battle against the army of the then Umayyad Caliph Abd al-Mālik ibn Marwān in 692, some twelve years after the events of Karbalā.[47]

Ḥusayn, in contrast, after receiving many letters of support from the Shīʿa of Kūfa and feeling unsafe in Mecca, abruptly left the city toward Kūfa in the middle of the Hajj season with the company of his family and a small group of followers. In their letters, the Kūfan Shīʿas, many of whom had fought for ʿAlī, asked Ḥusayn to join them as their Imam and leader to revolt against Yazīd. Right after the death of Muʿāwīyah, Sulaymān ibn Surad al-Khuzāʿi, a former disciple of Muhammad, ʿAlī, and Ḥasan, and a respectable Shīʿa of Kūfa, wrote the first of such letters to Ḥusayn (also signed by other leaders of the Shīʿa in Kūfa). The letter reads:

> Thanks be to God that your enemy and your father's enemy [Muʿāwīyah] is dead now . . . Now we are hearing that his cursed son [Yazīd] took power without the consensus of the community, and without knowing the traditions. We do not want to accept his claim for caliphate and will fight him with you. We were your father's friends and Shīʿa, and now we are your friends and Shīʿa. When you receive this letter come to us [in Kūfa] and become our ruler [*amir*], our Imam, and our Caliph. We don't have any ruler and Imam except Nu'man ibn Bashir [Yazīd's governor in Kūfa] who has no [real authority among the Shīʿa of Kūfa].[48]

Ḥusayn also sent his trusted cousin, Muslim ibn ʿAqil, to Kūfa to evaluate their readiness for the cause.[49] When he arrived in Kūfa, Muslim was initially impressed by the willingness of the vast majority of the Shīʿa to join Ḥusayn in his mission. He sent a messenger to his cousin asking him to hasten his travel to Kūfa. Meanwhile, in an unexpected turn of events, Yazīd sent ʿUbaydullāh ibn Zīyād as the new governor of Kūfa, and he swiftly and easily took control of the city and succeeded in arresting and executing Muslim and his prominent supporter, Hani ibn Urwa. The martyrdom of Muslim put an end to his mission in preparing Kūfa for Imam Ḥusayn's arrival, and consequently cast a deep shadow on the prospect of Ḥusayn's movement.[50] Already some important Shīʿa veterans, including his half-brother, Muhammad ibn Ḥanafīyyah, and his cousin, Ibn ʿAbbās, had warned him not to leave Mecca for Kūfa in opposition to Yazīd as they saw no chance of success for Ḥusayn. They thought Yemen would be a safer option for him since it was far away from Yazīd's Syria. However, Ḥusayn was determined to continue his way to Kūfa under any circumstances.[51] It is reported that, at his insistence to take the grave risk of going to Iraq, Ḥusayn, in response to Umm Salamah (a widow of Muhammad) referred to his dream of the Prophet and his previous premonition from his parents, ʿAlī and Fāṭimah, as well as Muhammad, that he was destined to be martyred and that there was no escape from that fate:

> By God, O mother, I shall be killed without any doubt. There is no escape from the predestined decree of God; there is no escape for me from death. Indeed, I know the day and hour, and the spot wherein I shall be killed. I know the place whereon I shall fall, and the spot in which I shall be buried, as I know you. If you wish that I show you my resting place and that of the men who will be martyred with me, I will.[52]

There is a report that after the martyrdom of Muslim, Ḥusayn was hesitant to continue his mission; however, the family of Muslim wanted to avenge his death and persuaded Ḥusayn to continue his march to Kūfa.[53] After arriving in Karbalā and confronted with a huge Umayyad army, most of them Kūfan soldiers, it was finally clear to Ḥusayn and his companions that there would be no victory for them. Hence, Ḥusayn offered to withdraw from his mission of going to Kūfa if they would let him go somewhere safe. ʿUbaydullāh ibn Zīyād refused Ḥusayn's request and ordered his army to attack Ḥusayn and his followers and kill everyone in his army in Karbalā. The battle lasted just a few hours on the tenth day of the month of Muḥarram in the year 680.[54] Almost all adult males in Ḥusayn's camp were killed in battle, except one of Ḥusayn's sons, ʿAlī ibn Ḥusayn Zayn al-'Abidīn (al-Sajjād), the heir and successor to Ḥusayn's Imamate. Zayn al-'Abidīn was reportedly sick and could not participate in the battle, so he, along with the women of Karbalā, was captured and sent to ʿUbaydullāh ibn Zīyād. Later, ibn Zīyād sent them with the decapitated head of Ḥusayn to Yazīd in Damascus.[55]

The martyrdom of the grandson of the Prophet at the hands of the grandson of the most important enemy of the Prophet (Abū Sufyān) just fifty years after Muhammad's death was a massive tragedy for all Muslims. Even the ruling Umayyad family was not happy with the tragic turn of events in Karbalā. Al-Ṭabarī narrates that, after the captives of Karbalā were sent to Yazīd, at their presence, he also showed his remorse for what had happened to the family of the Prophet and held a mourning ceremony for Ḥusayn in his house.[56] However, Yazīd's attempts to distance himself from those responsible for the killing of Ḥusayn were not effective and did not temper the resentment of the devastated family of the Prophet and their followers. Soon, Ḥusayn's martyrdom fueled anti-Umayyad uprisings that weakened the Umayyads' position in power, which ultimately resulted in their defeat in the revolution led by descendants of ʿAbbās, uncle of the Prophet, who formed the Abbasid Caliphate after the last Umayyad Caliph, Marwan ibn Muhammad, was killed in 750. The tragedy of Āshūrā was a turning point, particularly for the Shīʿa, as it was the single most important event in early Islam that defined the Shīʿa type of martyrdom forever. Some issues here must be discussed regarding Āshūrā.

Because of the utmost importance of the event in Islamic history, there are many historical and *ḥadīth* reports that cover every aspect of the martyrdom of Imam Ḥusayn and his followers in Karbalā. Most of them were written at least fifty years after the events, so they were not produced by first-hand witnesses or those involved in the events. Moreover, due to the sensitivity of Āshūrā for the broader Muslim community and the theological ramifications of the martyrdom of Imam Ḥusayn for the Shīʿa in particular, historical facts and myths are mostly inseparable in the narrative of the story and that makes an academic study of the events very difficult. However, as we are examining the Shīʿa "perception" of martyrdom, it is important to see how the Shīʿas understood Imam Ḥusayn's martyrdom and how they now use it to justify their religious and political stances. Hence, for the sake of this study, here I am not going to distinguish facts from myths to decipher what actually happened in Arabia, Iraq, and Syria around 680.

The martyrdom of Ḥusayn, as shocking as it was, happened in a remote place in less than a day. It was meant to be out of the public's eye. However, the tragic story ironically was publicized by the Umayyads themselves who brought the captives of Karbalā and let them scatter voices of discontent. The result was a widespread sense of guilt, particularly in Kūfa, where most of the Shīʿa had withdrawn their support from Ḥusayn after ibn Zīyād cracked down on Muslim ibn ʿAqil's mission and prohibited anyone from joining Ḥusayn. The sermons of Zaynab (Ḥusayn's sister) and ʿAlī ibn Ḥusayn, while in captivity in Kūfa and Damascus, were also effective in denying Yazīd the opportunity to turn the massacre of Karbalā in his favor and strengthen his power. In fact, the killing of Ḥusayn backfired badly and Yazīd was forced to free the prisoners and let them return to Medina.[57] In some reports the captives were even allowed to visit the graves of the martyrs in Karbalā on their way back to Medina.[58] In an effort to clear his name, Yazīd even blamed ʿUbaydullāh ibn Zīyād for the killing of Ḥusayn, and reportedly said to ʿAlī ibn Ḥusayn, "May God curse ibn Marjanah [ibn Zīyād], God knows if his [Ḥusayn's] fate were with me, I would have accepted whatever he requested and prevented his death, even if I had to lose one of my children, but God had a different plan as you saw."[59] Moreover, for three days, Yazīd let women mourn for Ḥusayn in his court.[60]

Ultimately, Yazīd was unable to clear his name for being responsible for the killing of Ḥusayn. The damage was done, and with the passive, yet effective, role of Zaynab and ʿAlī-ibn Ḥusayn in spreading the story of Āshūrā through lamentation, the martyrdom of Ḥusayn eventually became a symbol of resistance and a marker of identity for the minority Shīʿa. Later Imams adopted this passive strategy of opposing the status quo and the anti-Shīʿa policies of the Sunni Caliphs by holding and encouraging mourning gatherings for Ḥusayn every year on the day of Āshūrā.[61] The Imams encouraged their followers to perform pilgrimage to Karbalā on the day of Āshūrā as a sign of respect for his cause; and those who could not go to Karbalā were asked to weep and mourn for Ḥusayn at their homes together with their households.[62] The passive resistance in the form of mourning was not exclusively restricted to the martyrdom of Ḥusayn. Reportedly, the fifth Imam, Muhammad al-Bāqir, asked his son and successor, Jaʿfar al-Sādiq, to hold mourning ceremonies for ten years on the anniversary of his death (reportedly due to poison).[63] However, the tragic nature of the martyrdom of Ḥusayn and his family and followers, as well as the captivity of the women and children, made Āshūrā the symbol of oppression against the family of the Prophet, worthy of special attention by the Shīʿas. Many traditions suggest extraordinary rewards for weeping and commemorating the martyrdom of Ḥusayn. Shīʿa sources are replete with Muhammad's prophecies regarding Ḥusayn's martyrdom and the merits of being sad and mournful for his tragedy. One famous tradition from the Prophet asserts: "Verily, the martyrdom of Ḥusayn kindles such a fire in the hearts of the believers which will never extinguish."[64] I will discuss more about traditions on the martyrdom of Ḥusayn later in this chapter.

Another issue in the narratives of the events of Karbalā is that, despite the theological importance and significance of Ḥusayn's martyrdom for later generations of the Shīʿa, in the available sources, as far as I know, a direct reference to words such as martyrdom (*shahādah, istishhād*) or martyr (*shahīd*) is rare. Ḥusayn did not build a case for himself as a would-be-martyr other than merely embracing imminent death at the hands of the Umayyads. He did not draw a theological conclusion from his intention for martyrdom. Ḥusayn did use the terminology of martyrdom for himself and his companions on only three occasions. It was never expanded upon on what that would mean to the rest of the community. First, in a letter to the people of his tribe (*Banū Hāshim*) apparently written while he was in Mecca, he declared: "[W]hoever joins me will be martyred [*istashhada*] and whoever declines my request will not taste victory." Once more, on the night before Āshūrā, during his speech to his followers, Ḥusayn revealed what he had dreamt earlier that night: "And after that, I saw the Messenger of Allāh with a number of his disciples, and he told me, 'You are the martyr of this community, the settlers of the heavens and God's throne congratulate themselves for you are going to join them; you will be with me [tomorrow] night, so be hasty; an angel has descended from heaven to collect your blood in a green tube.'" And finally, on the day of Āshūrā, after the midday prayer in the heat of the battle, he encouraged his remaining followers to be patient: "[Y]ou, the nobles, this is paradise that is opened for you, its rivers have come together, and its fruits are ripe."[65] In contrast, reportedly, Ḥusayn repeatedly used expressions such as "death" (*mawt*),[66] "be killed" (*qutil, maqtūl, qatīl, madhbūḥ*),[67] "to kill" (*qatl*),[68] as he prepared his followers to come to terms with their eventual death if they joined his movement against the rule of Yazīd. Comparing this with the image of Ḥusayn as the ultimate martyr and the holiness of martyrdom in the path of God among the later generations of the Shīʿa in the following centuries after Āshūrā shows us how Āshūrā profoundly changed and reinterpreted martyrdom into something essential for the identity of the Shīʿa community.

Similar to Ḥusayn, his disciples in Karbalā, while eager to shed their blood in defence of their leader, did not paint, or at least envision, their death as an act of martyrdom bearing some extraordinary theological and eschatological significance as was later articulated in the Shīʿa works. Even in *zīyārat āshūrā*, the author(s) did not call the tragic death of Ḥusayn and his devoted family and followers "martyrdom." Considering the abundance of attention to the martyrdom of Imam Ḥusayn in the late Umayyad and early Abbasid periods, we can assume that, if the *zīyārat āshūrā* had been composed a hundred years later, it would have been written differently. There would have been a direct reference to the concept of martyrdom; at least, Ḥusayn would have been called *sayyid al-shuhadā* ("master of the martyrs"), instead of only his title *Abā Abdillāh.*

Certainly, the concept of martyrdom as dying for God was known to the people around Ḥusayn, but the tragedy of Karbalā made martyrdom a driving force with a theological significance for social and political changes. Martyrdom in the post-Āshūrā setting became a litmus test for identifying truth and falsity in the sectarian context. The desire for martyrdom and holding martyrs in high regard came from the Shīʿī understanding of martyrdom as witnessing the truth embodied in the path of the heirs of the Prophet (the Imams) through expressing love toward them and hatred for their enemies.[69] In other words, the moving death of Imam Ḥusayn and his disciples in Karbalā made a case for the Shīʿa, that dying in defence of the Imam and the *walī* of the time deserved to be called martyrdom (as if imitating the path of the Imams and following their footsteps was authentic Islam).

Āshūrā was, in fact, a turning point in how the Shīʿa pursued martyrdom as a strong weapon when facing relatively dominant adversaries. The martyrdom of Ḥusayn, the grandson of the Prophet, was so shocking in the eyes of the Shīʿa that it overshadowed all martyrs before and after him including his father, ʿAlī, as well as early martyrs like Ḥamzah; hence, he became synonymous with martyrdom and received the title of *sayyid al-shuhadā*, a title previously reserved for Ḥamzah. Another difference that Āshūrā made was that up until that time, even for the Shīʿa, martyrdom was seen mostly as a personal honor that one would long for. Āshūrā changed it forever by valuing voluntary martyrdom as a duty for the community of believers in times when the blood of martyrs is needed for the survival of the faith and redemption of the community. For the Shīʿa, the martyr's blood triumphed over the sword; it was a victory in defeat. The concept of martyrdom changed from being beneficial for the martyr in the afterlife to becoming a motivating factor in social and political movements. It turned out to be a vehicle of protest and a voice of discontent. Āshūrā (and the martyrdom of Ḥusayn) became a representation of lost opportunities for Muslims to make their community the one that the Prophet had envisioned; Āshūrā demonstrated what went wrong in Muslim history.

Preserved sayings of the martyrs of Karbalā are another fascinating topic in the study of martyrdom. In the tragedy of Āshūrā, Ḥusayn was a centrepiece surrounded by about a couple of hundred totally devoted followers. As mentioned before, there are many exaggerated and fabricated reports of the events of Karbalā that have been made mostly to arouse the emotions of the Shīʿa audience. Weeping and lamenting for Ḥusayn also gradually gained unparalleled religious and theological significance. Nevertheless, his tale of martyrdom is full of epic quotes that redefined martyrdom as a duty of believers in the face of grave injustice. In one of the most famous quotes we read that, on the day of Āshūrā, Ḥusayn said to his opponents: "Do you not see how right is not acted upon and falsehood is not prevented? Then let the believer desire the meeting with God, for I see death as being nothing other than happiness while life with the oppressors as humiliation."[70]

Shīʿī historians also depicted Ḥusayn's followers and family members as completely selfless heroes who sacrificed everything they had for the sake of their Imam. We find some interesting quotes from the martyrs of Karbalā, all competing to be the first to give their life before Ḥusayn and get martyred. ʿAbbās, half-brother of Ḥusayn, and second only to his older brother among the martyrs in terms of importance, is famously narrated shouting toward the enemies on the battlefield when he stormed to get water for children and women: "O self, there is no point in living after Ḥusayn, I don't want you to stay alive after him . . . even if you cut off my right hand I won't turn my back on my religion and my righteous Imam, son of the trustee and pure Prophet, the truthful

Prophet who brought the divine religion that attests the oneness of God."[71] Others have been recorded uttering similar epic slogans, wishing to fight for Ḥusayn until the last drop of their blood and be martyred for him, and then return to fight again and get martyred several times over.[72]

One of the most cited themes of the story of Āshūrā that appeared in the sayings of Ḥusayn and his family was the issue of the love of God in accepting his tragic fate. Ḥusayn's absolute trust in God and his calmness and joy of meeting God is the pinnacle of the story of Āshūrā which has been retold and stressed by Shīʿī orators for centuries. In a couple of late sources, it is reported that moments before Ḥusayn's death, while he was fatally wounded on the ground, he whispered to himself saying: "O' God, I am pleased with your wish, patient with your trials, submitted to your decree, there is no other (worshipped) Lord than you, O' helper of those in distress."[73] Reportedly, his sister Zaynab, in Ibn Zīyād's court on the day after Āshūrā, described the tragedy and martyrdom of Ḥusayn in a similar way by conceding to God's will: "I did not see anything but beauty."[74] This esoteric and mystical understanding of Ḥusayn's martyrdom through the lens of the pure love of God and absolute submission to his will particularly has become the dominant narrative in modern Shīʿīsm.

The immediate effect of the tragedy of Karbalā was the revolt (of penitents) in 684 by a group of the Shīʿa led by a respected former companion of the Prophet, Sulaymān ibn Surad Khuzāʿī, from the city of Kūfa where Ḥusayn was heading to lead an uprising against the Umayyad Caliphate. The primary goal of the group was to avenge Ḥusayn's blood. They were ready for martyrdom (if necessary) out of guilt for their failure to stand behind Ḥusayn in his mission against Yazīd;[75] hence, they named themselves *Tawwābūn* (repenters) and chose *yā lathārāt al- ḥusayn* ("Rise to avenge Ḥusayn's blood") as their slogan.[76] Before their revolt, the *Tawwābūn* visited the grave of Ḥusayn and wept for his martyrdom and for their part in the tragedy. This marked the first major public mourning practice for martyrdom of a Muslim. On Ḥusayn's grave, Sulaymān gave his followers a sermon and called Ḥusayn "martyr son of martyr."[77] Again, this was one of the early usages of the title "martyr" in a political context. In accordance with the Islamic traditions to seek forgiveness for the deceased,[78] Sulaymān also asked forgiveness for Ḥusayn, a clear contrast with the later depiction of Ḥusayn as the so-called infallible Imam, the *sayyid al-shuhadā*, and the intercessor of the community on the day of judgment.[79] However, there are elements in Sulaymān's speech that suggest a superhuman status for Ḥusayn, a kind of intermediary between God and his people as later became a principle in Twelver Shīʿīsm.[80]

An interesting issue regarding the martyrdom story of *Tawwābūn* is the novel concept of the relation between martyrdom, sin, and repentance, something that had no precedence in Islam. According to Islamic traditions, God will forgive the sins of the martyr.[81] Forgiveness for the martyr was essentially a side effect of their martyrdom. Nevertheless, martyrdom was never seen primarily as a remedy for guilt. No one opted for martyrdom because they thought they did something wrong and wanted to fix that. The *Tawwābūn* knew their movement would most likely end in defeat; yet they deliberately chose martyrdom as a form of purification for the sins they committed by abandoning Ḥusayn when he needed their support in Karbalā. In their visit to Karbalā, Sulaymān reportedly said:

> Oh Lord, we have betrayed the son of our Prophet's daughter! Pardon us for what we did in the past and relent toward us ... If you do not pardon us our sin and have mercy on us, then we are among those who are lost ... Praise be to God who, if he had wished, would have honored us with martyrdom with [Ḥusayn]. Oh my God, since you forbade us it together with him, do not forbid us it on his account after him.[82]

Their commitment to martyrdom resembles the golden calf's story where the Israelites killed each other because they failed in their faith to the God of Israel. The *Tawwābūn* wanted to exact revenge for Ḥusayn's martyrdom; however, instead of weeping for his loss, they were concerned with "the magnitude of the treason of the Kūfan Shīʿites and the need to repent from it"; hence, their willingness to shed their own blood.[83] They predictably failed to gain victory over the superior Umayyad army, and after suffering so many losses, including Sulaymān, the rest of their army of five thousand retreated to Kūfa.[84]

Following the *Tawwābūn*'s defeat, there was a rather successful revolt of Mukhtār al-Thaqafī in revenge for the martyrdom of Ḥusayn and his followers five years after the events of Karbalā in 685. Mukhtār was reluctant to join Sulaymān's revolt out of pragmatism since he did not believe in Sulaymān's competence as a war leader. Mukhtār had lobbied against Sulaymān's movement, arguing that he would lead his army into fruitless danger.[85] In his revolt, Mukhtār also chose *yā lathārāt al-ḥusayn* ("Rise to avenge Ḥusayn's blood") as his slogan, but unlike the leaders of *Tawwābūn*, he believed in martyrdom as a last resort and plotted his revolt meticulously and successfully. He managed to free Kūfa from the rule of the Umayyads for a few months and succeeded in killing most of the people responsible for the killing of Ḥusayn and his followers in Karbalā.[86] Mukhtār himself was finally killed in 687 in a battle with Musʿab bin al-Zubayr, a younger brother of 'Abdullāh ibn Zubayr, who led a partly successful non-Shī'ī rebellion against the Umayyad Caliphate.[87]

Mukhtār is remembered among the Shī'a as a great martyr, particularly because of his role in revenge for the martyrdom of Imam Ḥusayn, though he remained a somewhat controversial figure due to some disagreement about his true intentions and whether he was loyal to 'Alī ibn Ḥusayn al-Sajjād, the fourth Shī'ī Imam. However, the Imams mostly appeared to be pleased with his loyalty to the family of the Prophet and his actions against their enemies.[88] The case for the martyrdom of Mukhtār came from his courageous effort to kill the enemies of the Prophet's family, particularly Ḥusayn. Most later Shī'a uprisings near the end of the Umayyad Caliphate (except the revolt of Zayd which follows) did not build their rebellious attempts around avenging Ḥusayn's blood, rather, more generally, they made a case to return the Caliphate into the competent hands of the family of the Prophet (*al-riḍā min āl-i muḥammad*) as the rightful Caliphs (though with some disagreements over the identity of the person within that family).[89]

The revolt of Zayd ibn 'Alī, grandson of Ḥusayn and brother of the fifth Imam, Muhammad al-Bāqir, was another notable collective Shī'a attempt against Umayyad rule and resulted in another instance of Shī'ī martyrdom in 740. He was considered an Imam for the Zaydi Shī'as; Twelvers also generally respect Zayd ibn 'Alī as a righteous and learned scholar (not an Imam) and regard him as a respected martyr, though with some reservations. Zayd based his ill-fated uprising against Hisham ibn 'Abdulmalik, an Umayyad Caliph, on avenging the martyrdom of Ḥusayn, and on enjoining good and forbidding wrong (*al-'amr bi al-ma'rūf wa al-nahy 'an al-munkar*), similar to the intention of Ḥusayn in his revolt and martyrdom in Karbalā.[90] Zayd gathered his followers in Kūfa and started a Shī'ī uprising; but his revolt quickly faced defeat and he was killed in battle. The circumstances surrounding Zayd's martyrdom were also similar to that of his grandfather, Ḥusayn. Most of his initial supporters abandoned him. So, Zayd's small group of loyal followers faced the Umayyad army and lost the battle easily.[91] Because he was from the family of the Prophet, grandson of Ḥusayn, and son of the fourth Imam, 'Alī ibn Ḥusayn, his martyrdom gained a lot of attention and scrutiny later among the Shī'a. Again, the controversy over his status as a Shī'ī martyr stems from the obscurity surrounding his loyalty toward the Imam of his time, Ja'far al-Sādiq (in Twelver Shī'īsm). Some traditions highly praise Zayd's revolt and martyrdom, implying that he started his movement with Imam Sādiq's permission.[92] Some other traditions suggest that he acted on his own against the will of Ja'far al-Sādiq. According to those reports Zayd expected to be the Imam after his brother Imam Bāqir (like the Imamate of Ḥusayn after his brother Ḥasan) and even expressed his disappointment over the Imamate of Jaʿfar al-Sādiq.[93] Overall, Shīʿī traditions respect the personality of Zayd as a great and righteous member of the Prophet's family, and a martyr, even though the Imams were not totally in agreement with his political activism. In other words, the status of Zayd as martyr came from his close connections to the Imams, his well-known piety, and his supposedly pure intention to struggle in the path of the Imams.

Another early martyr-like figure among the broad and diverse group of the Shīʿa was Muhammad ibn ʿAbdullāh ibn al-Ḥasan al-Muthanna, better known as *al-nafs al-zakīyyah* ("the pure soul"), a descendant of both Ḥasan and Ḥusayn, the second and the third Imams, respectively. Muhammad was eager to assume the Caliphate and revolted against the Abbasid Caliph, Mansur (*al-nafs al-zakīyyah*'s former ally against the Umayyads), which resulted in his death (or martyrdom) in 762.[94] Because he was a very pious Muslim, and his name was also the same as that of the Prophet, Muhammad ibn ʿAbdullāh even gained the reputation of being the awaited Mahdī (since in some traditions al-Mahdī was regarded as bearing the name of the Prophet). He reportedly called himself al-Mahdī and took the oath of allegiance from his followers accordingly.[95] This claim of being the Mahdī put *al-nafs al-zakīyyah* at odds with his influential contemporary, Jaʿfar al-Sādiq, the sixth Imam, who categorically denied such a claim and refused to acknowledge his revolt; hence, Muhammad's death was not praised by Twelver Shīʿa as true martyrdom.[96] The point here is that his revolt and other later similar efforts were mostly political and not religious in nature. They were also interpreted by the mainstream Twelver Shīʿa as selfish activities for the sake of gaining political power rather than being a part of a Shīʿī specific agenda in defence of the Shīʿa Imams; hence, martyrdom generally did not completely fit those killed in such political endeavors.

The last major Shīʿa uprising during the historical periods of the Imams was by a group known as the "martyrs of Fakhkh" in 786. This revolt against the Abbasids was led by another descendent of Imam Ḥasan, Ḥusayn ibn ʿAlī ibn Ḥasan ibn Ḥasan ibn ʿAlī. Of all martyrdom incidents caused by uprisings against the Sunni Caliphs, the martyrs of Fakhkh were particularly praised by the Shīʿa Imams, both for their righteousness and their intention to hand over power to the Imams and their endeavor to enjoin good and forbid wrong. There are even some reports from the Prophet and Jaʿfar al-Sādiq that they paid tribute to the would-be martyrs of Fakhkh when they passed by the area of Fakhkh in Mecca. It is reported that Muhammad performed his prayers in Fakhkh and then cried.

When he was asked about the reason behind his crying, Muhammad said, "[D]uring my prayers Gabriel revealed to me that one of your descendants will be killed in this place, and a martyr killed along with him would be rewarded twice a normal martyr."[97] It is also narrated that Jaʿfar al-Sādiq's successor, Imām Mūsā al-Kāẓim, while seeing the decapitated heads of the martyr (Ḥusayn ibn ʿAlī ibn Ḥasan ibn Ḥasan ibn ʿAlī) in front of the then Abbasid Caliph, al-Hādī, praised their leader as "a righteous Muslim, who continually fasted and stood in prayer, enjoined what was good and forbade what was evil."[98]

In the transition from the military martyrdom of the Muslim conquests period to the sectarian martyrdom I discussed briefly above, there are two important points worth noting before moving to martyrdom in the modern period in the following chapters. First, martyrdom in the dominant Sunni Islam gradually lost its relevance as the Muslim conquests ended.[99] Hence, unsurprisingly, Islamic martyrdom, originally understood as violently dying for God on the battlefield, was expanded in Sunni traditions to include non-violent forms of death.[100] At the same time, for the Shīʿa, as the minority sect, the violent form of martyrdom thrives not through war by non-Muslims, but mostly at the hands of Sunni authorities who started to persecute the Shīʿa in order to suppress political opposition movements (as I reviewed some of the high-profile martyrdom cases above). Hence, Shīʿīsm sometimes is called by its followers the religion of revolt and martyrdom.

The famous early Zaydi Shīʿa historian, Abū al-Faraj *Isfahānī* (897–967), in his hagiographical work, *Maqātil al-tālibiyīn*, collected stories of the life and martyrdom of some 216 martyrs among the descendants of Abū Ṭālib (father of Ali, the first Imam) until his time in the fourth Islamic century. His long list starts with Jaʿfar ibn Abī-Ṭālib, a respected companion and cousin of the Prophet who was killed in the battle of Mūʿtah in 629. However, not all of them are considered martyrs within the Twelver Shīʿa tradition, and this is due to something that differentiates the theology of martyrdom between Twelver Shīʿīsm and other Islamic traditions. As touched on before, the real difference comes from the unique understanding of the principle of the Imamate in Twelver Shīʿīsm in which absolute religious and political authority is vested in the position of the Imamate that is supposedly occupied by divinely selected individuals (twelve, to be specific). Anything that goes against or contrary to the will and tradition of the Imams is considered unlawful and wrong. Being among sensitive issues, a political revolt would require the Imam's approval in the Twelver tradition; hence, not all deaths occurring during a political uprising by the Shīʿa could be termed martyrdom. So, while in Sunnism the concept of martyrdom is most commonly associated with the concept of jihad without any particular prerequisite other than pure Godly intention, theologically speaking, in Twelver Shīʿīsm, martyrdom, as is the case with jihad, first and foremost is closely linked to the concept of Imamate and should be defined as dying in the cause of the Imams. In other words, the authority of the Imams, or those appointed by them, is essential to determine the righteous form of jihad and martyrdom. Therefore, the more an act of martyrdom conforms to the Shīʿī concept of the Imamate and the Imams' teachings the more it is praised.

As is clear from the above discussion, my second point is that Muslim conquests after the Prophet were never fully backed by the Shīʿa, who considered the Sunni Caliphs illegitimate rulers of the community. Hence, those slain in the wars waged under the authority of the Caliphs were not held in high esteem by the Shīʿa as "true martyrs." In fact, from the Shīʿa point of view, true martyrs were those who were killed while struggling in support of, or under the direct leadership of, the Prophet or his divinely guided successors, the just Imams[101] (this was well documented in the Shīʿī *ḥadīth* collections, in chapters like "Under whom is jihad permitted?"). These include martyrs when the Prophet was alive (Ḥamzah chief among them), fighting martyrs who served in the armies of ʿAlī and Ḥasan, the first and second Imams and particularly those killed along with Imam Ḥusayn in Karbalā in 680, and finally, loyal Shīʿas who died or who were killed in prison or under torture by the Sunni authorities due to their faith. In fact, the issue of obedience to the divinely guided religious authority (Imam) has such importance in Twelver Shīʿīsm that, in effect, it measures the purity of one's faith and defines the greatness of his/her martyrdom. For this very reason, Shīʿas narrate traditions from the Prophet and the Imams stating that those who died while loving and following the heirs of the Prophet (the Imams) die as true martyrs.[102] In the next section, I will review some of these Shīʿī martyrdom traditions.

Shīʿa Martyrdom Traditions

When it comes to defining martyrdom in a general way and dealing with the question of who should be counted as a martyr and what their rewards will be in the afterlife, there are no discernible differences between the Sunni and Shīʿa traditions (for the most part). Most of the *ḥadīths* discussed in the appendix are also found in Shīʿī sources. Generally speaking, different categories of martyrs, all the requirements needed for one to be counted a martyr, and any rewards associated with martyrdom, including forgiveness, the power of intercession, and sexual rewards, are also found in Shīʿī sources. Again, we read things like a "drop of blood on the way of God" is second to none in terms of merit;[103] believers who suffer from diseases die as martyrs;[104] those who defend their family and possessions die as martyrs;[105] martyrs will not be put on trial in the grave;[106] for martyrs, dying is easy and sweet, and they will meet their heavenly partners (*hūrīs*) upon martyrdom;[107] martyrs will intercede for seventy or seventy thousand of their relatives, friends, and acquaintances;[108] and so on. In *tafsīr* works, we also see a similar pattern with no discernible differences between Sunni and Shīʿa understanding of martyrdom. As is the case with Sunni sources, some Shīʿī *tafsīr* interpret the Qur'anic terms *shahīd* and *shuhadā* mainly as witnesses to people's deeds on the day of judgment, and consider *shahīd* as "martyr" a post-Qur'anic development;[109] and some other *tafsīr* on verses 3:160 and 4:69 speculated that the term *shuhadā* used there could mean martyrs, since it is contextually acceptable.[110] So, I will not repeat those common martyrdom traditions here in detail and instead will try to explain what the Shīʿa sources add to the discussion from the sectarian perspective.

Basically, when we talk about martyrdom in Shīʿīsm, we mean the sectarian understanding of martyrdom. In some traditions, the righteous among the Shīʿa are considered martyrs regardless of their way of dying simply by virtue of their acceptance of and faithful adherence to the truth, which comes from obeying the Prophet and his successors (the Imams) in every aspect of their life. Generally speaking, this is the case for all believers according to Islamic martyrdom traditions (as will be discussed in appendix, all believers would die martyrs.), but in the Shīʿī understanding of the issue, believers are exclusively meant to be from the Shīʿa community. *Al-Maḥāsin*, an important early Shīʿa work (probably written in the third Islamic century during the later period of the Imams), narrates the following *ḥadīth* from Imam Ḥusayn on the merits of being a believer (a devout Shīʿa): "There is no one from our Shīʿa except they are a righteous martyr [*shahīd*]." When he was asked how this could be the case as most of the Shīʿa believers die on their bed, the Imam replied: "Have not you recited the book of Allāh, chapter *al-Hadid,* saying that 'And those who believe in God and his messengers—it is they who are truthful and are witnesses [*shahīd*] before their Lord'?"[111] Note that, in this tradition, the term *shahīd* mentioned in the verse means "martyr" since the person who asked the question from the Imam seemed to be confused as to how, while most of the Shīʿa died peacefully on their bed, they could be counted as *shahīd* ("martyr"). Dying from diseases and misfortune is also something that can be rewarded based on faith as in some *ḥadīths* a Shīʿa suffering from poor health or natural calamities qualifies for martyrdom or even gets the rewards of up to a thousand martyrs: "There is no Shīʿa of us that gets misfortunes or diseases and is patient with that except Allāh secures rewards of one thousand martyrs."[112]

The issue of following the path of the Imams is clearly highlighted in numerous Shīʿī traditions as a major criterion for being martyr; it is usually mentioned in the forms of "staying with our issue" (*ʿalā ʿamrinā*) or "this issue" (*hādhal-ʿamr*), which refer to those among the Shīʿa who adhere to the path of the Imamate and *wilāyah* wholeheartedly and sincerely, and particularly firm believers of the promised al-Mahdī.[113] A very interesting *ḥadīth* from Imam Sādiq (with some variations) regarding the importance of the Imamate and *wilāyah* in the Shīʿī theology reads: "Whoever dies while steadfast on our issue is like someone who is under the tent of the *Qāʾim* [al-Mahdī], or even like the one who is fighting with his sword alongside al-Mahdī, or even like the one who gets martyred while serving him, or even like the one who gets martyred serving the Prophet."[114] Remaining a firm believer (in the principle of the Imamate) during the Occultation of Imam al-Mahdī is the highest challenge, according to some Shīʿī traditions; hence, such a believer would get the highest honour, the rewards of one thousand martyrs of the battles of Badr and Uḥud (which are typically considered to be the purest martyrs in Islam).[115]

Sectarian literature shows the preponderance of its followers. Similarly, martyrdom in Shīʿī sources is treated as something authentically belonging to the Shīʿa and their privilege. So, in this light, of all Muslims, only the Shīʿa are truly eligible for the title "martyr," whereas all other so-called martyrs, at best, have gone astray and wasted their lives or, at worst, are seen as enemies of the true Islam. This means that even in a fight with a sworn enemy of Islam (such as pagans of the early Islam), martyrs of the Shīʿa would be superior in ranks to those martyrs coming from other traditions as if they are the real martyrs while others are the counterfeit, or, at the very best, inferior to them. In a tradition ascribed to Imam Sajjād (the fourth Imam) cited by the early Shīʿī *tafsīr*, *Furāt al-Kūfī*, we see this kind of distinction between martyrs of different traditions: "A martyr of us [family of the Prophet] is better than ten ordinary martyrs, and a martyr from our Shīʿa is better than seven[116] martyrs from other traditions."[117] In a similar tradition attributed to the Prophet, he tells his daughter Fāṭimah seven exclusive characteristics of his family: "Our Prophet, your father, is the best of the Prophets, our successor, your husband [ʿAlī], is the best of the successors, our martyr, your uncle Ḥamzah, is the best of the martyrs, and there is someone from us who has two wings that can fly with them in heaven, and he is your cousin Jaʿfar ibn Abītālib, and the *sibṭs*[118] of this community are from us [your sons Ḥasan and Ḥusayn], and their Mahdī is one of your decedents."[119]

In Shīʿa piety, no one is comparable to the Prophet and the Imams; likewise, not even martyrs can surpass them in terms of merit and significance. Hence, according to a popular tradition, it is believed that all Imams have died as martyrs, so they hold the positions of martyr and Imam simultaneously: "[T]here is none of us but killed a martyr (by sword or poison)."[120] Moreover, the Qur'anic verses with the terms *ṣiddīqūn* ("truthful") and *shuhadā* ("witnesses") are generally considered as primarily referring to the Imams. For example, a prophetic tradition explains that in verse "those whom God has blessed, the Prophets, the truthful ones, the witnesses [martyrs], and the righteous" (Qur'an, 4:69), the truthful is ʿAlī, and the witnesses (martyrs) are Ḥasan, Ḥusayn, Ḥamzah (the Prophet's uncle), and the other Imams.[121] Hence, remembering them and performing the devotional acts of *zīyārah* (pilgrimage, which basically involves saluting the Imams and asking for intercession or even resolving mundane needs) are commonly justified by referring to verse 3:169 that reads: "[Martyrs] are alive with their Lord, well provided for."[122]

Visiting the tombs of martyrs is highly encouraged in Shīʿī sources, particularly those of the Imams, and more specifically, the shrine of Ḥusayn and other martyrs of Karbalā who are considered the martyrs par excellence that every devout Shīʿa yearns to be with, as they repeatedly recite the famous section of the *zīyārat wārith*: "How we wish we were with you so we would earn a great achievement" (*Ya laytanā kunnā maʿakum fa nafuḍa fawḍan ʿaẓimā*). According to a long tradition from the eighth Imam, ʿAlī ibn Mūsā al-Rida, reciting that phrase results in getting the rewards of those martyred with Ḥusayn. Moreover, visiting the shrine of Ḥusayn or weeping for his martyrdom would wipe out all minor and major sins. Cursing those responsible for the tragedy also would put the person in the company of the Prophet in paradise. The Imam also asked the Shīʿa to weep for Ḥusayn whenever they happen to be sad: "If you have to cry over something, then do so over Ḥusayn for surely, he was slaughtered in the manner in which a ram is slaughtered."[123] In another narration from Jaʿfar al-Sādiq, the sixth Imam, visiting the grave of the "lonely martyr" (Ḥusayn) is equivalent to performing twenty pilgrimages to Mecca.[124] There are many other *ḥadīths* on the merits of visiting the graves of the Imams while paying proper attention to their position as martyrs and righteous Imams of the community that must be obeyed. Some traditions even guarantee rewards equal to that of a thousand pilgrimages to Mecca, a thousand martyrs of Badr and Uḥud, a thousand of those fasting, and a thousand accepted *ṣadaqahs* ("voluntary charity") for pilgrims of Ḥusayn's shrine.[125]

There is no dearth of such traditions linking extraordinary rewards and consequences of commemorating Ḥusayn's martyrdom. Many of these appear to be fabricated tales attributed to the Imams by those who benefited from the expanding and lucrative business of Āshūrā since the rise of the Safavid dynasty (1501–1736), that established Twelver Shīʿism as the mainstream tradition in Persia, and particularly after the 1979 Islamic revolution in Iran. Those fabricated and exaggerated traditions may not have been composed during the first couple of Islamic centuries by Muhammad and the Imams, yet they have had a lasting impact on the way the Shīʿa community understands martyrdom and theological issues related to it.

2

Martyrdom Revival in Twelver Shīʿīsm

Diverging Paths: Martyrdom in Modern Sunnism vs. Modern Shīʿīsm

For the majority Sunni Muslims, the postconquest era, except for the Crusades and Mongol conquests periods, meant no more viable possibility for martyrdom. By contrast, being the minority sect, the Shīʿite Muslims had more exposure to martyrdom at the hands of Sunni rulers. However, after the disappearance of the twelfth Imam and the beginning of the indefinite Occultation period, Twelvers found themselves in a puzzling situation. They turned to quietism and the practice of *taqīya* that had been encouraged by the Imams during their later period. The Shīʿi jurists then generally avoided sanctioning confrontations with Sunni states. As I will discuss later, toward the modern period, an increasing number of Shīʿi jurists embraced political activism and legitimized acts of martyrdom in the service of Shīʿa-oriented governments. Similarly, martyrdom became more achievable within the Sunni part of Islam as Muslims started to confront the colonial powers since the nineteenth century. The twentieth century and the postcolonial period particularly became fertile soil for theorizing a modern take on jihad and martyrdom in both Sunni and Shīʿa worlds.

There is no clear-cut answer to the question of when Islamic civilization fell behind the Christian world. We can say that, symbolically, the power balance between Islam and the West turned in favor of the European powers starting with the Ottoman Empire's failure to capture Vienna for the second time in 1532.[1] We can also assume that the process was completed after the Peace of Westphalia in 1698 (which ended the European wars of religion) and the beginning of the colonialization of Muslim lands.[2] As for the question of how the West got past the Islamic world and became the dominating power, Jared Rubin offers a plausible explanation by highlighting different political-economy equilibrium. Rubin's argument is that, unlike the situation in Western Europe after the Reformation, the religious establishment in the Muslim lands kept the power of legitimizing rulers. That power gained them leverage at the political and economic bargaining tables and eventually caused the slowdown of economic growth in the Muslim world compared to the leading Western countries.[3] Whatever the reason behind the decline of the Islamic world in the modern period, Western imperialism and the subordination of Muslims to the rule of "infidels," due to the inability of the Ottoman Empire to maintain the political power of the Caliphate system, turned bitter to the taste of Muslim leaders and activists, particularly since for centuries memories of the early Muslim conquests had been glorified.[4] Therefore, in the early decades of the twentieth century as the Ottoman Caliphate dissolved and nationalists undermined Islamists, it was inevitable to see renewed attention to the jihad and martyrdom traditions that for long had been buried inside the vast Islamic corpus.

Heading toward the early twentieth century, the Muslim world saw several uprisings or liberation movements against Western hegemony. Those included Indian Muslims' resistance against British colonialism,[5] Algerian resistance against French forces,[6] the Mahdist movement in Sudan,[7] Egyptian revolt against British rule,[8] and the Libyan uprising against Italian colonialism.[9] That being said, the anti-colonial movements in the late ninetieth and early twentieth centuries were mostly inspired by nationalism and had less to do with full-fledged jihad and Islamic ideals. Muslim leaders often usurped the vocabulary of jihad to agitate their fellow Muslim compatriots to join them in their anti-colonial or liberating causes. Perhaps the first widely accepted modern calls for jihad happened in the case of Palestine's 1936–9 revolt where Muslim leaders used the language of jihad to get the attention of Muslims around the world against the Zionists' occupation of the so-called "holy lands" in Palestine.[10]

Despite the lack of genuine and widespread Islamic motives in early modern movements, political shifts and unrest in the Muslim world created fertile conditions for the revival of jihad and martyrdom-seeking. In Daniel Brown's words, "If medieval Muslim scholars lacked the opportunity, the necessity, or the desire for physical martyrdom, modern Muslim experience has provided all three in abundance. Western ascendancy, the colonial experience, and the political and economic dislocation that followed in their wake have led modern Muslims to reopen the questions of Jihad and martyrdom. For some Muslims, the modern experience has clearly presented both an enemy worth fighting with and a cause worth dying for."[11] In light of those changes, Sunni thinkers responded more quickly and coherently than their Shīʿa counterparts. However, since Shīʿīsm was originally born as a resistance movement and grew from the blood of its vast number of revered martyrs, most importantly Imam Husayn, it was only a matter of time before Shīʿa Islamists caught up with, if not surpassed, Sunni Islamists in theorizing and utilizing martyrdom as an effective weapon in local and regional conflicts.

The modern understanding of jihad and martyrdom and their theoretical and theological developments in Sunni Islam were largely shaped in the twentieth century after the abolition of the Ottoman Caliphate by the Turkish revolutionaries in 1924 and the backlash over the increasing influence of Western culture in the Muslim world. Even though the Caliphate system had practically become just a name without real authority over Muslim affairs in the vast Ottoman territories, the end of the Caliphate shook the Muslim world to its core. In fact, the Caliphate was still seen as a respected traditional institution and a symbol of *ummah* ("the community of believers"); hence, the abolition of the Caliphate was not seen as a positive development for traditional Muslim thinkers and activists.[12] From the political point of view, with the decline of the Caliphate, and as the Ottoman Empire gradually lost territories to the European powers, the Young Turks advocated a pan-Islamic policy to gain broader support from Muslims around the world to, consequently, "rescue simultaneously the Caliphate and the empire."[13] At the same time, some Arab nationalists advocated for the return of the Caliphate to the Arabs. The outcome of the First World War and the establishment of the Turkish National Movement sealed the fate of the Ottoman Caliphate and made the transition of the Caliphate to the Arab world unlikely. The Sharif Husayn of Mecca was the only Arab leader who could become the next Caliph, but his connection to Great Britain was a big negative point in Muslim eyes, especially among Muslims in India and Egypt.[14]

After the abolition of the Caliphate, Muslim intellectuals struggled to come up with an alternative to the institution of Caliphate so that the idea of *ummah* could continue its relevance. One common understanding was that the Caliphate system deviated from its ideal status under *al-Rāshidūn* ("the Rightly Guided Caliphs"). So, inspired by proto-Salafīs like Jamāl al-Dīn al-Afghānī (1838–97) and Muhammad Abduh (1849–1905), there were calls for the return to the Golden age of Islam (a largely ambiguous term). Among the thinkers who wrote on the issue of the Caliphate system and the future of the Muslim world, Muhammad Rashid Rida (1865–1935), a Syrian editor of the periodical *al-Manar*, was very influential. Rida saw the ethnic-based nation-state ideas in a negative lens, and the removal of the Caliph's political authority and its eventual abolition as "the beginning of a larger assault against Islam."[15] Nevertheless, because of practical reasons, lack of cooperation among regional Muslim powers, and the absence of any legitimate candidate for the Caliphate position, Rashid Rida reluctantly agreed with abolishing the Caliphate for good. In its place, he envisioned a modern concept of the Islamic state.[16]

The increasing influence of Western culture in Muslim societies and the rise of despotic local rulers following the disintegration of the Ottoman dynasty were two factors in particular that revived the discussion around jihad and martyrdom among the growing body of Salafī Islamists. Hassan al-Bannā, the founder of the Muslim Brotherhood, was among the first to present jihad as an obligatory duty for all Muslims, and warned those Muslims who abandoned jihad that they would face "humiliation and disgrace on earth and punishment in the hereafter."[17] References to martyrdom were also common in his writings. Al-Bannā's main concern was the growing influence of Western culture on social organizations and the everyday lives of Muslims. He "desired a common Muslim front in order to deal with the social problems which threaten the foundations of Islam."[18]

Later, Sayyid Qutb, the ideologue of the Muslim Brotherhood, emerged as an outspoken critic of those who only accepted defensive jihad as legitimate and argued that Islam had an aggressive global mission to submit all tyrannical and unjust systems under the rule of Islam. Qutb considered martyrdom an essential part of achieving Islam's global mission and believed Muslims should fight for the glory of Islam to the point of martyrdom.[19] His signature argument was that "Muslims had lost their way and lived in a state of moral 'ignorance' (*jahiliyya*)"; hence, they had to return to the jihadi mindset and free Muslim societies from the yoke of Western materialism.[20] Similarly, Abul Aʿla Mawdudi envisioned the creation of an Islamic state according to Islamic principles. Mawdudi's attraction to jihad came from his desire for a global revolution to "fight against the evil forces of the world . . . in order that evil and contumacy should be wiped out and God's law should be enforced in the World."[21] He argued that distinguishing between defensive or offensive jihads was nonsense; in Mawdudi's words, "these terms are relevant only in the context of wars between nations and countries."[22] According to Mawdudi, "Islamic Jihad is both offensive and defensive at one and the same time. It is offensive because the Muslim Party assaults the rule of an opposing ideology and it is defensive because the Muslim Party is constrained to capture state power in order to arrest the principles of Islam in space-time forces."[23]

Another influential figure in the radicalization of Sunni Islam was 'Abd al-Salām Faraj (1954–82), who participated in the 1982 assassination of Egypt's

Anwar Sadat for signing a peace treaty with Israel. He is often cited as a pioneer militant Islamist who glorified jihad and martyrdom in the contemporary Sunni world. His obsession with jihad was to the point that he released a tract on the subject with the attention-grabbing title, *al-Farīḍa al-ghāʾiba* ("[jihad,] the forgotten duty"). Faraj was outspoken in his criticism of the Al-Azhar's largely conservative and traditionally trained "*ulamā*", accusing them of intentionally neglecting jihad. In his argument for the necessity of jihad, he mainly focused on the Qur'an's so-called sword verses (9:5 and 2:216) and considered several other verses that call for "conciliation and forbearance with one's adversaries" to be abrogated by them. For Faraj, the priority of Islamists should be the fight against the so-called "near enemy," that is corrupted Muslim governments. However, the shift toward fighting the "far enemy" (particularly the U.S. and the Soviet Union), that caught the attention of Western media and politicians, was a later development among Sunni jihadists and it was fully implemented by Al-Qaida in the 1990s.

In summary, while the first half of the twentieth century and its prolific Islamists created the ground for theorizing jihad and Islamic activism, the second half actually saw those ideas being implemented and giving rise to a radically violent understanding of jihad and martyrdom among Sunni Salafīs. The post-Second World War period, the beginning of the Cold War, and the rise of pan-Arabism created volatile conditions in the Middle East. In addition, the creation of the state of Israel in 1948, and later the humiliating defeats of the Arab states in the 1967 and 1973 Arab-Israeli wars and the failure of the project of Arab nationalism, helped radicalize Sunni Islamists. But, for both Sunni and Shīʿa worlds, 1979 in particular was a turning point in how ideas on jihad and martyrdom became widespread. The two factors that brought that change were Iran's Islamic revolution that was followed by eight years of devastating war with Iraq, and the Soviet Union's invasion of Afghanistan that started more than a decade-long vicious civil war and created political mayhem in the country. An indirect consequence of those conflicts was the U.S. military adventure in the Middle East in the 1990s that further caused the emergence of radical ideas on Islamic jihad and martyrdom, especially among Sunni Salafīs. I will closely examine the case of Iran and its war with Iraq in the following sections. Here I review some points on the Afghanistan crisis as a catalyst that facilitated the rise of global jihad.

The Soviet Union's invasion of Afghanistan that started in December 1979 was in support of the then newly founded communist government of the People's Democratic Party of Afghanistan (PDPA) that was struggling with both internal rivalries and Muslim anti-government armed groups. While it was meant to be a short operation, the Soviet army found itself drowned in a decade-long war of attrition against a coalition of diverse factions of Afghan fighters that became known as the Mujahideen, and who received financial and military training primarily from the U.S., the U.K., Pakistan, Iran, Saudi Arabia, and China. Basically, the Soviet-Afghan war became a defining episode of the Cold War era that eventually triggered the dissolution of the Soviet Union in 1991. The Soviet Union's invasion of Afghanistan also became a highly sensitive issue for Muslims around the world. It was seen as an invasion of Muslim lands by unbelievers (*kuffar*), a classic cause for waging jihad. By the mid-1980s, Afghanistan had become the destination for Muslim foreign fighters who wanted to join the Afghan Mujahideen in their jihad against the Soviets. Coming mostly from the Gulf region and North Africa, it was estimated that the community of Afghan Arabs reached around 7,000 fighters by 1992.[24] The Afghan war then brought together ingredients that put jihadi Salafī groups at the forefront of world politics in the following decades. When the war ended, it left the veteran foreign fighters, many of them uprooted from the politics and culture of their home countries, motivated to take on another global mission to fulfill their jihadi tendencies and confront the Western powers, particularly the United States. So, while the phenomenon of Muslim foreign fighters was not particularly a point of concern for Western intelligence services in the 1980s, it turned out to be a very sensitive security issue and a shared problem for Western countries involved with Muslim politics.[25]

A key inspirational figure responsible for reviving jihad and martyrdom in the Sunni world was Dr. Abdullah Azzam (1941–89). Azzam's importance and his wide sphere of influence came from the fact that he was a complete package: a Palestinian/Jordanian cleric, an al-Azhar alumnus, a prolific writer and public speaker, a Muslim Brotherhood veteran, and a Salafī Muslim at heart.[26] To understand the inevitable contemporary developments in the concept of martyrdom and Sunni jihadi movements, we have to examine Azzam's ideas and involvement in jihad activities; hence, I will go into some detail on Azzam's life. Abdullah Azzam's jihadi mission was shaped by his Muslim Brotherhood roots, his fascination with Sayyid Qutb's radical ideas, the Israeli occupation of Palestine (particularly since the Six Day War of 1967), and his disillusion with the secular nature of the leftist Palestine Liberation Organization, as well as the failure of the Arab states in their support of the Palestinian cause and their enmity with Islamists.[27] His many writings and international lectures were instrumental in attracting young Arab Muslims to the Palestinian cause and jihad in Afghanistan. More explicitly and unapologetically than any other Muslim scholar or Islamist before him, Azzam advocated for military jihad. He even issued a fatwa making jihad in Afghanistan an individual duty for Muslims worldwide, paving the way for the contemporary global jihadi movements.[28]

Following the Six-Day War, Azzam left Palestine and for some years lived in Jordan, Egypt, and Saudi Arabia before moving to Pakistan in the early 1980s to participate in the Afghan conflict. His mission was to unify diverse Afghan factions in their fight against the Soviets. In 1984, Azzam founded Services Bureau in Peshawar to facilitate Arab fighters joining the Afghan jihad. The Services Bureau also produced and distributed internationally *al-Jihad*, a periodical that resulted in a dramatic increase in the number of Afghan Arab volunteers. Many of them later joined various Islamist groups, embraced life in jihad, and participated in other conflicts in Bosnia, Algeria, Chechnya, Iraq, and Syria.[29] Most importantly, Azzam was the one who persuaded Osama Bin-Laden to devote his time to the jihad cause in Afghanistan and recruited him as the main financier of the Services Bureau. Bin-Laden's wealth and connections in Saudi Arabia helped Azzam bring more Arab volunteers to Peshawar. Bin-Laden was tasked with setting up training camps for the Arab volunteers. Still, later he distanced himself from the Services Bureau and built a more serious military training camp called *al-Ma'sada* in late 1986 that became the foundation of Al-Qaida (founded in 1988).

Azzam then truly can be called the father of modern global jihad, though, as Meir Hatina has observed, he was only preoccupied with Afghanistan and Palestine and wanted to "create a strong base for Islam, rather than a sweeping global jihad."[30] Nevertheless, Azzam facilitated the beginning of a global and uncontrollable trend in jihad by writing about the theology and ideology of jihad in Islam, and establishing an organization for the logistics of recruiting volunteer fighters from the Arab world. The foreign fighters who went to Afghanistan got accustomed to their life under jihad and ideologically became stateless; hence, after the end of jihad in Afghanistan, they were ready to participate in other conflicts or join Al-Qaida in its global war against the U.S. and other Western powers involved in Muslim affairs in the Middle East. However, what Azzam started was not in a vacuum. By early 1980, pan-Islamism was fast becoming a popular trend in Arab countries as pan-Arabism failed to connect with deeply religious Arab Muslims. In addition, by the 1980s, the Muslim Brotherhood had expanded its international organization and created a global network of Islamists to get involved in Muslim politics.[31] In that fertile environment, using his solid religious credentials and connections among

Islamists, Azzam acted as a catalyst in escalating the global jihadi movement in the Middle East.

Azzam was also instrumental in reviving the lure of martyrdom among Sunni Islamists and Salafī fighters. He glorified memories of martyred Mujahideen in Afghanistan by dramatizing and retelling miraculous stories about martyrs from before and after their martyrdom. The way he treated martyrdom in terms of miracles associated with martyrs, although it had parallels in Shīʿism and Sufism, was almost unprecedented in the mainstream Sunni world; though, in his depiction of martyrdom, Azzam was careful not to be accused by hardline Sunni Salafīs of being influenced by either of those traditions.[32] In *Signs of the Merciful*, Azzam's bestselling book published in 1983, he focused on elaborating the eyewitness accounts of miracles experienced by Mujahideen on the battlefield. He also wrote stories of martyrs' miracles, including "their blood smelling of musk, their bodies not decomposing at all, and rays of light emanating from their graves."[33] The Muslim Arab audience generally found those stories about miracles in jihad and the tales of martyrs interesting to read. As Thomas Hegghammer noted, *Signs of the Merciful* "was the single most influential book in terms of inspiring Arabs to go to Afghanistan in the 1980s."[34] In his later writings, Azzam started writing hagiographies of martyrs (mostly Afghan Arabs) and published them regularly in his *al-Jihad* magazine. The hagiographies were full of references to miracles of martyrs.[35] In November 1989, Azzam himself was assassinated in a highly sophisticated car-bomb plan. He turned into one of the jihadi movement's greatest martyrs, and soon people retold stories about miracles that appeared following his martyrdom, such as the strong smell of musk coming out of his body.[36]

One important consequence of Abdullah Azzam's call for jihad and martyrdom came from his fatwa issued in 1984 that the Afghan jihad was an individual obligation that did not need state, parental, or any other authority's permission. Azzam concluded the text of his fatwa with a rhetorical question: "Have you heard, Muslims, If the [duty of] jihad is individual, the father does not [give] permission to the child, nor the husband to the wife, nor the master to the slave nor the creditor to the debtor?"[37] Not only was this the first explicit fatwa in the modern era that asked foreign fighters to join the jihad, ironically, it also caused the fragmentation of authority within the Sunni Salafīs. In fact, by declaring jihad an individual obligation, Azzam discredited any sort of authority that prevented Muslims from joining jihad.[38] Making individual Muslims solely responsible for their decision on joining jihadi activities, in effect turned the Sunni religious establishment, such as al-Azhar which had already lost most of its influence among radical Islamists, totally irrelevant in the eyes of action-minded young Muslims who joined the Afghan jihad and the subsequent conflicts in the Muslim world. In addition, Azzam did not envision any controlling structure for overseeing the actions of foreign volunteer fighters, so they remained free agents who could turn radical and step in any direction.[39] Azzam himself soon faced the consequences. As the number of foreign fighters dramatically increased, he found himself with diminishing authority and influence to control all volunteer Afghan Arabs and prevent them from joining extremist groups or exercising excessive violence. This was also the case with his fruitful relationship with Bin Laden. Azzam persuaded Bin-Laden in the first place to commit full-time and wholeheartedly to the Afghan jihad. However, Bin-Laden eventually broke away from the Azzam's Services Bureau to found Al-Qaida and train action-minded Arab fighters who were ready to go to extreme lengths in their jihadi aspirations.

The Afghan and foreign fighters found themselves with increased confidence and pride as they succeeded in pushing the invincible Soviet Army out of Afghanistan, a feat that was completed in February 1989. For them, it was a huge accomplishment considering that the Red Army's withdrawal from Afghanistan eventually contributed to the breakdown of the Soviet Union.[40] With the Soviets gone, Muslim fighters finished their mission by defeating Kabul's communist government in 1992; the honeymoon, though, was short-lived. Immediately after the resignation of the communist government in March 1992, a vicious civil war broke out between different Afghan Mujahideen factions that ended up with the Taliban taking over most of the country from 1996 until the U.S. invasion of Afghanistan in 2001. However, the mayhem followed by the civil war and later the Taliban's rule created opportunities for Al-Qaida to expand its training camps and develop and execute radical martyrdom operations on a global scale.

Azzam's role in the rise of global jihad among contemporary Salafīs then cannot be overemphasized. He was also the last among the high-ranking traditionally trained "*ulamā*" who were directly involved and highly influential in jihadi circles. So, Azzam's dramatic martyrdom in November 1989 left the jihadi movement on its own without a universally respected scholar of his caliber. To a large extent, Azzam was the father figure and moderate face of the jihadi movement in the Sunni world who tried, but ultimately failed, to unify various factions among Muslim fighters in Afghanistan; certainly his assassination, an event that has remained a mystery, did not help. It is hard to imagine how jihadi groups would look like today had he survived, but the fact is that, since his death, Salafī jihadists have become more radical, more sectarian, and have exercised unjustifiable violence toward civilians and their enemies.

Jihad, Martyrdom, and State-Building

There is no doubt that the Soviet invasion of Afghanistan profoundly shaped the future of the Middle East and Central Asia. The Afghan war created a perfect cause for jihad. Thanks to the efforts of the charismatic Abdullah Azzam and his associates at the Services Bureau, the culture of jihad and martyrdom rapidly spread through the region. The Afghanistan experience perhaps had the same effect on the rise of martyrdom-seeking in the Sunni world as Iran's 1979 Islamic revolution and the eight-year war with Iraq did on martyrdom in Shīʿīsm. However, they had different characteristics and went in their own directions. The main point of difference came from the location of authority. The supreme religious and political authorities have come together in the case of the contemporary Twelver Shīʿīsm. After the revolution, Iran was turned into a strong state with a central and powerful religious authority that, for the most part, has represented the Shīʿa in the Muslim world and orchestrated Shīʿī movements in the region through its proxies in Lebanon, Iraq, and Syria. Iran's religious leaders have created a unifying and popular brand of Shīʿīsm that emanates a particular understanding of jihad and martyrdom that, while rich in Shīʿī symbols and myths, serves the religious and political agenda of the country's Supreme Leader. The same situation is nowhere to be found in the Sunni world.

Within the Sunni sphere, despite the wishes and efforts of Abdullah Azzam and other Islamists before and after him, the Sunni world has never had a legitimate Islamic state representing the majority of Sunnis worldwide, as is the case with the position of Iran for the Shīʿas. Claims of righteousness and leadership have been a matter of dispute in the Sunni world. Not even the influential Wahhabi "*ulamā*" in Saudi Arabia, with ties to political power far more than any other Sunni country,[41] have been able to exert religious authority over the rest of the Muslim world in the same way that Iran's Supreme leader appears on the eyes of the Shīʿa worldwide. The Saudi kingdom also assumed the title of *Khadim al Haramain al-Sharifain* ("Custodian of the Two Holy Mosques"), particularly after Iran's Islamic revolution, aimed at drawing attention to the "religious dimension" of the kingdom and posing itself as the center and leader of the Muslim world.[42] In practice, though, that grandiloquent title has not brought home the respect and authority that the monarch might have wished for. In fact, since al-Qaida emerged, jihadi-Salafī movements have been developed and influenced by Wahhabi ideology, which originated from and has been aggressively promoted by Saudi Arabia. However, the Saudi kingdom and contemporary jihadi movements have been at odds over competing claims of true Islam's guardian.[43] In fact, the relationship between jihadi-Salafī groups and the ruling family of Saudi Arabia has gone from sore to bitter enmity. While al-Qaida has been critical of the Saudi state, the Islamic State went a few steps further and openly declared war against the Saudi kingdom as its most important enemy by calling it the "head of the snake."[44] The Saudi state has even found itself under pressure from part of the Saudi "*ulamā*". Their issues with the state have ranged from their objection to Saudi support of the U.S. troops' presence in the country to their accusation of the state distancing itself from jihadi-Salafī ideals.[45] The point here is that the distrust and sometimes enmity between the Saudi kingdom, as the strongest Sunni state, and jihadi-Salafī groups highlights the complex situation in the Sunni world that prevents unifying ideas on jihad and martyrdom emerging from a leading Sunni state.

The problem of authority in the Sunni world, compared to the situation among the Shīʿa, partly stems from the fact that Sunnis formed the absolute majority of Muslims worldwide: 87–90 percent are Sunni Muslims whereas only 10–13 percent are Shīʿa Muslims.[46] Moreover, while the majority of Shīʿa Muslims live in just four countries (Iran, Pakistan, India, and Iraq), Sunnis are spread throughout the world with diverse cultural and religious orientations that cannot be unified under a single state/religious authority. That being said, neither is Twelver Shīʿīsm a monolithic tradition nor does Iran's Supreme Leader have influence and authority over all Shīʿa Muslims worldwide. Still, as a powerful and the only Shīʿa state, Iran acts and is seen as the leader and the guide for the Shīʿa. That means ideologies of jihad and martyrdom in contemporary Shīʿīsm have been shaped by the Islamic Republic in a top-down fashion. That is to say, the clerical establishment, as the so-called representative of the hidden twelfth Imam, has had the prerogative power to drive those ideas forward.

The mostly conservative nature of traditional Sunnism has also contributed to the fragmentation of authority within the Sunni world. Sunni high-ranking "*ulamā*", with the notable exception of the fourteenth-century Ibn Taymiyyah and his followers, generally accepted the legitimacy of Muslim governments unless the ruler acted openly against Islamic rules. That position put the traditional Sunni establishment at odd with action-minded and idealist Islamists. The decentralized and fragmented authority in Sunni Islam has profoundly affected how ideas develop among Sunnis. The inability of the traditional and conservative Sunni religious establishment in regulating the contemporary Sunni Islamist circles and jihadi movements has turned ideas on jihad and martyrdom more radical, diverse, and uncontrolled than is seen in the Shīʿa world. In the past several decades, a number of groups with competing ideologies and political agendas emerged among Sunni Islamists, from Tablighi Jamaat to the Muslim Brotherhood and its factions to various Salafī movements and extremist groups like al-Qaida, the Taliban, and ISIS. Few of them have had roots in or the support of al-Azhar or other Sunni religious establishments and their traditionally trained high-ranking "*ulamā*".[47]

As for Twelver Shīʿīsm, unlike their counterparts in the Sunni world, Islamists have arisen from or have deep ties with religious seminaries that have been at the center of resistance against secular governments during the last couple of centuries in Iran and Iraq. There are two widely different interpretations regarding the Occultation and the position of the Shīʿa. We can distinguish them broadly by apolitical and political orientations. The apolitical section of the Shīʿī "*ulamā*" and their followers keep themselves aloof from politics and political activism as they consider it a dirty space that should be avoided in the absence of the infallible Imams. The rationale behind their apolitical stance is that they do not consider anyone, including the most learned of the community, to have the absolute authority of the Imams who supposedly guide human beings in their "external" lives and "acts" as well as their "spiritual" lives.[48] Of course, there is a broad spectrum of apolitical traditionalists that have various degrees of attitude toward political activism. But, overall, apolitical traditionalists cast a shadow of illegitimacy over all governments during the Occultation of al-Mahdī. The point with contemporary Twelver Shīʿīsm that makes it more homogeneous and less conservative, compared to modern Sunnism when it comes to ideas on jihad and martyrdom, is that the majority of politically active groups, whether in Iran, Iraq, Lebanon, or other places in the region, act under the influence of the religious leaders of the Islamic Republic. While the quietist approach was the norm for centuries following the disappearance of the twelfth Imam, since the start of the Islamic revolution in the mid twentieth century, the political body of the Shīʿa jurists who decisively prevailed in the religious seminaries has shaped the political life of the majority of the Shīʿa.

Unlike the apolitical Shīʿa, the politically conscious Shīʿī Islamists, as was the case with Ayatollah Ruhollah Khomeini who led the Islamic revolution, tend to go as far as radically changing the entire society and state by adapting them to the ideal of Shīʿīsm, that is a society being guided and governed by the pious and the learned of the community. To this end, the dominant idea has been

Khomeini's theory of *wilāyat-i faqīh*, that is, to approve the same absolute religious and political authority of the Prophet and the Imams in the administration of Islamic government for the qualified ruling jurist. It is basically a transitional plan aimed to prepare the ground for the return of the twelfth Imam to lead his world revolution. Therefore, the acquisition of political power for their religious purpose is a core part of their theology, and so are the ideas of jihad and martyrdom to that end. All this highlights the earlier point that, unlike the status quo among the Sunni Islamists, Twelver Shīʿī Islamists are more or less tied to Iran's office of the *wilāyat-i faqīh*, currently held by Ayatollah ʿAlī Khamenei. Therefore, it is fair to say that, when it comes to the practices of jihad and seeking martyrdom, Sunni jihadists are fragmented, each group or individual acting as a free agent driven by their sense of individual duty toward fighting in the path of God and dying on that path as a martyr; in that way, they are only loyal to their group's leader (*amīr*) without following universally accepted doctrines and ideologies that can tie them organically to other groups. On the other hand, Twelver Shīʿī Islamists are authority-oriented, as the culture of emulating the authority of the Imams and high-ranking "*ulamā*" (the Imams' general deputies) lie at the heart of their tradition. As stated above, they are not acting in their own isolated bubble; most follow one general line of ideology coming from the position of *wilāyat-i faqīh*. However, there are still some factions that act independently and often in defiance of the Islamic Republic, like the Iraqi cleric Moqtada al-Sadr who has his own political agenda, or even Ayatollah ʿAlī Sistani who is now the highest-ranking Shīʿa jurist (with a vast body of followers) who cannot be forced to follow the lead from Iran's Khamenei.[49]

There is also another point of difference between the culture of jihad and martyrdom among Sunni and Shīʿī Islamists, and it comes from having role models and the expression of emotion toward them. There is no shortage of universally revered martyrs in the Twelver Shīʿī tradition, thanks to their long history of being a minority sect. That gives the Shīʿī believers a strong sense of togetherness and belonging to a unified community in debt to the blood of their great martyrs, above all Imam Ḥusayn (the master of all martyrs). Additionally, the public display of emotion in mourning martyrs has been a norm among the Shīʿa Muslims, and it is doctrinally recommended when it comes to the commemoration of the martyrdom of Imam Ḥusayn and the rest of the family of the Prophet. This is in direct contrast to how Sunni Islamists (most being Wahhabi or Salafis) act and commemorate their respective martyrs, given that weeping, extreme kinds of public mourning like self-flagellation, praying at gravesites of martyrs, venerating them and asking them for intercession are not sanctioned in the Wahhabi doctrine. Those acts are considered wrong forms of innovation due to their association with the concept of *shirk* (idolatry). So, while generally Shīʿī fighters do not hesitate to cry and show sadness for their fellow martyrs, as part of the ritual of commemorating them, most Sunni jihadi groups avoid displaying public emotions for their fellow martyrs and see that as a sign of weakness.[50] However, Abdullah Azzam's well-received publications of martyrologies and stories of miracles of martyrs made Sunni jihadists more receptive to the emotional side of martyrdom.[51]

Bearing in mind the things discussed above, we can simplify the development of martyrdom in modern Shīʿīsm in relation to that of modern Sunnism. From its beginning, martyrdom was developed to be the backbone of the Shīʿī tradition, thanks to its status as a minority sect for much of its history. While it is doctrinally different from Sufism, the tradition has grown to share some mystical and esoteric aspects of Sufism associated with the concept of *wilāyah*, at least in their core understanding of it.[52] The difference in the case of Twelver Shīʿīsm is that the *wilāyah* functions exclusively through the Prophet and after him through the chain of the twelve Imams. The Imams are considered to be the reason the world was created and without them "the universe would crumble, since [they are] the Proof, the Manifestation, and the Organ of God, and [they are] the Means by which human beings can attain, if not knowledge of God, at least what is knowable in God."[53] So, according to the belief system of Twelver Shīʿīsm, Islam is a meaningless set of rituals without the *wilāyah* of the Imams and at the same time *barāʾah* ("dissociation") from their enemies.[54] With this in mind, we can understand the importance of martyrdom in the path of restoring the rights of the Imams and defeating their enemies, and the commemoration of Imam Husayn's martyrdom in particular, in the eyes of pious Shīʿa believers. In other words, martyrdom in Twelver Shīʿīsm became the proof of one's adherence to the so-called principles of *wilāyah* and *barāʾah*. However, as the Occultation of the last Imam occurred and Twelver Shīʿī tradition went into the period of soul-searching to figure out what to do in the absence of the Imam, the once de facto religion of martyrdom was turned into a relative quietist tradition until the early modern era.

On the other side of the spectrum, particularly following the end of the Muslim conquests and the Crusades, martyrdom-seeking lost its relevance for Sunnis. However, the revival of martyrdom in the Sunni world appeared earlier than its revival among the Shīʿa. I can come up with a couple of reasons here. First, colonialism affected the Sunni-populated regions of the Islamic world earlier and more directly, resulting in several Sunni liberation political movements. Second, the collapse of the Ottoman Caliphate left Sunnis and their thinkers and leaders with an identity crisis. Consequently, Sunni Islamists started revising their ideas on jihad and martyrdom to respond to the rapidly changing political landscape and the rise of secular nationalism in the former Ottoman territories and colonies. While the Muslim Brotherhood, as a major post-Caliphate social and political movement, was founded in 1928, it took some twenty years before a Shīʿī version of the Brotherhood called *Fadāʾiyān-i Islam* ("Devotees of Islam") appeared in Iran. *Fadāʾiyān-i Islam* was founded by Navvab Safavi (1924–56), a charismatic young cleric, on a much smaller scale than the Muslim Brotherhood. Even then, they did not have a credible ideologue and thinker of the caliber of the likes of Sayyid Qutb, Hassan al-Bannā, Rashid Rida, or Abul Aʿla Mawdudi. Not surprisingly, *Fadāʾiyān-i Islam* and later Iranian revolutionaries translated the writings of Sayyid Qutb into Farsi. The influence of early-twentieth-century Sunni thinkers and Islamists on the development of Iran's Shīʿī thought could also be seen in Ayatollah Khomeini's views on Islamic government. While in exile in Iraq, he gave a series of lectures in the 1970s that later were turned into a book called "Islamic Government: Governance of the Jurist" (*Hukūmat-i islāmī: wilāyt-i faqīh*) and became the basis for the Islamic Republic. As Hamid Enayat has observed, Khomeini's thought on modern Islamic government had striking similarities with the views of Rashid Rida that were published decades earlier:

> [I]n both, the *"ulamā"* have prime responsibility for leading the popular struggle for establishing the new state; *ijtihād* is the main intellectual means of upholding and reviving the *Sharīʿah*; the head of state is distinguished more by his jurisprudential and exegetical competence than his political skills; sectarianism is discarded in favour of an irenic, "unitarian" Islam just as nationalism is deprecated in the name of universalism; and perhaps most important of all, resisting the cultural offensive of the West is the implied objective of any political, educational and legal reforms. The only significant difference between the two is that while the Sunni scheme has an air of finality about it, the Shīʿī model is, even if tacitly, temporary, since it is not consciously aimed to supersede the doctrine of the Return of the Imam.[55]

Nevertheless, as it follows, the modern Shīʿī discourse of jihad and martyrdom found its own distinctive form through the works and writings of Iranian thinkers likes ʿAlī Shariati, Ayatollah Murteza Muṭahharī, and Ayatollah Maḥmūd Ṭāleqānī, who were the prominent ideologues of the 1979 Islamic revolution.

They presented the modern interpretation of martyrdom through rediscovering and reimagining the story of Āshūrā and the martyrdom of Imam Ḥusayn. As the political landscape drastically changed in the Middle East with Iran's revolution, the rise of the only Shīʿī state with a messianic orientation in the Muslim world and the devastating eight-year war between Iran and Iraq that produced numerous martyrs redefined the discourse of martyrdom in the Muslim world with a Shīʿī flavor. Iran's Islamic revolution was the first of its kind in the Muslim world that successfully toppled a strong and secular regime and established an independent Islamic government. The Sunni Islamists of the time, then, at least briefly, turned to Iran as an inspiration before the sectarian differences resurfaced. The Islamic Republic's focus on developing a culture of martyrdom-seeking among its population, as well as its regional ambitions to export Islamic revolution, along with the rise of the Iran-backed Hezbollah in Lebanon in the early 1980s and its usage of suicide-bombing attacks as a strategic weapon to force the foreign troops out of the country, set a new model for Islamists to follow. Therefore, in part, the contemporary Shīʿī discourse of jihad and martyrdom can be credited for the rise of martyrdom-seeking among Sunnis during the Afghan war and the advent of suicide bombing (martyrdom operations) in the Sunni jihadi groups of the late 1980s and early 1990s, especially Hamas and al-Qaida. I will now focus on the development of martyrdom in Twelver Shīʿīsm since early modern Iran and will go into detail to discuss the recent sectarian dynamics in the Middle East that brought to light a messianic understanding of martyrdom in the Iranian brand of Shīʿīsm.

Changing the Gears: Reviving Martyrdom Among the Shīʿa

Historically speaking, the early Shīʿī struggle to secure political power for the Imams or other members of the Prophet's family subsided after a series of setbacks (most notably the tragedy of Karbalā). As a result, the would-be-called Twelver Shīʿīsm had turned into quietism by the time the eleventh Imam (Ḥasan al-ʿAskarī) died/was martyred at a young age (28) in 874. The lack of an apparent heir to the eleventh Imam, or as the followers of the Imam understood it, the Occultation of the twelfth Imam (al-Mahdī), forced the Shīʿa into a long and everlasting phase of passive waiting for the return of the Imam at the end of time. Hence, most of the post-Occultation Shīʿī authorities ruled out the lawfulness of fighting and political activism in favor of the *taqīya* practice ("dissimulation") in the absence of an infallible Imam. *Taqīya,* particularly as envisioned by the sixth Imam, in its original meaning was understood as "keeping or safeguarding of the secrets of the Imams' teaching."[56] That also meant that, when the time was not ready (before the rise of al-Mahdī), any sort of uprising against the Sunni governments would be problematic and against the will of the Imams because it would endanger the Shīʿa community. Therefore, actively seeking martyrdom was not encouraged by the Imams in the later period of their presence.[57] In a tradition narrated from Imam Jaʿfar al-Sādiq in the introduction of *al-Ṣaḥīfat al-Sajjādīyya* (the collection of some prayers which were composed by ʿAlī ibn-Ḥusayn, the fourth Imam), it is even stated that "before the rise of our al-*Qā'im* [Imam al-Mahdī] not one of us folk of the house [*Ahlul-Bayt*] has revolted or will revolt to repel an injustice or to raise up a right, without affliction uprooting him and without his uprising increasing the adversity on us and our partisans."[58] The renowned seventeenth-century Twelver Shīʿa scholar, Al-Ḥurr al- al-ʿĀmilī, in his influential *ḥadīth* collection, *Wasā'il al-Shīʿa*, has a chapter titled "The ruling of uprising with the sword before the return of al-Qā'im," and collected *ḥadīths* that prohibit political activism without the consent of the Imam or during the Occultation. He cites a *ḥadīth* from Imam al-Sādiq warning the Shīʿa that "any raising of the flag before the appearance of *al-Qā'im* would be the flag of evil."[59] This kind of apolitical stance, until fairly recently, has more or less been the consensus among the Shīʿa scholars. Hence, for the most part, the traditional Shīʿī martyrdom (that is, dying for the cause of the Imams in an uprising against the Sunni Caliphate system) subsided; or at least one would argue that active martyrdom was not recommended and sanctioned by the Shīʿa scholars. So, as reviewed in the previous chapter, in *ḥadīth* collections written after the Occultation, more and more traditions appeared emphasizing the waiting for the return of the Imam being more precious than martyrdom in the path of God.

The lack of legitimate Shīʿī fighting martyrs in the later period of the Imams and during the first centuries of the Occultation did not mean the Shīʿa had no more martyrs to remember and revere. In fact, passive martyrs who did not take arms in a sectarian cause shined in that period; most notably among them several Shīʿī scholars ("*ulamā*") who lost their lives for spreading Shīʿite beliefs. Some of those scholars later became known and remembered mainly with the title of "martyr": "the first martyr" (*Shahīd al-awwal*), Muhammad Jamāluddīn al-Makkī al-ʿĀmilī, m. 1385; "the second martyr" (*Shahīd al-thānī)*, Zayn al-Dīn al-Juba'i al-ʿĀmilī, m. 1558; and "the third martyr" (*Shahīd al-thālith),* Qazi Nūrullah Shūshtarī, m. 1610. ʿAbdul Ḥusayn Amīnī, a great twentieth-century traditionalist Shīʿa scholar, best known for his magnum opus *al-Ghadīr fī al-kitāb wa al-sunna wa al-adab*,[60] wrote a book on the hagiographies of martyred Shīʿa scholars from the fourth to the fourteenth Islamic centuries. The book is called '*Shuhadāʾ al-faḍīlah*' ("Martyrs of virtue") and includes the martyrologues of 130 scholar-martyrs. In the biographies of the scholar-martyrs, Amīnī depicted them as passive martyrs in the sense that they were allegedly wrongfully killed merely because of their faith and status as "Shīʿa scholars" or because of their proselytizing activities or their efforts to disseminate the Shīʿa beliefs. In the preface, Amīnī described the work as a "history of the martyrs among our great scholars who sacrificed everything in the way of religious truths."[61] He borrowed the phrase "[those] who sacrificed everything" (*alladhīna badhalū mahajahum*) from the end of *zīyārat ʿāshūrā* where the reciter repeats the phrase while in *sujūd* ("prostration"):

> O' Allāh! To you belongs the praise, the praise of those who are thankful to you for their tribulations. All praise belongs to Allāh for my intense grief. O' Allāh, grant me the blessing of the intercession of Ḥusayn on the day of appearance (before you) and strengthen me with a truthful stand in your presence along with Ḥusayn and the companions of Ḥusayn—those people who sacrificed everything for Ḥusayn, peace be upon him.[62]

In the *Zīyārah*, the martyrdom of the companions of Ḥusayn is defined as sacrifice for Ḥusayn (that is, the Imam of the time), which is purely a Shīʿī understanding of martyrdom. In Amīnī's understanding, those martyred scholars did the same by sacrificing everything in the way of religious truth (that is, the Imamate and *wilāyah* of the twelve supposedly *infallible* Shīʿa leaders). Since in Islamic *ḥadīth* collections the merit of a religious scholar is considered more than that of the blood of martyrs,[63] the scholar-martyrs are usually held in high esteem, second only to the martyrs of the Prophet's family.[64]

Although prior to the modern period, most Shīʿa scholars took the *taqīya* practice seriously during the absence of the Imam, political realities made them come up with a way to legitimize the use of violence, if needed, without violating the quietist posture. Hence, prominent Shīʿī jurists of the early Occultation period, such as Abū Jaʿfar al-Ṭūsī (995–1067), known as *Shaykh al-ṭāʾifah*, the father of jurisprudence and founder of the Shīʿa seminary of Najaf, ruled for the legitimacy of *defensive jihad* in the absence of the Imam to protect the Shīʿa faith.[65] There were many conflicts between Shīʿa and Sunnis that turned into violent confrontations and sometimes resulted in scores of casualties from both sides. Those tensions occurred particularly when the Shīʿa managed to establish their own states (Buyid, 934–1062, and Safavid, 1501–1736), or with the rise of a hardline Sunni state like the Seljuq Empire, 1037–1194.[66]

The Buyid rulers initiated public Āshūrā mourning rituals for the first time in Islamic history. Ibn al-Athīr tells us that on the day of Āshūrā in 963, Muʿizz al-Dīn, a Buyid ruler, ordered Baghdad's marketplace to be closed. He asked men and women to go to the public places in mourning and to avoid drinking water during the day to honor the sufferings of Imam Ḥusayn and his martyred family and followers.[67] With the rise of the Seljuqs, Āshūrā public processions and mourning were banned again (before gaining much more attention and publicity during the Twelver Shīʿī Safavid dynasty). In that period, the ban on Āshūrā rituals and pilgrimage to Karbalā resulted in sporadic violent clashes between devout Shīʿī mourners and Sunnis. For instance, it is reported that in 1049, a Sunni–Shīʿī deadly clash occurred in Baghdad at the beginning of the Seljuq period.[68] A year later, a group of the Seljuq-backed Sunnis attacked the Shīʿī section of Baghdad (*al-Karkh*), burned the area and killed some of the Shīʿa.[69] There were several more reported incidents of such sectarian violence in the medieval period.[70]

Starting from the sixteenth century, the Muslim world was divided into two powerful opposing camps: the Shīʿī Safavid dynasty and the Sunni Ottoman Empire. This division resulted in a series of regional wars and conflicts between the states for almost a century. Soon after the rise of the Safavids in Iran (1501), a significant Shīʿī and pro-Safavid rebellion occurred in the Ottoman Empire territories by the Turcoman tribes of the Taurus mountains in 1511, which resulted in the persecution of pro-Shīʿite groups and later sparked major conflicts between the Ottoman and Safavid states.[71] The battle of Chaldiran in 1514 was particularly devastating for the Safavids as they were defeated by the Ottomans and lost their capital (Tabriz) to the Sunni Turks before recapturing it in 1602, ending a long period of hostilities and semi-sectarian conflicts between the two states.[72] Nevertheless, it is hard to find any enduring and important references to martyrdom as a result of those conflicts. To my knowledge, no prominent and revered fighting martyr has been remembered or revered during the Occultation period up until the modern era when martyrdom was reinvented as follows.

Before the modern period, the martyrdom paradigm in Shīʿīsm was primarily defined by the tragedy of Karbalā and the martyrs of the formative period of Shīʿīsm. All later martyrs emulated the martyrs of Karbalā as their role models. However, since none of the early Shīʿī uprisings and political movements (including Imam Ḥusayn's) met with long-term success toward the end of the formative period of Twelver Shīʿīsm and particularly with the Occultation, the collective mindset of the Shīʿa was that of being *oppressed*; hence, "martyrdom" was seen as the greatest weapon of the oppressed, mostly as a last resort in their struggle to defend the legacy of the Imams. As the Shīʿa community came to terms with the absence of the Imam, the concept of martyrdom almost became a thing of the past; it was even eclipsed by the idea of *taqīya* in terms of importance. Martyrdom was overshadowed by the then *unparalleled* merit of waiting passively and piously for the return of al-Mahdī. The twelfth Imam supposedly went into hiding for fear of his life. Essentially, he avoided Imam Ḥusayn's kind of martyrdom, as did the Shīʿa in his absence. It was believed that the time was (and still is) not right for the form of idealism that Twelver Shīʿīsm had championed: a global Islamic state ruled by an infallible and divinely guided "God's caliph" (*khalīfat allāh*).[73] Moreover, by the time the Occultation began, the Twelver Shīʿī Imam had been envisioned as a divinely guided person, and "the most virtuous and perfect" of human beings; one who had the responsibility of guiding people in their "external" lives and "acts," as well as their "spiritual" lives.[74] In Twelver Shīʿīsm's doctrine, the living Imam was recognized as "the witness for the people [*shahīd*], and he was the gate to God (*bāb allāh*) and the road (*sabīl*) to him, and the guide (*dalīl*)."[75] Theologically speaking, with all these extraordinary virtues of the Imam, in his absence during the Occultation, no one could step in and take his duties; therefore, some of the social and political Islamic traditions, such as jihad, which required the presence and approval of the divinely inspired Imam ceased to be practiced.

With the Occultation turning into a painful reality for the Shīʿa, one that is expected to continue for a long and indefinite period, some Shīʿī theologians (as I discuss later) felt the necessity to be more politically active and to try bringing Muslim societies closer to the ideals of Shīʿite Islam; hence, they abandoned the long-held quietist tradition. They justified their involvement in politics by virtue of being general deputies of the Hidden Imam. The jurists envisioned themselves "as the acting sovereigns and guardians of the religion and community during the Occultation of the Imam."[76] This "general viceregency" on behalf of the Imam meant there would be someone who could call for and legitimize the act of martyrdom; hence, martyrdom became important again despite the absence of the Imam.

Peaking in the twentieth century with the 1979 Islamic revolution in Iran, Shīʿī idealism came closer to Sunni realism as jurists stepped in to undertake the roles that were traditionally reserved for the infallible Imam. To some extent, the transformation of Twelver Shīʿīsm into a politically conscious tradition and the reviving of its culture of martyrdom in recent decades came as a "natural response" to the paradox of Shīʿīsm, which was "a deeply political theological doctrine that lacked a direct political expression."[77] The politicization process that completed with the revolution, however, was a result of the long-term development of Shīʿī political thought, as well as the consolidation and centralization of religious authority that began during the Safavid period. Yet, Shīʿī jurists could not completely embrace Sunni realism and act independently on their own religious judgment as the "inescapable presence of the Hidden Imam" always limited the "theological grounds for the designation of leadership"[78] (Fradkin, 2009).

The first major engagement of Shīʿī jurists in politics came during the wars between the Iranian Qajar dynasty and the Russian Empire (1804–13 and 1826–8) that eventually resulted in defeat and the loss of some territories for Iran. In those wars, the Qajar royals approached prominent "*ulamā*" of the time to secure their support by construing the conflict with the Russians as a jihad against unbelievers, making the casualties of the war martyrs. Those jurists who sanctioned jihad against the Russians were also pioneers of the theory of *wilāyat-i faqīh* ("guardianship of the jurist") that later would be developed and implemented in the Islamic Republic of Iran by Ayatollah Khomeini.[79]

The "*ulamā*" carefully crafted their fatwas in favor of jihad with the Russians to assert their religious authority over the Qajar king, Fatḥ-Alī Shāh (1797–1834). For instance, Shaykh Jaʿfar Kāshif al-Ghitā' (1743–1812), the de facto leader of the Shīʿa of Iraq and Iran, counted the Shah of Qajar as his agent and authorized him to wage jihad against the Russians and called the faithful to embrace martyrdom to save the lands of Islam. In his fatwa in the first round of the conflict between the two countries (1804–13), he addressed the Shīʿas of Iran and Iraq, urging them to help the Qajar Shah to repel the Russians from the north of Iran:

> ... So, sell your lives for a very high price that is saved for you in paradise ... Rise to help the believers so that you gain heaven. Haven't you supplicated God during the month of Ramadan that martyrdom is our ultimate wish? ... Haven't you repeatedly said '*how we wish we were with the martyrs of Karbalā?*' Then do not contradict your saying; know that those killed in Azerbaijan in defence of the core of the Islamic land and for the protection of the believers are like the martyrs of Karbalā and in seek of God's favour.[80]

It was among the first instances of referring to the martyrdom of Imam Ḥusayn and the extreme sectarian emotions attached to it in order to motivate people to make the necessary sacrifice for a certain religious/political cause. The fatwa went on with further references to martyrdom, trying to convince the religious audience to participate in jihad against the Russians. Kāshif al-Ghitā' maintained that due to the inability of the "*ulamā*" to wage jihad on their own, the Shah of Qajar would be like his deputy and should lead the jihad on his behalf (who was, at the same time, acting on behalf of the Imam). Trying to assert his authority, Kāshif al-Ghitā' then continued with putting himself in the position of the Hidden Imam by attributing the power of intercession to himself and claiming to be the de facto chief commander of the army: "Whoever from the Qajar's army that is killed [in the battle with the Russians] is like being killed in our army; and whoever obeys him [in this matter] will be as if they obeyed us; and whoever refuses to obey him will be sorry and deprived from our intercession on the day of judgment."[81] This was a bold statement on jihad and martyrdom under the authority of clerics, and elevated the position of the so-called general deputies of the Imam (top jurists) by attributing some of the traditionally exclusive qualities of the Imam to his deputies. It meant that people would die under the flag of the top jurist (or religious authority) and become martyrs. What made that fatwa important and influential for later generations was that it was coming from one of the most prominent jurists of the time. Although the organization of *Marja'iyyat* ("source of imitation") shaped later at the top of the Shīʿite hierarchy with the universal leadership of Shaykh Morteza Ansari (1781–1864),[82] Kāshif al-Ghitā' enjoyed an almost peerless and unprecedented leadership over the Shīʿa world. This meant that, for the first time during the Occultation, a leader of the Shīʿa world issued a decree and called for active martyrdom.

However, this development of making the jurists into authorities who could legitimize jihad and martyrdom on behalf of the Imam was not possible without the triumph of the Uṣūlīs (the rationalists) over Akhbārīs (traditionalists), largely because of the efforts of the Kāshif al-Ghitā's mentor, Muhammad-Bāqir Wahid-Bihbahānī (1704–91).[83] Ever since the Uṣūlīs' triumph, there has been a growing number of jurists who have used their position as "deputy of the Imam," and the authority associated with that, to mobilize the faithful for jihad-like activities. Kāshif al-Ghitā' was not alone in issuing fatwas on jihad and martyrdom in fighting the Russians; his pupil, Sayyid Muhammad Mujāhid (1766–1826), was particularly active in urging the Qajar Shah and the Shīʿa of Iran to wage jihad against Russia in the next round of the territorial conflict between Iran and Russia (1826–8). He called for martyrdom and moved to Iran from Najaf to be personally on the frontline of jihad and encouraged other "*ulamā*" to join him in the fight with Russia, hence his title of "Mujāhid."[84] With Iran failing to capitalize on its early progress due to some internal power struggles and losing ground against the Russians, he subsequently withdrew from his "jihad" mission and literally "died of grief."[85]

The fighting martyrs during the Russo-Persian conflicts formed a kind of new category of martyrdom in Shīʿīsm. During the presence of the Imams, the would-be revered martyrs fell on the battlefield (or in prison) in support of the living Imam as the rightful successor to the Prophet, and their martyrdoms were sanctioned by the Imams (either explicitly or implicitly) for that reason. With the Occultation, as mentioned before, that kind of active martyrdom due to participation in an armed struggle was less and less practiced, and most jurists adopted the quietist position. Hence, scholar-martyrs who were killed mainly with the charge of adhering and scattering the teachings and traditions of the Imams were typical of martyrs during that period. However, by the time of the Russo-Persian wars, the theology of jihad and martyrdom had changed considerably as the Shīʿa jurists embraced political activism in cooperation with (pro-)Shīʿite governments in order to strengthen the Shīʿa community in a hostile environment. Hence, the jurists' call for defensive jihad and martyrdom was no longer for the defense of the legacy of the Imams or hastening the return of the Hidden Imam, rather (first and foremost) it was for the protection of the Shīʿī country; it was meant to keep the (only) Shīʿī country of the time (Qajar Iran) independent and secure from the invasion of foreigners (the Russians).

The participation of the "*ulamā*" in defensive jihad and their call for martyrdom during the Russo-Persian wars, however, did not go smoothly. The stance of the "*ulamā*" was met with some controversy. Moreover, because of their fatwas for jihad and martyrdom, the pro-jihad clerics found themselves in a difficult position following the back-to-back defeats at the hands of the Russian army. Some felt that the "*ulamā*" had gone too far with their religious zealotry and single-handedly pushed the country into disastrous wars (particularly the second war).[86] Moreover, the "*ulamā*" were accused of being responsible for the defeat as they withdrew from the battlefield after the Persian forces had started to lose ground.[87] It was also reported that when Sayyid Muhammad Mujāhid retreated from the frontline to the city of Tabriz, he was not treated well by its religious population. The reason was that a popular preacher, along with some other Shīʿa fighters from the city, had been "martyred" during the battle, and people held Mujāhid accountable for the defeat and the loss of their loved ones.[88] Despite the not-so-successful mobilization of the Shīʿa population of Iran for participating in jihad and embracing martyrdom against the Russians, it was just the beginning and a lesson to learn for the Shīʿa establishment to assert its authority over the religious segments of the society more systematically.

The twentieth century was a turning point in the development of the concept of martyrdom for both Sunni and Shīʿa. The fragmentation of religious authority arguably plagued the traditional Sunni establishment more than that of the Shīʿa. Salafīsts (or Islamists in general), who took the lead in the fight against unbelief, were (and still are) mostly lay believers who were disappointed with the corruption or the inability of the traditional "*ulamā*" to stand up against injustice and un-Islamic rules.[89] Therefore, the Sunni Grand Muftis of Al-Azhar and elsewhere somewhat lost their grip over the Sunni population around the Muslim world and became relatively irrelevant in the fight against Western countries' hegemony over the Muslim world. On the contrary, Twelver Shīʿīsm's religious establishment has remained more or less at the center of religious and political movements in the last couple of centuries. This difference between the way Sunnism and Shīʿīsm responded to modern developments in the Islamic world resulted in two different approaches toward martyrdom. While Islamists and independent Muslim warriors in the Sunni world took matters into their hands and embraced jihad and martyrdom as individual duties in order to re-establish the rule of God, Shīʿī martyrdom was orchestrated and valued by the religious establishment. Furthermore, after the Islamic revolution in Iran, martyrdom became part of the state's agenda and served as a legitimizing factor for the Islamic government.

In contrast with the trend of martyrdom among the Sunnis, since the beginning of the twentieth century until the Islamic revolution in Iran, most of the well-known Shīʿa martyrs were clergy members from different ranks. Even since the revolution, when the number of Shīʿa martyrs in Iran skyrocketed, many of the influential and iconic martyrs have been clerics. Needless to say, giving them the martyr title has an ideological tone. According to the Islamic Republic's official narrative, some of the most prominent martyrs before the revolution include the following: Shaykh Faḍlullāh Nūrī (a controversial figure, executed by the Constitutionalists in 1909); Shaykh Muhammad Khīyābānī (executed in 1920 during the rebellion against the central government in the Qajar era); Mīrzā Kūchak Khān (died of frostbite during a rebellion against the Qajar government in 1921, officially regarded as a martyr in Iran after the revolution); Sayyid Ḥasan Mudarris (died in exile in 1937); and Sayyid Nawwāb Safavī (the pioneer of militant Shīʿī fundamentalism, executed in 1955 by the Pahlavi regime for terrorist activities).

Of all the martyrs mentioned above, Shaykh Faḍlullāh Nūrī and Sayyid Ḥasan Mudarris stood out partly because Ayatollah Khomeini, the ultra-charismatic leader of the Islamic revolution, admired them the most and shaped his political career by following their footsteps. Nūrī's execution (or martyrdom) came after his uncompromising opposition with the constitutionalists who demanded the rule of law and equality of all citizens before the law. He found it to be fundamentally against Islam. In a fatwa released at the peak of the civil war in 1909, he condemned the whole idea of constitutionalism as something that the seculars had used to revoke Islamic Sharia law in favor of Western-inspired legislation. He thought it would be his duty to stop constitutionalism by any means. By this, he implied that he was ready to give up his life, if necessary, and remain steadfast during that "big trial [*fitnah*] of the end of time, and the huge test for Muslims wherein the grown-ups are feeble, and the young grow."[90]

Mudarris was also a role model and paradigmatic martyr for Khomeini because of his tenacity in the face of the despotic anti-clerical rule of Reza Shāh Pahlavi (1925–41). Mudarris was elected to the national parliament several times and became the most outspoken critic of the Shah's policies before being forced into exile in a small city in northeast Iran where he was murdered/martyred in 1937. In post-revolutionary Iran, both Nūrī and Mudarris are officially regarded martyrs/heroes and, as has become customary in the Islamic Republic regarding other martyrs, some highways, streets, hospitals, and schools have been named after them. A picture of Mudarris is even depicted on the back of the 100-Rial banknote. His martyrdom anniversary is also celebrated as Parliament Day in Iran.

Khomeini on several occasions hailed Nūrī and Mudarris as "great martyrs." As for Nūrī, Khomeini called him "a crusading [*mujahid*] jurist of high status," who was martyred because he opposed the separation of religion and state, and insisted on the supervision of *mujtahids* over the lawmaking process of the state.[91] Shaykh Abdul Hossein Amīnī in his *Shuhadā' al-faḍīlah* also included Nūrī as one of the prominent scholar martyrs of the twentieth century. The description of his martyrdom in Amīnī's words is interesting: "[Nūrī] was martyred by the hand of injustice and enmity, [he] sacrificed [himself] in the way of *da'wah* (calling) to Allāh, sacrificed in the way of religion, sacrificed in the way of [enjoining good and] forbidding wrong, sacrificed in the way of nobleness and religiosity."[92] Khomeini maintained high regard for Mudarris as well, calling him "our great martyr . . . to whom titles cannot do justice":

> It is necessary in this age of flourishing of the Islamic revolution, to commemorate the prominent *mujāhid*, prolific committed Muslim and magnanimous scholar who lived in the dark age of suffocation of Reza Khān. At a time when pens had been broken and tongues tied and throats squeezed, he did not spare expressing

> the truth and invalidating the wrong. In those days, the right to life had been stripped of the people of Iran, the arena of foray for affronting hectors was open across the country and the hands of his evil mercenaries throughout the country were stained in the blood of liberal ones of the country especially the "*ulamā*" and people from different walks of life. This weak-bodied scholar with a thin body and great fresh spirit invigorated by faith and purity of heart and a tongue sharp as the sword of Haydar-Karrar [reference to Imam ʿAlī] stood against them and shouted the truth. He disclosed their crimes, straitened the chances of Reza Khān and ruined him. Finally, he sacrificed his life for the cause of dear Islam and the noble nation. He achieved martyrdom by the hand of the monarchical headsmen and his soul joined his pure ancestors. In fact, our great martyr, the late Mudarris, to whom titles cannot do justice, was a brilliant star on the firmament top of a country that had become dark as a result of the oppression and tyranny of Reza Shāh. Unless one has experienced those times, one cannot appreciate the value of this noble character. Our nation is indebted to his services and sacrifices.[93]

The praises for Nūrī and Mudarris are significant and show another nuanced transition in the development of martyrdom. For the likes of Khomeini, those martyrdoms were two contemporary, high-profile cases of sacrifice for the principles of enjoining good and forbidding wrong (*al-ʿamr bi al-maʿrūf wa al-nahy ʿan al-munkar*). In Khomeini's understanding, Nūrī's and Mudarris's martyrdoms were significant as they gave up their social and religious positions and prestige and stood firm on Islamic principles and voiced against injustice, tyranny, exploitation, and un-Islamic trends with all their capacities. Nūrī became the ally of the Qajar Shah against the constitutionalist rebels after he saw the despotic rule of the Shah would be much less harmful than the secular and anti-clerical demands of the constitutionalists. And Mudarris was a great and admirable martyr in Khomeini's view because he had no fear of losing his respectful status (as a member of parliament) and even his life in the face of the tyrannical rule of Reza Shāh, something that Khomeini himself later emulated in his opposition to Muhammad Reza Shāh.

Reopening of the Gates of Active Martyrdom: Historical Background

The fever of martyrdom in the Shīʿa world came into the spotlight with the beginning of Ayatollah Khomeini's movement in 1963 in opposition to the Pahlavi regime which led to the establishment of the Islamic Republic in 1979. This came after the Shīʿa top jurists had adopted quietism following their disappointing involvement in politics and Iran's constitutional revolution, a failed attempt to Islamize the lawmaking process in the early twentieth century. The execution of Shaykh Faḍlullāh Nūrī by the victorious constitutionalists shocked the religious establishment (both pro- and anti-constitutionalist camps in Iraq and Iran). The bitter division in the clerical body during the constitutional revolution was followed by the exclusion of the "*ulamā*" from the political arena by the secular governments, particularly during the reign of Reza Shāh (1925–41), who was keen to dismantle and loosen clerical authority in all aspects of society. With Reza Shāh's de-Islamizing policies, even the authority of the clerics in the educational sector and the judiciary branch of government was significantly reduced.[94] The result was the retreat of top jurists to their pedagogical and scholastic role confined within the boundaries of religious seminaries and mosques.

With the revival of quietism in the early twentieth century, extreme political activities and calls for active martyrdom were looked upon with skepticism. The leading jurists of the time prohibited clerics from engaging in any sort of activity which gave the authorities the excuse to further crackdown on the public practice of religion. Ayatollah Seyyed-Hossein Burūjirdī, the sole leader of the Shīʿa of his age, similar to his predecessor and the founder of Qum Seminary, ʿAbdulkarīm Ha'irī-Yazdī (1859–1936), was silent on all sensitive political issues.[95] In response to critics of his reluctance to be politically active, Burūjirdī once said: "Some people criticize me for not interfering in politics. The reality is that when I was in Najaf, I observed the involvement of Ākhūnd Khurasānī and Nā'īnī [two leading pro-constitutionalist jurists] in politics and saw the result. Consequently, I became very sensitive about this issue ... Since we are not well versed in political issues, I am afraid we will be tricked and stopped from achieving our main objectives."[96] Burūjirdī particularly condemned the radicalism of *Fadā'īyān-i islām* ("Devotees of Islam").[97] In 1949, Burūjirdī invited some 2,000 clergymen to attend a conference in Qum to envision the future of the religious establishment. By his demand, the clergy "adopted a firm non-interventionist position which prohibited all members of the clergy from joining parties and trafficking in politics."[98] This was in line with the original definition of *taqīya*, and the long-held position of quietism adhered to by the Shīʿa during the later period of the Imams and after the Occultation where certain provocative acts and behaviors (including political activities and actively seeking martyrdom) had been prohibited due to their potential for endangering the Shīʿa community and compromising the Imams' mission and legacy.

With the death of Ayatollah Burūjirdī in 1961, reformists in the religious establishment found an opportunity to propose reforms in the sociopolitical doctrine of Shīʿīsm in order to address the problems of modern society. In 1961, a volume of essays, *An Inquiry into the Principle of Marjaʿīyat and the Religious Institution*, was published by some prominent religious scholars of the time. It was widely circulated among the younger generations of the "*ulamā*" and university students. This was the first major scholarly effort to transition from quietism to political activism. What the authors had in mind[99] "would have led to the emergence of an autonomous religious institution which might effectively have challenged the state's domination of that institution since the Safavid period."[100] The emerging unified politically conscious and self-controlled religious establishment claimed authority on both religious and political fronts, would act and behave like the infallible Imam, and exercise the same kind of lasting religio-political authority that traditionally had been reserved only for the Prophet and the twelve Imams. Therefore, theologically, there were more degrees of freedom for the subjects of jihad and martyrdom.[101]

The impact of the reformed religious establishment on the Shīʿī concept of martyrdom has been significant. No longer was calling for martyrdom necessarily a defensive last-resort strategy to repel foreign threats to the lands of the Shīʿa. Martyrdom was seen as a decisive multipurpose weapon on its own. It was transformed into a mobilization tool in any religiously motivated violence or protest, and a means to strengthen the authority and legitimacy of the religious establishment. Hence, rather than discouraging the act of martyrdom, the Shīʿite leaders started to embrace it to its full capacity. The powerful and emotion-packed message that martyrdom carried with itself was needed to reignite devotion and faith to the Shīʿa leadership.

With the Islamic Republic in Iran and the merging of state and religion together, there were no more excuses for practicing the long-accepted tradition of *taqīya* that had prohibited actively seeking martyrdom for centuries. Even sixteen years before the Islamic Republic, at the early stages of Khomeini's movement, he had signaled the end of the practice of *taqīya*. In response to the allegedly brutal and deadly state-sponsored attack on a famous religious school (*fiyḍīyyah*) in Qum, in 1963, Khomeini argued that, in situations where the principles of Islam were in danger, *taqīya* was *ḥarām* ("not permissible"); the faithful should be ready to shed their blood for the defense of Islam in such cases.[102] Hence, later, with the Islamic Republic in place, Khomeini called for martyrdom as a sacred means to preserve Islam. His definition of Islam, however, was closely linked to the ideology of the Islamic Republic; so, with the defense of

Islam, he actually meant the Islamic Republic. On numerous occasions, he maintained that the preservation of the Islamic state from inside and outside threats was, in fact, the preservation of Islam and it was the most important duty of Iranian Muslims.[103]

It is noteworthy, however, that even after the death of Ayatollah Burūjirdī and during the heat of the revolution when an entire generation of clergy was politicized, some groups of senior traditionalist "*ulamā*" in Iran and Iraq still questioned Ayatollah Khomeini's break with the idea of *taqīya*, his political activities, and his call for martyrdom in an effort to establish an Islamic state. This was a task, they argued, which was traditionally reserved exclusively for the Hidden Imam to fulfill when the time was right.

The most vocal critic of Khomeini's political activism was the Najaf-based top jurist of the time, Ayatollah Abul-Qāsim al-Khoei (1899–1992). In his view, although the learned of the community ("*ulamā*") were in charge of the affairs of religion, their guardianship (*wilāyah*) on behalf of the Hidden Imam was limited to organizing and overseeing some necessary religious obligations,[104] the practice of which could not be ceased, such as receiving Islamic taxes (*khums* and *zakāt*)[105] and using them in appropriate ways.[106] Therefore, some key functions of the Imamate, including legitimizing (offensive) jihad and martyrdom should be halted until the Imam's return. For al-Khoei, there was no theological justification for assuming absolute authority (*wilāyah*) for the "*ulamā*" on behalf of the Imam. In this sense, what those traditionalists generally considered as a legitimate involvement of "*ulamā*" in political activities during the Occultation of the Imam was "limited to [the] idea of protecting the interest of the Shīʿī community."[107] Hence, calling for martyrdom had to be limited to defensive purposes, as the "*ulamā*" did during the wars with the Russian Empire in the Qajar era. In Iran, as was the case in Iraq, most of Ayatollah Khomeini's peers and seniors were skeptical of his political adventure. They were especially cautious about becoming responsible for the blood of the so-called martyrs of the revolution if they publically encouraged their followers to engage in revolutionary activities.[108]

Despite the reluctance of top-level jurists in sanctioning the political activism of Ayatollah Khomeini and his few like-minded peers, Twelver Shīʿīsm was poised for sweeping changes by taking a more socially and politically conscious attitude toward the contemporary issues around it. Had it not been for Khomeini and the younger generation of the clergy's revolutionary activities and their call for sacrifice and martyrdom for the greater good of the society (like what happened in the Sunni world), lay thinkers and activists would have taken the lead, particularly in response to social justice issues of the time, while the "*ulamā*" took a back seat. Nevertheless, one lay thinker had a tremendous influence on both university and religious seminary students by eloquently borrowing the communist language of the time for his reinterpretation of the principles of Shīʿīsm: ʿAlī Shariati (1933–77).

A Sorbonne-educated social scientist, Shariati is widely regarded as an ideologue of the Islamic revolution.[109] A lot has been said about the indisputable role of Shariati in popularizing the idea of the Islamic revolution and making Khomeini's ideas of the Islamic state look appealing to the university students of his time.[110] Shariati's epic narrative of Imam Ḥusayn's martyrdom depicted Shīʿīsm as the religion of martyrdom and rebellion against the corrupted inheritors of Islamic culture. His contribution to the development of the Shīʿī concept of martyrdom came with ruthlessly criticizing the long-practiced political passivism embodied in the idea of *taqīya* by calling it "total irresponsibility; the uselessness of all action under the pretext of the Imam's absence."[111] Shariati's contribution to reigniting the fever of martyrdom came from his efforts to bring back Imam Ḥusayn's martyrdom from the piles of history books and passive traditional mourning rituals for his martyrdom to the everyday lives of the Shīʿa by depicting his martyrdom as one of "fighting and dying for a just cause."[112]

Shariati's understanding of the Shīʿī concept of martyrdom had two equally important parts driven from the martyrdom of Ḥusayn and the captivity of his sister, Zaynab: first, the actual martyrdom (he called it "blood") when the martyr (despite having legitimate excuses not to give up his life) consciously chooses death as his "weapon of jihad for the sake of great values which are being altered";[113] secondly, "the message" that should be borne "to the whole world," and it should be "the eloquent tongue of this flowing blood and these resting bodies among the walking dead [those who refused to become martyr for the sake of their world]," as Zaynab did with regard to the martyrdom of her brother (a mission perhaps harder than that of Ḥusayn's).[114] For Shariati, Shīʿī martyrs "committed a Ḥusayn-like act," while the rest "must perform a Zaynab-like act. Otherwise, they are followers of Yazīd."[115] For Shariati, martyrs commit self-sacrifice when they do not see the point of living with injustice, knowing that values are compromised. In his left-leaning ideology, there was almost the binary of good and evil with no middle ground; a believer must choose either to die (martyrdom) or (in the case that martyrdom is not an option) become a messenger of the martyrs; otherwise, that individual would be in the camp of evil. Therefore, Shariati depicts martyrdom as something at the heart of history, beginning with the tale of Cain and Abel; Cain martyred Abel, and thus history began with the confrontation of good versus evil.[116]

Shariati's powerful and emphatic lectures with a novel reinterpretation of the Shīʿites' ideals and their legendary leaders and martyrs was the best thing that a revolution could ever have needed in a deeply religious society. While he did not survive to witness the peak of the revolution and its success, his call for martyrdom and ability to make it appealing to his audience in a world fascinated with the Marxist idea of class struggle was a strong motivation for young and educated Iranians to join the wave of the Islamic revolution and make sacrifices for its success. Following his death in 1977 in mysterious circumstances at the age of 43 in the U.K., he became known as "the martyred teacher" and "the teacher of martyrdom."[117]

As Shariati tried to change the perception of the Shīʿa regarding martyrdom, and Ḥusayn's martyrdom in particular, to make the idea of seeking martyrdom relevant to the everyday life of his people, others followed with their narratives of Ḥusayn martyrdom. One such thinker was Ayatollah Niʿmatullāh Salehi-Najafābādī (1923–2006). He was the author of a highly controversial book called *Shahīd javid* ("The Eternal Martyr"), first published in 1968, in which he criticized the traditional narrative of Imam Ḥusayn's movement. Given that Salehi-Najafābādī denied "the Shīʿite tradition which endows the Imams with occult wisdom which enables them to peer into the future, the gap between his portrayal of the potentially fallible Imam and the traditional portrayal of a supernaturally wise Imam was so much the greater."[118] In Salehi-Najafābādī's view, the traditional understanding of Imam Ḥusayn's martyrdom "is only good for making people weep. It is supernatural, presenting no model for believers to follow."[119] Instead, he proposed the idea that Ḥusayn's martyrdom was the result of a calculated political move to take the Caliphate from the Umayyads. Ḥusayn did not leave his hometown, Medina, seeking martyrdom for the sake of the love of Allāh, rather he was tempted by the letters of support he received from the Kūfan Shīʿa, to go there and establish a government.

In this reading of events, once the Kūfans withdrew their support, Ḥusayn had no choice but to die honorably and not to surrender without gaining any tangible benefit for the Muslim community. Therefore, unlike the traditional reading of his martyrdom account, Ḥusayn did not intend to be killed in Karbalā at the beginning of his movement; rather, he first tried for political gain in Kūfa, but when the plan did not go well, and later after his peace talks failed, he proudly accepted martyrdom.[120] Salehi-Najafābādī even made a bold point by arguing that martyrdom is not essentially valuable; it is the defending of religion that

God asks from us and not martyrdom. In other words, martyrdom is a means to defend religion, not a goal in itself and one should not opt for martyrdom in the first place, even though they might end up getting martyred along the way.[121]

Another influential view on martyrdom came from Ayatollah Murteza Muṭahharī (1919–79), again an ideologue of the Islamic revolution and the right-hand man of Khomeini during the course of the revolution and beyond until his assassination/martyrdom in the early months of the Islamic Republic. In Muṭahharī's words, martyrdom "is the death of a person who, in spite of being fully conscious of the risks involved, willingly faces them for the sake of a sacred cause, or, as the Qur'an says, *fī sabīl allāh* (in the way of God) … *Shahādat* is heroic and admirable, because it results from a voluntary, conscious and selfless action. It is the only type of death which is higher, greater and holier than life itself."[122] His take on martyrdom was that the great cases of martyrdom in Twelver Shīʿīsm were of the nature of reforming the *ummah* ("community") of the Prophet. In his view, the principle of "enjoining good and forbidding wrong" (and not establishing a government as Salehi-Najafābādī had argued) was the main motive for Ḥusayn to accept martyrdom. Ḥusayn's rationale was that only through shedding his blood could other Muslims understand the extent of corruption that had plagued the community of the Prophet. In seeing martyrdom this way, Muṭahharī focused his attention on the epic and heroic (*ḥamāsī*) side of martyrdom in Twelver Shīʿīsm.[123] So, unlike Salehi-Najafābādī's view that martyrdom has no merit in itself, Muṭahharī thought of martyrdom as an agent of change, a heroic act with far-reaching consequences in reforming the wrong in society.

3

Revolution, War, and Martyrdom

The 1979 Islamic Revolution and the Power of Martyrdom

The Islamic Republic opened a new chapter in the history of Twelver Shīʿism. Its unforeseen creation, however, shocked not only the region and the world powers but the Shīʿa leaders themselves, who had not expected to achieve a revolution so quickly, and they had little theoretical and theological preparation to take the helm of the first real Shīʿite state. Ayatollah Khomeini's *Islamic Government*, written while he was in exile in Najaf, was not a blueprint for how to rule an Islamic government in practice; instead, it was a start at giving the theory of *wilāyat-i faqīh* serious thought. Even though his students and like-minded "*ulamā*", most notably the Iraqi-based Muhammad Bāqir al-Sadr (1935–80) and Ḥusayn-ʿAlī Muntaẓirī (1922–2009), wrote commentaries on Khomeini's idea of Islamic government, the whole notion was new and vague for the Shīʿa. It needed polishing through some years in practice before it could become a comprehensive political philosophy suitable for modern times. That meant the new Islamic government was prone to religious and political crises and went through one conflict after another, domestically and internationally. Nevertheless, surprisingly for outside observers, the new Islamic state survived all the turmoil and passed through each crisis stronger than before. The leadership had found the recipe for success by relying on the revolutionary zeal of the people and fully utilizing the power of martyrdom, both as a legitimizing factor to strengthen the pillars of the state and as an extremely strong motive to mobilize people with a broad spectrum of political orientations on a large scale to preserve the outcome of the revolution and the newly created popular government.[1]

A major incident of mass martyrdom that led to the revolution happened on Friday, September 8, 1978, in Jālih Square in Tehran when the Shah's armed forces opened fire on the protestors who had violated martial law. The casualties/ martyrs were later officially reported by the Islamic Republic's Martyrs

Foundation to number eighty-four persons.[2] However, at the time, the religious leaders (and even the Western media) reported hundreds or thousands of martyrs in a massive one-day massacre in Tehran. The religious leaders also claimed that the armed forces responsible for the killings were Zionist agents, a claim that enraged the devout Shīʿa population even more.[3] The revolutionaries were quick to call that day "Black Friday," and the square was renamed "Martyrs' Square." The anniversary of the massacre is held officially every year by the Islamic Republic via the broadcast of special TV programs and the installation of propaganda billboards. The anniversaries are to remind the people of the importance of that tragedy; they are meant to depict the blood of the martyrs as a turning point in the victory of Islam over *ṭāghūt* ("arrogant," or "false god"), a term made popular by Khomeini in reference to the Shah and his followers. In fact, the shock of the Black Friday massacre, assisted by the exaggerated numbers of martyrs, helped seal the fate of the Pahlavi regime. Leading to the incident, Khomeini had penned a letter to his followers and encouraged them "to die in order to defeat the enemy of the people." For the revolutionaries, the massacre and its aftermath was another example that demonstrated the victory of martyrs' blood over the sword.[4]

In the eyes of the religious leaders, the September 8 tragedy was reminiscent of the Āshūrā massacre, and the martyrs of Jālih Square followed in the footsteps of the martyrs of Karbalā. Ayatollah Maḥmūd Ṭāleqānī (1911–79), a highly charismatic leader of the revolution and second only to Khomeini, made the connection between those martyrs and the celebrated early martyrs of the Shīʿa. At the first anniversary of the event, just two days before his death, Ṭāleqānī, in the Friday Prayer held beside the graves of the martyrs of September 8, defined martyrdom as a redeeming and transcending act that would make a mundane and sinful human being into an inspiring and god-fearing soul worthy of the highest respects; the would-be martyrs by closing themselves to the point of martyrdom find so much spiritual power that would free their self from the constraints of the material world, and, in doing so, they even lead other people to ascend toward God, essentially saving a nation fallen into immorality and corruption (a sort of redemptive power traditionally linked to the martyrdom of Ḥusayn). On another occasion, Ṭāleqānī depicted the martyr as someone "who operates above this lowly world"; a person who in the final chapter of their life gets rid of "worldly attachments" and becomes "a *shahīd* even before [they become] a martyr [that is getting killed]."[5] Ṭāleqānī saw the martyrs of Jālih Square in this light and put them in the same category as the martyrs of Karbalā. In his view, they were martyred for the freedom of all human beings from the arrogance of the global *ṭāghūt*; they were martyred for reviving "progressive virtues and rulings of the Qur'an and Islam," which had been neglected in the materialistic and imperialistic world.[6]

Iran–Iraq War and the Love of Martyrdom

The widespread appeal of martyrdom during Iran's Islamic revolution was certainly a reason behind its success, yet the real need for martyrdom was felt once the Islamic Republic was established in 1979. From the viewpoint of the religious establishment that succeeded in taking control of the revolution and subsequently the state, self-sacrifice/martyrdom was all that the newly created Islamic state needed to secure its continued existence in the face of the hostile *other* (the so-called West). However, nothing like the Iran–Iraq War (1980–8) was as effective in institutionalizing the culture of martyrdom and the mass inclination to seek refuge in the sacredness of becoming a martyr. Having emerged fresh from the revolution, the people of Iran were not in the mood to let a foreign invasion of their country occur without putting up a fight. This made the country, which had been so divided into factions and prone to civil war, become united against the Ba'athist[7] Iraq invasion of Iran, which according to Iran's leaders was fully backed by the West.[8] Ayatollah Khomeini and other religious leaders of the revolution actually benefited from the state of war as it consolidated their authority by virtue of being able to rely on the already rich Shī'ī tradition of martyrdom to mobilize the deeply religious Iranian society and make people sacrifice themselves for the independence of the country. The fact that Khomeini was an ultra-charismatic leader and had a strong background in mysticism helped give martyrdom a fresh and robust mystical dimension.

Martyrdom has always been a subject of interest to Muslims for its promise of sweet, otherworldly rewards delineated in *ḥadīths* and traditions. Martyrdom has also long been praised for the precious sacrifice that the martyr makes in the path of God and his religion. Moreover, martyrdom has been seen as the price a Muslim willingly pays for the defense of national territories from the threat of foreign and non-Muslim invasion. Nevertheless, Khomeini should be credited with successfully popularizing the esoteric meaning of martyrdom as a subject of love on its own. In Khomeini's illustration, the love of martyrdom, which comes from the love of God, appears to be the main motive for giving up life. In that mystical understanding, the martyr receives an unparalleled blessing by becoming closer to God; hence, martyrdom becomes the goal of someone who loves God.[9] Early on, in the first months of the war, in a meeting with workers of the Martyr Foundation (*Bunyād-i shahīd*) and a number of the martyrs' families, Khomeini praised martyrdom in mystical terms by highlighting a part of a famous tradition that reads: "A martyr looks at the face of God."[10] He then went on to expand on this point:

> According to this narration that has been recorded, God, the blessed and exalted, manifests himself to the martyr when he attains martyrdom, just like he did in the case of the Prophets, because the martyr has given his all in the way of God. This is the last stage in one's ultimate perfection . . . the categories of the Prophets and martyrs have been placed on the same level in that just as the exalted one manifests himself to the Prophets, so does he to the martyrs. The martyr, too, beholds God's visage by removing the curtain, just as the Prophets had done. This is the last stage one can possibly attain. This last station of the Prophets is the gift bestowed on martyrs. They, too, will reach this final stage according to the limits of their existence.[11]

Khomeini's definition of martyrdom in love language can be best seen in his message to the Iranian nation after the war ended:

> As for the martyrs, nothing (enough) can be said. The martyrs are the light of the candle of the meeting of the friends. The martyrs are in their drunken cachinnation and in the happiness of their union "*with their Lord they have provision.*"[12] They are among the "souls at peace" who have been addressed by God, thus: "Enter thou among my bondmen! Enter thou my garden!"[13] Here is the talk about love and affection. In describing it, the pen will stop from inscribing by itself.[14]

In Khomeini's view, martyrdom was not just a means to get some fantastic rewards in the afterlife or a by-product of joining a jihad for religious or national purposes; instead, it was a real target and the most appealing goal for the faithful.[15] The way he defined martyrdom made it mainly a spiritual adventure in the pursuit of God without taking into account its worldly consequences. He seemed untroubled by the vast number of martyrs and wounded Iranian soldiers during the war that ended without gaining victory other than pushing back the Iraqis to their borders. He had already maintained in his message to announce the acceptance of UN Resolution 598, which ended the war with Iraq:

> Martyrdom in the way of God is not a concept to be compared with victory or defeat in battle. The station of martyrdom is itself the pinnacle of servitude to God and wayfaring in the world of spirituality. We should not degrade martyrdom to the extent of saying that, in exchange for the martyrdom of the

children of Islam, Khurramshahr and other cities were liberated. All these definitions of martyrdom are wrong assumptions of nationalists.[16]

Thus, for Khomeini, martyrdom, like true human love, was something beyond rational calculations; the death of the martyrs may or may not pave the way for the victory of their people, and this is totally fine since what really matters is the incredible spiritual pleasure of becoming a martyr.

Although this mystical attitude toward martyrdom was not a new development in the understanding of martyrdom (as it had its roots in classic *ḥadīth* works), the credit goes to Khomeini for making it relevant for a whole nation as he was in a position that could easily influence people's thoughts and worldview. Someone charismatic and enigmatic like Khomeini, who returned victoriously from the fifteen-year exile and was received by his people as if al-Mahdī had come, had the luxury of ruling the hearts of millions of zealot Shīʿas, who, by calling him "Imam," were ready to totally submit to the views and wills of the Messiah-like leader of their revolution.

The subtle change in the perception of martyrdom created a whole new kind of enthusiasm for martyrdom in Iran which was reflected in the formation of a popular paramilitary volunteer militia known as the *Basīj* ("mobilization"). The *Basīj* was formed by Khomeini's order in 1980 originally as a civil force to help rebuild the country after the revolution. Nevertheless, the *Basīj* became a very large and strong organization during the war, responsible for recruiting and training hundreds of thousands of volunteer fighters (many of them young school students), who had responded to Khomeini's call for martyrdom and joined the ranks of the Islamic Revolutionary Guard Corps (IRGC).[17] Khomeini envisioned the *Basīj* as a powerful ally to put his Islamic ideals into practice. In Khomeini's words, the *Basīj had* to become a "twenty-million army to safeguard the Islamic Republic and the beloved country, protecting it against the dangers of the transgressing superpowers."[18] Initially, many among the *Basīj* volunteers (called *Basījīs*) were illiterate or with low education; and a part of the reason they turned to *Basīj* and participated in the war was to escape from the hardship of their day-to-day lives.[19] However, seeking martyrdom and submitting to God was the dominant culture with which the *Basīj* had been created. Hence, *Basījīs* usually called themselves "martyrdom lovers" (*āshiqān-i shahādat*).[20] Khomeini was clearly proud of his achievement in developing the *Basīj*, labeling the organization "the sincere army of God":

Basīj is a pure and fruitful tree whose blossoms give out the aroma of spring, the freshness of certainty and the story of love. *Basīj* is the school of love and the

> academy of martyrdom. Its anonymous martyrs, whose followers have recited on top of its towering minaret the call to martyrdom and valor. *Basīj* is the locus of the barefooted and ascension of the pure Islamic thought whose trained ones have gained name and fame in having no name and fame. *Basīj* is the sincere army of God whose organizational account has been endorsed by the *mujahidin* from the beginning up to the end. [21]

In many of the hagiographies of the Iran–Iraq war martyrs published in Iran, longing for martyrdom is seen as the most dominant characteristic of the martyrs. For example, it is reported that before martyr Mahdī Ziynuddīn (a young major general who was killed in the Iran–Iraq War in 1984) married his wife, he told her about his priority in life which was to get martyred: "You should know that I am a married man. I married the war and the front lines. You will be my second wife. Martyrdom is the end of my path. If I survive the war without getting martyred, I will go anywhere that is a war between truth (*ḥaqq*) and false (*bāṭil*) to get martyred there."[22] The theme of treating martyrdom as a priority in life continues to be common among ultra-devoted *Basījīs* forces. I will discuss the current situation later in this work.

The love of martyrdom entails dying consciously and purposefully, something that has become widespread since the revolution in Iran. Before the Islamic Republic, Shariati was instrumental in changing the paradigm from seeing martyrdom as a by-product of jihad into the focus and center of attention as the deliberate way of dying in a heroic and liberating fashion. Martyrs, as Shariati explained, sacrificed themselves to deliver a message to all of humanity; their martyrdom was a thoughtful act, and they sacrificed themselves for "thought" and, in doing so, they became "thought" themselves.[23] Shariati juxtaposed two types of martyrdom by comparing the martyrdom of Ḥamzah and that of Imam Ḥusayn: "In the first case, *shahādat* [martyrdom] is a negative incident. In the latter case, it is a decisive goal, chosen consciously. In the former, *shahādat* is an accident along the way; in the latter, it is the destination."[24]

Khomeini championed the conscious attitude toward martyrdom in his inspirational speeches to mobilize people to give up their lives for the sake of Islam and the Islamic revolution. For Khomeini, seeking martyrdom was a deliberate act by the lovers of God; martyrs were the flag-bearers of the caravan of salvation. In a speech delivered to the families of the martyrs at the beginning of the war, Khomeini maintained that the martyrs with their conscious choice to shed their blood led others in the way of salvation: "They were the leaders and have now left our presence and have attained salvation while we have lagged behind on this path and could not pace up with the caravans and tread their paths. We are all from God; the entire universe is from God and is his manifestation, and the entire universe shall return to him. Thus, it is better that one chooses a voluntary return to God through martyrdom for him and for the cause of Islam."[25]

Shariati's distinction between two types of martyrdom and Khomeini's take on the issue highlight the extent of the departure from the passive martyrdom paradigm of the past, which pushed the boundary of martyrdom toward suicide. In other words, in the new martyrdom paradigm that emerged out of the Iran–Iraq war, heroism was defined by the active desire and determination for martyrdom that required taking extreme and irrational risks for the sake of the love of God.[26] This martyrdom-seeking culture has been cultivated and educated among young *Basījīs*. Since the end of the war, there have been propaganda tours just before the Persian New Year (late March) which take the religiously motivated youth, especially school-aged and university students to visit the war zones in the south and southwestern Iran and to commemorate the heroism of martyrs and soldiers during the eight-year war with Iraq. These caravans are called *Rāhīyān-i nūr* ("Passengers of Light"). The visitors walk in the so-called "holy lands," where one would find signs and relics of the martyrs everywhere. In these guided tours, the visitors indulge themselves in an atmosphere of martyrdom, heroism, and jihad for the sake of Islam. Most of the visitors, particularly the young ones who do not have memories of the war, idolize some of the most famous martyrs (e.g., martyrs Chamrān, Hemmat, Bākerī, Bāqerī, Jahān-Ārā, Bābāī, to name a few). A tableau installed in an area of the war zone (see Figure 3.1) is self-explanatory and motivational, and it shows the state's determination in popularizing the martyrdom-seeking culture. The message is simple and strong; it reads: "Remember! We all die unless we get martyred." This is exactly what Shariati and Khomeini had preached before; that is to say, what that really matters is to become a martyr; otherwise, life is in vain or ordinary at best.

The war with Iraq was demonstrated by the religious leaders (notably Khomeini) to be the continuation of the Āshūrā movement. Hence, the Iranian side was depicted as the truth (*jibhi-yi ḥaqq*), and the Sunni Baʿathist Iraqi side was the false front (*jibhi-yi bāṭil*), even though the majority of Iraq's population and part of its army was Shīʿite. Saddam Ḥusayn, then the Iraqi president, was also labeled as the Yazīd of the time by Iranian propaganda. The state media purposefully dropped the "Ḥusayn" in Saddam's name and replaced it with "Yazīd" to vilify Saddam's image.[27] Often, the term *kāfir* ("infidel") was also added at the end of Saddam's name to make the war with Baʿathist Iraq look like a jihad against unbelievers.[28] Khomeini even called Saddam's forces in the war "the

Figure 3.1 War zones propaganda. Source: http://bayanbox.ir/view/6737303656775689026/shahīd-s-mohajer.blog.ir.jpg.

devil's soldiers" and proclaimed that their fate would be hell.[29] Before the war, the Shah was called "Yazīd" by the religious revolutionaries and Khomeini enjoyed an Imam Ḥusayn-like reputation.[30] This trend proved to be popular in the Iranian post-revolution political literature. The holder of the position of *walī-i faqīh* (now Ayatollah ʿAlī Khamenei) is treated like Imam Ḥusayn, and the enemies of the Iranian brand of Islam are called the "Yazīds of the time" (*Yazīdiān-i zamān*).

The war with Iraq quickly became more connected to the tragedy of Karbalā and the sufferings of the other Imams. After the initial phases of the war, where the Iraqi forces had occupied some Iranian territories, Iran was able to recapture its soil and even started penetrating inside Iraq. In the later period of the war, Khomeini's stance was to continue the military mission to topple Saddam and free Iraq from his despotic rule. Because the shrine of several Imams, including Imams ʿAlī and Ḥusayn are in Iraq, the war was also seen as jihad for the sake of the Imams and to free their shrines (especially Karbalā) from Sunni rule. The love of martyrdom had been intertwined with the love of the *Ahlul-Bayt* ("Prophet's family"). Hence, the most common headbands Iranian soldiers wore had the names and titles of the *Ahlul-Bayt* such as *Ya Ḥusayn, Ya Zahrā, Ya ʿAlī,* and *Ya Mahdī.* As part of the state strategy to connect the war to Imam Ḥusayn's movement and depict its martyrs like the martyrs of Karbalā, there was a popular chant among Iranian soldiers saying, "Karbalā, Karbalā, we are coming [for your liberation]" (*karbalā, karbalā, mā dārīm mīyāyīm*). Ten of Iran's military operations against Iraq were named "Karbalā" (Karbalā 1 to Karbalā 10). Other Karbalā-related operation names were *Ḥusayn ibn ʿAlī, Thār Allāh,*[31] *Āshūrā, Muḥarram,*[32] and *Muslim ibn ʿAqil.*[33] For the *Basījīs* seeking martyrdom, the war meant responding to Imam Ḥusayn's famous call for support just before his martyrdom: "*Hal min nāṣirin yanṣurunī?*" ("Is there anyone to help me?").[34] Hence, *Labbayk yā ḥusayn* ("We are at your service, O' Ḥusayn") was another common headband title during the war, and the chant was a declaration of one's readiness to become a martyr for Ḥusayn. So, typically in posters and murals, martyrs were painted with the image of Imam Ḥusayn being present at the scene of martyrdom to take the new martyr with him to paradise.[35]

"The night of the operation" (a commonly used reference in memos of the war veterans) was very special for many of the volunteer *Basījīs*, because, for them, it was the reminiscence of the night of Āshūrā; so they became extremely emotional and, similar to the martyrs of Karbalā, spent the night praying to God and weeping for their sins and the plights of Imam Ḥusayn. Prior to any operation, preachers and *marthīya khwāns* (also known as poets of the *Ahlul-Bayt*) were sent to the front lines to prepare the soldiers emotionally and spiritually for martyrdom by reminding them of the sufferings of Ḥusayn and other martyrs of the *Ahlul-Bayt*. Some first-hand documentaries and reports show the genuine pre-operation Āshūrā-related emotions and mourning rituals coming from their ostensible zeal for martyrdom.

The desire for martyrdom and the degree of detachment from the material world were so high in some of the soldiers that one would feel they were, indeed, walking martyrs. As the youngest Iranian commander during the war, Ḥasan Bāqerī (martyred in 1983 at the age of 26), before an operation in one of his latest interviews, told a TV reporter that "all brothers are eagerly counting the hours until the start of the operation. And the spirit of self-sacrifice and martyrdom-seeking is so high among [the soldiers of Islam] that an hour is an hour [even one hour sooner is better]."[36] Bāqerī's quiet, somber demeanor is the first thing one would notice in the video, a typical trait of many martyrs during the war. He never looked at the camera or the interviewer; rather, he gazed down during the entire interview as if he were living in a higher world disassociated from the social etiquette of normal people in the material world.

The Iran–Iraq war was also a turning point for Muslims in terms of blurring the line between martyrdom and suicide. In accordance with the unprecedented zeal for martyrdom, during the war, Iran allegedly used the so-called human-wave attack tactic to overwhelm the Iraqi forces and their superior warfare with the sheer number of soldiers on the ground ready to die if needed, hence resulting in a substantial number of martyrs after each operation. Two operations (Karbalā 4 and Karbalā 5, both in 1986) were examples of the human-wave attack with the casualties rapidly reaching thousands of martyrs and wounded soldiers in each operation. Eyewitnesses say that after one of those offensives, piles of Iranian soldiers' bodies littered the ground for miles, many of them children of about 15.[37] However, Iranian officials have denied the allegations of Iran's use of the human-wave tactic in the war; a senior staff member of the *Centre for Documents and Research on the Sacred Defense* called this a "baseless" and "laughable accusation."[38] Despite this refusal, it is widely believed that the Iran–Iraq War introduced a new approach to martyrdom for the entire Muslim world to follow. The problem of suicide bombers among the Sunni Islamists such as Al-Qaida and Hamas is said to have its roots in the Iran–Iraq War.[39]

The Islamic Republic enjoyed having tens of thousands of volunteer forces (*Basījīs*) who were ready to die under the leadership of Khomeini, a charismatic and Imam-like religious figure. In accordance with Khomeini's teachings, Iran's strategy was martyrdom first, victory second; the love of martyrdom was what drew many of those volunteers to the front lines, not the desire for worldly victories or patriotism. Khomeini put the priority on performing the "duty" (*waḍīfih*) and not seeking the desired "result" (*natījih*): "All of us are bound to perform our duty and obligation, and not wait for the result."[40] Khomeini's successor and the current *walī-i faqīh*, Ayatollah ʿAlī Khamenei, later backed this idea and clarified Khomeini's words by saying that "the person who acts according to obligations in order to reach the desired results will not feel regretful even if he does not achieve the desired results."[41] That "duty first" approach led the *Basīj* and other armed forces of IRGC to, fearlessly and with complete trust and belief in the so-called "Imam's line" (*khatt-i imām*), embrace martyrdom and take serious risks to hurt the Iraqi forces and push them out of the occupied territories of south and southwestern Iran.

The zeal for martyrdom in the early years of the war and the state propaganda around it resulted in a high number of child martyrs as well. There are no verifiable independent statistics of the exact number of children who joined the *Basīj* forces and got martyred. However, according to the *Center for the Propagation and Preservation of the Values of the Sacred Defense*, of 190,000 martyrs (in their estimate), more than 33,000 were school children.[42] Other sources claim up to 90,000 children were martyred during the war.[43] Moreover, according to other unverifiable statistics, there were 7,054 martyrs aged 14 or under and 65,575 martyrs aged between 15 and 19.[44] Recruiting children became easier with Khomeini's fatwa in 1982, in which he declared that volunteer children no longer needed parental permission to join the *Basīj* forces on the front lines.[45] Child soldiers, after a few weeks of training, were mostly used in situations where a bulk of soldiers was needed for an operation. Hence, many of those child martyrs voluntarily sacrificed themselves in human-wave attacks or exploded themselves to clear the way in a minefield for other soldiers to take the offensive.[46]

The most paradigmatic child martyr was a 13-year-old boy from Qum, Muhammad Husayn Fahmideh, who performed a suicide attack to stop an Iraqi tank column. The incident happened just a month after the war's outbreak on October 30, 1980, when the Iraqi forces were on the verge of occupying the city of Khurramshahr. In order to stop an Iraqi tank column's advance through a narrow route in the city, he reportedly wore a grenade belt and threw himself under the first tank, killing himself, disabling the tank, and causing the other tanks to retreat. His martyrdom is believed to be the first case of a suicide attack in the modern Muslim world (both Sunni and Shīʿa) and inspired others to embrace this kind of martyrdom, which later became known as a "martyrdom operation" (*ʿamalīyāt-i istishhādī*). A major reason that Fahmideh became a martyrdom icon in Iran was the message of Ayatollah Khomeini in praise of his suicidal martyrdom: "Our true leader is that [thirteen]-year-old boy—whose tiny heart is much larger than hundreds of our pens and words—who threw himself with a grenade under the enemy's tank and destroyed it, and attained the sweet blessing of martyrdom for himself."[47] Khomeini's words immediately became an inspiration for other students to join the ranks of soldiers seeking martyrdom and set the tone for other soldiers to emulate Fahmideh, knowing that the way to victory would come through sacrifice. Khomeini's praise of the sacrifice made by Fahmideh was written on the walls of schools and mosques throughout the country, and the story of his martyrdom was taught in schools. Since then, the anniversary of the martyrdom of Fahmideh has been named the "Day of Student *Basīj*" on the official calendar of Iran.

The eight-year war produced too many martyrs in Iranian society. Official reports in Iran estimate that there were 200,000 martyrs, though other estimates present even higher numbers going up to 600,000 Iranian casualties during the war (directly or indirectly).[48] Almost everyone in Iran knew at least one martyr among their relatives and friends. As for the motivation for others to flock to the war zones voluntarily, ready for self-sacrifice, martyrdom had to be revered and remembered. Martyrdom became the most prestigious status one could get in the revolutionary society of Iran. The martyrs' families were supposed to be proud of gifting the martyrs to the country and Islam. In their last wills (*waṣīyat nāmih*), martyrs commonly urged their parents/wives to be proud of their sons'/husbands' achievement of martyrdom. Many of the martyrs' parents were genuinely happy with their "offerings" and wished they had more sons so they could see them becoming martyrs, as well.[49]

The martyrs' last wills were mostly similar in content and typically demonstrated their desire and anticipation of the joy of martyrdom.[50] According to a study of 100 martyrs' wills performed by Muhammad Hussein Shā'irī, the love of God was the dominant motivation for martyrdom.[51] In other words, they mostly saw martyrdom as the way to get closer to God. The martyrs saw Imam Ḥusayn as the best role model for the seekers of God; hence, his name or a reference to his martyrdom appeared in almost every martyr's will. A famous wartime chant (which is found in the martyrs' wills) read: "*Ḥusayn ḥusayn shu'ār-i māst, shahādat iftikhār-i māst*" ([shouting] "Ḥusayn! Ḥusayn! is our chant, martyrdom is our pride").[52] In many of the last wills written by the famous martyrs of the war that I personally examined, the martyrs also urged their fellow countrymen to follow Ayatollah Khomeini (better known as "Imam") word for word and stick to the principle of *wilāyat-i faqīh* as the only way to preserve Islam and the revolution. In the political literature after the revolution, this is known as "the protection of the blood of martyrs" (*ṣīyānat-i khūn-i shuhadā*).

According to Shā'irī's study, the martyrs saw Khomeini as the heir to the Prophet and the Imams. For them, the love of Khomeini was equal to the love of al-Mahdī, the hidden twelfth Imām, which itself was the sign of the love of God. This is coming from the perplexing logic of Shī'īsm, which is best demonstrated in a famous supplicant called by different names such as *Ma'rifat imām al-'aṣr*: "O' Allāh, let me know you; for if you do not let me know you, I will not know your Prophet. O' Allāh, let me know your Messenger; for if you do not let me know your Messenger, I will not know your proof. O' Allāh, let me know your proof [*al-ḥujjah*, the Imam]; for if you do not let me know your proof, I will deviate from my religion."[53] In other words, the knowing (*ma'rifah*) of the Imam is the cornerstone of religion, and it guarantees that one already has belief in God and his Prophet. In post-revolutionary Iran, this line was extended to include the *walī-i faqīh* as well. So, martyrs in their wills attested to their devotion to Khomeini and his Islamic mission and counted their blood as offerings to that mission. This was known for them as the criterion of true faith, which was branded *islām-i nāb-i muḥammadī* ("pure Muhammad's Islam"). Popular chants uttered by the soldiers and reflected in the martyrs' wills were also indicative of their devotion to Khomeini and their genuine wish to get martyred for him: "*Rahsipārīm bā khomeini tā shahādat*" ("We are heading [ahead] together with Khomeini until martyrdom");[54] "*Mā hamih sarbāz-i tuyīm khomeini, gūsh bi farman-i tuyīm khomeini*" ("O Khomeini, we all are your soldiers, O Khomeini, we are awaiting for your order").[55] After Khomeini, these chants remained and have been tweaked to address the current *walī-i faqīh*, ʿAlī Khamenei. While "Khamenei" replaced "Khomeini" in some of the mentioned chants, the general term *wilāyah* (the guardianship of the Imam and the *walī-i faqīh*) is mostly used in chants; a commonly seen chant written on posters and in weblogs is "*Bā wilāyat tā shahādat*" ("Along with *wilāyah* till martyrdom").[56]

Facing the more sophisticated and superior Iraqi army, Iran needed to rely on its larger population; hence, the culture of martyrdom had to be rooted deep in the society for a mass mobilization of volunteer fighters to occur. Although Khomeini and other religious leaders of the Islamic Republic depicted the war as the war between Islam and *Kufr* ("unbelief"),[57] they did not officially call for jihad because traditionally, as I discussed earlier, there have been reservations about the legitimacy of waging jihad in the absence of the twelfth Imām.[58] Moreover, the war was between two Islamic countries and, more than that, two countries sharing the majority Twelver Shīʿa population, so not everyone was comfortable with participating in a war in the form of jihad under the authority of Khomeini, especially after 1982 when Iran recaptured all of its occupied territories and went on the offensive. The Islamic Republic's religious leaders presented the conflict with Iraq first and foremost as self-defense, and secondly, as a liberation mission to free the holy cities of Iraq and its Shīʿa population from the despotic rule of the Baʿathist Saddam. Hence, the war was labeled as the "Sacred Defense," or the "Imposed War," so that the Iranians would feel obliged to defend their country from the Iraqi invasion regardless of their political and religious orientations.

The memories of the revolution and martyrs were fresh in Iran and had the potential to produce a huge number of volunteers ready to die in a defensive war, something that Saddam and his allies had underestimated. A large-scale strategy was implemented to cultivate the value of seeking martyrdom among people (most importantly students). The state produced cultural products, including war-related movies and TV programs, heroic and emotional songs and posters, and other forms of propaganda to encourage a culture of martyrdom among the youth. The streets of Tehran (and other big cities in Iran) literally became an open museum of martyrs. The commemoration of war martyrs became a part of daily life. Paintings of martyrs were the first things one would notice walking around the city. The large, realistic paintings, which were mostly based on personal portraits and were accompanied by their names and sometimes part of their last will or a quote from Khomeini on martyrdom, made the citizens relate to the martyrs and their cause.[59]

Moreover, martyrs made a celebrated return home as their emotion-packed funerals attracted large crowds, many of whom did not know the martyrs personally but participated as their religious and national duty to honor the martyrs. Official news headlines reporting the martyrs' funerals usually read something like *Tajdīd-i piymān ba ārmānhāyi imām wa shuhadā* ("the renewal of the pledge to the ideals of the Imam (Khomeini) and martyrs").[60] During the war, in almost every neighborhood, there was a special booth for honoring a recent martyr of that area. The booths were usually decorated with lights and small pieces of glass and mirrors, and normally had pictures of the new martyrs beside a photo of Khomeini. Frequently, there was an audio cassette of a Qur'an recitation, *rawḍa khwānī* for Imam Ḥusayn, or war-related songs playing from the booths.

During the Iran–Iraq conflict, motivational chants and songs played a significant role in making the atmosphere heroic and motivational for the soldiers before each operation. The songs helped to ignite the flames of martyrdom inside them. They are also reliable sources for understanding the beliefs advocated by the Islamic Republic. These war chants and songs usually highlighted the values of martyrdom. They were intended to develop the love of martyrdom among the people so that they would be ready for any form of self-sacrifice advocated by the religious leaders of the Islamic Republic. Karbalā and Imam Ḥusayn were common themes that appeared in most of the chants and songs. Caravans dispatching soldiers to the war zones were usually labeled *kārwān-i karbalā* ("Karbalā caravans"), which was also reflected in the chants and songs. Getting to Karbalā was one of the main motives for wearing the robe of martyrdom; the soldiers went to the war listening to such songs as: "We will give our lives to conquer Karbalā";[61] "I have heard the sound of your call; I have chosen your path O' brother; O' caravan of Karbalā I am joining you";[62] "Whoever is longing for Karbalā, *Bismillāh* (get ready)! Whoever has excitement, *Bismillāh!* If you have been yearning for martyrdom in your heart, this caravan goes to Karbalā, *Bismillāh!* A caravan is ready for the lovers of Ḥusayn, if you are now ready to get (blessed) *Bismillāh!*"[63]

For the Iranian soldiers, as already had been highlighted by Shariati, seeking martyrdom was a response to Imam Ḥusayn's timeless call for devoted supporters:

"Is there anyone to help me?" They responded to that call with the chant of "*Labbayk yā ḥusayn*" ("At your service, O' Ḥusayn"), which was repeated in the war songs, too. For them, an important purpose of the Iran–Iraq war was to avenge Imam Ḥusayn's blood; something that since the later period of the Imams traditionally had been reserved for al-Mahdī, the hidden twelfth Imam. Hence, the Iranian army envisioned itself similar to the army of the Hidden Imam, as it was evident from a famous wartime song: "O army of the master of time (the Hidden Imam) Get ready! Get ready! For a war without mercy! Get ready! Get ready!"[64]

This messianic interpretation of war has had a deeper root in the Islamic revolution because the whole country is thought to belong to Imam Mahdī; hence, the *walī-i faqīh* has been the acting ruler of Iran and will remain so until the Imam's return at the end of time. In 1981, soon after the revolution, in a speech to state officials, Khomeini maintained that Iran's master was no one but the Hidden Imam: "You should be engaged with your work in a big heart, without fearing any of these problems [referring to the wave of assassinations of Iran's president and prime minister, Muhammad-'Alī Rajai and Muhammad-Jawād Bāhunar, and some other high-ranking officials of the Islamic Republic in 1981], as Islam is your stronghold, God is your support and the owner of this country is the Imam of the time."[65] This was, in fact, meant to reaffirm that anyone killed for the cause of the Islamic revolution would be a martyr. Traditionally, martyrdom in Twelver Shī'īsm was defined as giving up life in the service of the Prophet or the infallible Imam. The logical conclusion of this line of thought is that, as the acting owner of the country, the deputy of the Hidden Imam and the holder of the *walī-i faqīh*'s office (Ayatollah Khomeini and, today, Ayatollah Khamenei) defines righteousness; and therefore, martyrdom will be defined by sacrificing one's life in accordance with the *walī-i faqīh*'s intentions (better known in the political literature of the Islamic Republic as *manwīyāt-i rahbari*). Hence, the war songs picked up this idea and put Khomeini in the Hidden Imam's position: "Whoever says *labbayk* to Khomeini's orders, swear to God he goes in Ḥusayn's way. Whoever obeys the Spirit of God's orders (Khomeini's orders), *bismillah* (get ready for the war)*!*[66] Whoever is longing for Karbalā, *bismillah!*"[67] Another famous song reads: "You soldiers ready to give your lives, now is the time of courage. O the army of God's Spirit [Khomeini], the hour of martyrdom has arrived. O the army of God's Spirit, the hour of bravery has arrived. See how the forces of Islam stretch to infinity. To throw back the enemy, get ready! Get ready!"[68] Similarly, the chants of "*Labbayk yā khomeini*" came along with the chants of "*Labbayk yā ḥusayn*" and "*Labbayk yā mahdi.*"

4

Civic Martyrdom

Lest We Forget: Iran's Postwar State of Martyrdom

The war with Iraq changed Iran's cultural and political scene forever. Apart from the high costs forced upon the country and its people during the long and bloody conflict, for the Islamic Republic's leaders, the war was ultimately a blessing when seen in terms of revolutionary Islamic ideology. The war exposed the power of the institutionalized culture of martyrdom in holding back an enemy that was "armed to the teeth."[1] The current supreme leader, Ayatollah ʿAlī Khamenei, has been determined to make sure the memories and values of the martyrs of the revolution and the war period (i.e., deep faith, strong devotion, and determination) stay alive and be transmitted to the next generation. In his speeches, Khamenei sees martyrs as "role models" who should be introduced to the youth.[2] He also called war-disabled veterans (known in Persian as *jānbāz*, literally meaning "one who has given up life") "living martyrs" who "bear witness to the glorious struggle and great endeavors of the Iranian nation."[3]

In Khamenei's view (which defines the strategy of the Islamic Republic), the veneration of martyrs and the values of martyrdom are necessary to counteract the waves of cultural attacks coming from the West, where martyrdom is depicted in a negative way as a dogmatic residue of the intolerant traditions of the past. He maintains that values of jihad and resistance against the "bullies of the world" and the "global arrogance" come from the culture of martyrdom, which should be transferred to the new generation.[4] In particular, he has backed the program of the *Rāhīyān-i nūr*'s caravans as one of the best ways to cultivate the culture of martyrdom and disseminate its values.[5] Martyrdom essentially has become the cornerstone of revolutionary ideology and a source of power in the Islamic Republic. In Khamenei's words, martyrdom is the concept that reveals "the greatness of the revolution."[6] He maintains that the concept of martyrdom in the Muslim world was boosted by the "miracle of the Islamic revolution"; at the same time, Islam and the revolution's future and success depend on the willingness of the people to embrace martyrdom if necessary.[7]

Non-War-Zone Martyrs

All the state propaganda around the value of martyrdom shows how much it has evolved from being a purely religious phenomenon to a largely political concept. Martyrdom in Iran is now a state-sponsored term used in any sort of death occurring due to one's participation in the 1979 revolution or the so-called "imposed war" with Iraq, acts of terrorism, assassination, or any fatal incident involving a public servant on duty. However, the key criterion here for any death (either violently or due to an accident) to be labeled martyrdom in the postrevolutionary political literature is that the person's life and career should have served the interests of the Islamic Republic. The most notable martyrs not related to the war (passive form of martyrdom) have been the assassinated high-ranking political or military officials of the Islamic Republic and other victims of terrorist attacks in Iran or abroad; they have been martyred mostly at the hands of the People's Mojahedin Organization of Iran (*Mujāhidīn-i Khalq*), better known in state propaganda as *munāfiqīn* ("hypocrites"), or by Sunni extremists and Salafī groups based in neighboring countries. Martyrs of the scientific community (mostly nuclear scientists) are among the recently emerged cases of martyrdom. Those so-called "nuclear martyrs" were scientists involved in Iran's nuclear program who were assassinated separately from 2009 to 2011. Given the sensitivity and importance of the nuclear program for Iran's leaders, the nuclear martyrs have been vibrantly pictured alongside the martyrs of the eight-year war with Iraq. Ayatollah Khamenei sanctioned them as martyrs of high status: "Iranian scientists were martyred in the way of God . . . their martyrdom prepares the ground for the progress of Islam."[8] According to Sādiq Zībākalām, a Tehran University professor and a mostly tolerated, outspoken critic of the Islamic Republic's policies, the highlighting of the nuclear martyrs is in line with state sponsorship of resistance against Western powers: "The state wants to glorify those heroic struggles against the Western powers to show that we have been through much trouble and misery, and we did not give in."[9]

Much like early Islam after the period of Muslim conquests, the state-sponsored concept of martyrdom was expanded to include non-violent ways of dying following the Iran–Iraq war; state leaders have celebrated many sorts of passive, non-war-related cases of martyrdom. Examples include martyrs of the press (*shuhadā-ye aṣḥāb-i risānih*), such as the casualties of the crash of a military transport aircraft of the Iranian Air Force on December 6, 2005, in which thirty-nine journalists from state-run media outlets lost their lives en route to cover the news of a series of military exercises in southern Iran. The journalists' death was widely described in state media as martyrdom. Another more recent case of a much-publicized claim of martyrdom occurred during the Plasco building incident in Tehran on January 19, 2017, where sixteen firefighters died while trying to control a fire that eventually caused the collapse of the building. The immediate reaction to the loss of the firefighters was that they were martyrs. Khamenei praised the firefighters and officially called them "martyrs": "In one way this incident is tragic, yet in another way, it is a source of pride, and those individuals are the martyrs of the path of difficult services and hazardous responsibilities; they will never be forgotten, God willing."[10] This expanded understanding of martyrdom was best delineated by Khamenei as he pushed the country to make developments in every possible way following the destructive war with Iraq. In a public speech, Khamenei tried to present a more inclusive definition of martyrdom suitable for peace periods:

> The culture of martyrdom means the culture of making efforts with one's own resources for the sake of furthering those long-term goals which are shared by all people. Of course, in our case, these goals are not particular to the people of Iran. Rather, these are goals for the entire world of Islam and the whole of humanity. If this culture is firmly established in society, it will become the exact opposite of Western individualism which is based on selfishness.[11]

Ayatollah Khamenei's effort to encourage his people to work harder at every level with the religious language of martyrdom more than anything else shows how deeply Iranian religious society is obsessed with the concept of martyrdom so that values of the society need to be explained in this way. For a Shīʿīte nation that constantly lives with the vibrant and always fresh memories of the martyrs of Karbalā and other religious leaders, who sacrificed themselves for the glory of the tradition and the good of the community, martyrdom is synonymous with greatness and good deeds. Since the end of the war, martyrdom, in essence, has become something like the highest medal of honor, a title given to honor outstanding services to the community.

Rainbow Martyrdom: Politics of Blood

The use of the term "martyr" is so widespread in Shīʿīte Iran that even secular groups have no objection to using it. It is part of the spoken vocabulary, which does not necessarily connote a dogmatic meaning for nonreligious people. It is becoming like another common Islamic expression: *inshā allāh* ("If Allāh wills it"), which is now used virtually by everyone in Muslim societies (religious or secular), meaning "hopefully." Martyrdom has a very positive connotation; hence, similar to sectarian martyrdom discussed before, when the ideological *wilāyat-i faqīh*-based Iranian state appropriates the term to describe its heroes, rivals (including adherents of other forms of Twelver Shīʿīsm that do not approve of the *wilāyat-i faqīh*) highlight their own fallen heroes as the real martyrs. The most recent case of such contrasting claims of martyrdom occurred during the civil unrests following the disputed 2009 presidential election. The opposition so-called Green Movement's propaganda and reformist news sites called those protesters who died in the notorious (now closed) Kahrīzak detention center south of Tehran or during the street protests "martyrs of the Green Movement."[12] Of all casualties of the Green Movement, Neda Āqā-Sultān, a 26-year-old philosophy student from Tehran who was shot dead during a street protest, became a symbol of the Green Movement martyrs, as the haunting 90-second footage of her death was uploaded on the Internet and shared extensively on Facebook and Twitter, causing quite a stir.[13] The so-called Green Movement martyrs were perhaps the first cases of so-called martyrdom in recent years that defied the Islamic Republic's definition of martyrdom, namely dying for the cause of *wilāyat-i faqīh*-based Islam.

In response to the followers of the Green Movement, pro-government propaganda dismissed the opposition groups' martyrdom claims by comparing them to the murder of the third Sunni Caliph, 'Uthman ibn Affan, in 656, which gave Muʿāwīyah a pretext to launch a revolt against the rule of the reigning Caliph and first Shīʿa Imam, ʿAlī ibn Abī Ṭālib. Muʿāwīyah reportedly used 'Uthman's bloody shirt to gain popular support for his mission under the rubric of avenging the blood of 'Uthman from ʿAlī and his followers.[14] Accordingly, in 2009, many of the pro-government news websites and weblogs accused the opposition groups of plotting the martyr-like death of Nidā Āqā-Sultān. Similar to what Muʿāwīyah did against ʿAlī with his allegedly false accusation regarding the death of 'Uthman, they argued that foreigners supported layers of the Green Movement by calling Āqā-Sultān and other victims of the unrest martyrs, and they intended to hurt "the ʿAlī of the time" (referring to ʿAlī Khamenei who, to his followers, resembles Imam ʿAlī in many ways).[15]

As for the appropriation of the term "martyrdom" after the Iran–Iraq war, a recent trend has been that of love and extreme affection toward the supreme leader (*ʿishq bi rahbar*). Ayatollah ʿAlī Khamenei is increasingly called "Imam

Khamenei" by his devout followers (similar to the way Ayatollah Khomeini has been called "Imam"); and because of his resemblance to Imam 'Alī, seeking martyrdom for the sake of *Imām Khamenei* is now a trend among passionate *Basījīs/Hezbollahis*.[16] It seems that the dynamic of Khomeini–Khamenei for the followers of the *wilāyat-i faqīh* is similar to that of the Prophet and Imam 'Alī for the Shī'a. While the Prophet's leadership was indisputable among his people, the Caliphate/Imamate of 'Alī was disputed and challenged. This caused 'Alī's reputation in Shī'ī resources as the oppressed (*maẓlūm*) Imam. In a similar way, while the charismatic Khomeini was essentially the undisputed leader of the revolution and subsequently the Islamic Republic until his death in 1989, Khamenei had a rough path to assert his authority over the Iranian people with varying tastes of religiosity and political inclination. Hence, in their inner discussion, ardent devotees of the Ayatollah often blame segments of the Iranian population and some of the state officials and political elites derogatorily called *khawāṣṣ-i bī baṣīrāṭ* ("ignorant members of the elite") for disrespecting the *walī-i faqīh* and making Khamenei oppressed and alone by disregarding his rule and guidance. As a result, perhaps more pronounced than the *Basījīs*' zeal in seeking martyrdom for the love of Khomeini, ultra-devoted followers of Khamenei are entirely ready to sacrifice themselves for him; so chants like "*jānam fadāyi rahbar*" ("I will sacrifice my soul for my leader")[17] are routinely heard in government-sponsored political gatherings and demonstrations.

Another popular chant by the devotees of *walī-i faqīh* in support of Khamenei makes a reference to Imam 'Alī and his loneliness even among his followers in Kūfa: "*Mā ahl-i kūfih nīstīm 'alī tanhā bimānad*" ("We are not like the people of Kūfa to let 'Alī become alone").[18] This allegory aims to convey a menacing message to the deniers and enemies of the *walī-i faqīh*: unlike the people of Kūfa who betrayed Imam 'Alī (by failing him in his war with Mu'āwīyah) and his sons, namely the Imams Ḥasan (by forcing him into a truce with Mu'āwīyah) and Ḥusayn (by failing to support him in the tragedy of Karbalā), they are eager to sacrifice themselves in support of Ayatollah Khamenei ("the 'Alī of the time," as they call him). A symbolic and extreme way to show their support of the *walī-i faqīh* until their last drop of blood has been to show up in demonstrations and political rallies wearing white burial sheets while chanting "*khuni ki dar rag-i mast, hadiyyih be rahbar-i mast*" ("the blood in our vessel is a gift to our leader").[19] This readiness for martyrdom had already been demanded by Khamenei himself in 2000 by implicitly putting himself in Imam Ḥusayn's position. In a speech to a large group of youth, Khamenei said: "Thanks to the great Islamic revolution, neither America nor any superior power (if emerged) can force on the Islamic world something like the incident of the Imam Ḥasan's peace treaty. Here if the enemy put too much pressure, the Karbalā incident will be repeated."[20]

Sensitivity toward things that are considered "principles" has undergone a metamorphosis in recent decades in Iran. It is now actually a common trait in most of the Islamic world as Muslims usually do not forbear from showing their strong resentment or anger toward anything that seems an insult to Islamic principles. The controversies surrounding Salman Rushdie's novel, or the Danish and French cartoons of the Prophet, are among the most famous examples of Muslims' uncompromising attitude toward things that are considered sacred in Islam. In Iran, the so-called "principle" of *wilāyat-i faqīh* goes even further because of the added political sensitivity attached to it. For the zealot revolutionaries and younger generations sympathetic to the ideals of Imam Khomeini and the Islamic revolution, any violation of core principles derived from those ideals cannot be tolerated.[21] In these circumstances, possible death would not be a deterrent for the faithful to launch an uncompromising resistance to put an end to the practice of wrongdoing; and anyone dying in this path is a martyr. These martyrs are called "martyrs of enjoining what is right and forbidding what is wrong" (*shahīd-i ʿamr-i bi maʿrūf wa nahy-i az munkar*). The prohibition of wrongdoings can be in its basic form (that is, going against immoral sins) as was the case with a much-publicized injury incident and later "martyrdom" of a *Basījī* (ʿAlī Khalīlī) in 2011 in which he was the victim of a knife attack after allegedly trying to prohibit the attackers from publicly listening to un-Islamic music and sexually harassing two women. His martyrdom caused significant outrage among religious segments of the society, resulting in the passing of a law in Iran's Islamic Consultative Assembly which made it unlawful to stop someone from performing the duty of enjoining what is right and forbidding what is wrong; and accordingly, an offender would be sentenced to imprisonment or probation without a chance of parole.[22]

As Shīʿīte faith and state politics have become intertwined in Iran through the agency of the *wilāyat-i faqīh*, the application of enjoining what is right and forbidding what is wrong has gone beyond the prohibition of simple moral sins and encompassed the political sphere in the form of the preservation of the system (*hifḍ-i niẓām*). Ayatollah Khomeini set the tone early after the revolution and requested absolute diligence to make sure the system remains in place at any cost: "The question of preserving the Islamic Republic system in this era ... is among the most important rational and religious obligations which nothing can hamper."[23] The preservation of the system of the *wilāyat-i faqīh* is such an important religio-political duty that not only do the military forces of the country protect the frontiers in their capacity as the "armies of the Hidden Imam," but also the intelligence ministry's operatives, which anonymously and quietly protect the system, are understood as *sarbāzan-i gumnām-i imām-i zamān* ("nameless soldiers of the Hidden Imam"). Hence, exactly like martyrs of the military forces, fallen intelligence operatives are considered martyrs, though in a state of anonymity. The Islamic Republic leaders count the martyrs of the intelligence community among the "oppressed martyrs" (*shahīdān-i maẓlūm*) due to their anonymous status, which deprives them of having proper public burials like other martyrs;[24] also because the term "nameless soldiers of the Hidden Imam" has gained a bad press in opposition media, often referring to repressive undercover forces responsible for torturing and killing dissidents.[25] Ayatollah Khamenei, in response to the opposition's cynical references to the intelligence ministry's operatives, described their work as *mujāhidat-i khāmūsh* ("silent sincere effort"), emphasizing the holy qualities required from anyone who is involved in jihad, hence their status as martyrs in case of death on duty: "The silent and sincere efforts on the part of the Ministry of Intelligence requires fighting carnal desires, paying attention to God, and strengthening the sense of abstinence and piety."[26]

5

Martyrdom Reimagined

Martyrdom Out of the Borders

The end of the Iran–Iraq war left the lovers of martyrdom among the *Basīj* and *Hezbollahi* forces heartbroken as it meant there was no further opportunity for getting martyred. The feeling of having missed the caravan of the martyrs has been a common regret of many among war veterans. A much-recited long poem with a very sad and somber tone (performed by the renowned *rawḍa khwān* of the war, Sādiq Āhangarān) best describes this feeling of regret for missing martyrdom:

> The light-winged [martyrs] flaunted and passed away; they called me hapless and passed away. Don't close the gates of the garden of martyrdom; [you, the martyrs!]—don't laugh at us from the other side [heaven]. Martyrdom was heaven's ladder; martyrdom was a ladder to heaven; why did they take away that ladder? Why did they block the path to heaven? . . . You ascended; I'm still on the earth; brother, I'm shame-faced; I'm ashamed; I once had a white horse; martyrdom once was the prospect . . . Tell me, who stole my white horse? Who stole my hope? They prayed for me to remain in prison; they prayed for me to remain astray; I don't have the patience to stay; I don't have patience for agony.[1]

Even though after the war martyrdom was not completely out of reach for its seekers, nothing for them was like rolling in the blood in a true jihad in the path of God, that is, struggling in the path of God under the command of his caliph (or the caliph's deputy) on earth. Hence, those desperate for martyrdom looked elsewhere to participate in regional conflicts with Islamic/Shīʿa interests to protect. Lebanon has been a point of interest since the early years of the Islamic Republic. After the Israeli invasion of southern Lebanon in 1982, Hezbollah ("party of Allāh") was formed following the reorientation of former Lebanese Shīʿa groups under the spiritual leadership of Shaykh Mohammad Ḥusayn Faḍlallāh (d. 2010) and with the support of Iran. With the formation of Hezbollah, the Shīʿītes of Lebanon commenced a vigorous and successful resistance against Israel and the presence of Western forces in Lebanon. Hezbollah started life as a resistance movement against foreign occupiers in Lebanon, but it later tried to champion the Palestinian cause on behalf of Iran. The formation of Hezbollah as Iran's protégé fitted into Khomeini's mission to export the Islamic revolution to other Muslim countries in the Middle East and elsewhere.[2] Moreover, it opened up another opportunity for the Iranian Shīʿas to partake in jihad-like activities, that is fighting non-Muslim enemies outside their borders.[3]

The Israeli invasion happened just after the liberation of Khurramshahr, which was a turning point in the Iran–Iraq War and put Iraq on the defensive for the rest of the war. This led many in Iran's Revolutionary Guard to turn their attention to Lebanon as a genuine front for the jihad against the enemies of Islam by sending 1,000–3,000 trained Revolutionary Guards to fight Israel.[4] However, Khomeini soon opposed the idea of sending Iranian troops to Lebanon by calling it a trap and a Western conspiracy to turn Iran's attention away from Saddam Ḥusayn's invasion so as to let him gain a victory over Iran.[5] Hence the famous chant "The road to Jerusalem goes through Karbalā" (*Rāh-i quds az karbalā mīguzarad*)[6] became Iran's de facto ideological strategy for the rest of the war. In a speech to the Friday Prayer leaders, Khomeini expands on his thought about focusing mainly on the war with Iraq until a decisive victory: "We want to liberate Quds, but without delivering Iraq from this sinister party, we cannot do it. We consider Lebanon to be part and parcel of us, yet liberation of Iraq is a prelude to the liberation of Lebanon. We should not abandon the preliminary steps and trace the main question, devoting everything to it, while Iraq finds the respite to strengthen its foothold."[7]

Hezbollah's declaration of existence basically came through some thirty-six suicide attacks (called "martyrdom operations," inspired by the tales of the Iranian soldiers' self-sacrifices during the ongoing war), which caused the death of 659 foreign troops between 1981 and 1986.[8] The attacks were effective in forcing the U.S. and French troops out of Beirut. With the same strategy, Hezbollah succeeded in forcing Israel to finally withdraw its troops from southern Lebanon in 2000.[9] The suicide attacks were supported by the majority of the Lebanese population as defensive measures. Moreover, the suicide attackers were well received as martyrs by Lebanon's Shīʿa community. The community's support for martyrdom (following the Islamic revolution in Iran) was instrumental in the willingness of would-be suicide bombers to shed their blood for a higher purpose.[10] This particular form of martyrdom, where the attackers blow themselves up to hurt the enemy, mostly diminished among the Shīʿa both in

Iran and Hezbollah. However, the Sunni Hamas organization appropriated the idea from Hezbollah fighters and has used it extensively since the beginning of the Palestinian Intifada (particularly since the second Intifada in 2000) before Al-Qaida took the suicide-bombing specialist crown in spectacular fashion through the 9/11 attacks.[11]

Unlike its Sunni version, of all the suicide attacks performed by Lebanese Shīʿī groups, few have targeted civilians because prominent Shīʿīte jurists have been reluctant to issue a fatwa regarding the permissibility of killing non-combatant civilians in "martyrdom operations." However, most classic Shīʿa jurists permitted killing innocent civilians in jihad if the enemy used them as a shield and the victory over the enemy had to be achieved by killing the civilians first.[12] Regarding the issue of Palestinian resistance against Israel in particular, a few jurists have sanctioned killing Israeli civilians in martyrdom operations with some reservations. In his fatwa, the Iranian Ayatollah Muhammad Fāḍel Lankarānī (1931–2007), for instance, implicitly permitted killing Israeli citizens through martyrdom operations. His reasoning was that Palestinians were defending themselves: "The issue of Palestine is an issue of defence, and self-defence and the defence of the essence of Islam by any means are permissible [even through killing civilians if needed]."[13] He later expanded on his reasoning by saying that: "If a thief tries to rob your home, you will fight with him even if he brings his wife and children ... In fact, the Israeli occupiers have martyred Palestinian children on their mothers' laps and destroyed their homes ... But based on the Islamic thought, it is necessary that Palestinian fighters [*mujāhids*] perform jihad and fight with the Israeli army and civilians who support the Zionists."[14] Nevertheless, when it comes to fighting hostile Sunni Salafīsts, the Shīʿa jurists generally prohibit killing innocent civilians by martyrdom operations.

Shrine Defenders

With the escalation of sectarian conflicts, especially in the wake of the collapse of Saddam's regime in 2003, however, the Shīʿites (mostly civilians) became the main target of suicide attacks; the victims have been hailed as martyrs. With the beginning of the Syrian civil war in 2011 and subsequently the rise of the so-called Islamic State (ISIS), the state of affairs changed in the dynamic of suicide attacks (martyrdom operations). While Sunni Salafī groups still conducted the overwhelming majority of martyrdom operations in Iraq and Syria against Shīʿa militias and civilians, in December 2013, *Al-Monitor* reported that Shīʿa suicide bombings were on the rise, although they avoided targeting civilians as much as possible.[15] Perhaps this had to do with a fresh opportunity that the Syrian conflict brought for the devout Shīʿa in the region to achieve martyrdom in a jihad-like confrontation against the anti-Shīʿa coalition of Salafī Sunnis. The following reported saying of Iran's Supreme Leader highlights that new opportunity for martyrdom and explains the rise of martyrdom-seekers among the Shīʿa in Syria. According to *Al-monitor*'s interview with a Hezbollah commander, before officially announcing Hezbollah's participation in the Syrian war in 2013, its leader (Ḥasan Naṣrallāh) visited Ayatollah Khamenei in Tehran. Reportedly, Khamenei declared: "Syria is the second Karbalā. This means that we must sacrifice our lives for this cause, as did Imam Ḥusayn in Karbalā."[16]

Syria has played a significant role in the history of Shīʿīsm since ʿAlī assumed the Caliphate and faced his Syrian-based rival Muʿāwīyah. In 680, it was Yazīd, the second Umayyad Caliph, who put Syria at the center of a big controversy by being responsible for the long-lasting and emotion-packed tragedy of Karbalā that changed history and made martyrdom a cornerstone and defining factor of Shīʿīsm. If one fast-forwards, since 2011 Syria has been in the spotlight again, and become a Karbalā-like conflict zone for the Shīʿa, this time around Ḥusayn's sister: the heroine and messenger of the martyrs of Karbalā, Sayyida Zaynab, whose shrine is in Damascus.[17] In the recent case, however, the players have changed roles: the Syrian government, affiliated with Alawites (distant cousins of Twelver Shīʿītes), is now assuming the position of defending *Ahlul-Bayt*.[18] Meanwhile, among the armed opposition groups, or the so-called rebels, there are powerful factions (Salafī jihadists) who consider Shīʿīsm and Sufism deviations in Islamic history and their practice of revering religious figures and glorifying tombs and historical buildings as a severe case of *shirk* (idolatry).[19]

The Syrian crisis started in 2011 during the so-called Arab Spring and turned violent when the Syrian president, Bashar al-Assad, refused to recognize the opposition's peaceful demonstration and began to crack down on any resistance to his government. What really caused the brutality and complexity of the Syrian civil conflict, compared with other Arab countries that had experienced popular uprisings since 2011, was that the conflict in Syria escalated into a full-fledged proxy war involving many countries and various Islamist groups. Each of these had its own regional and ideological interests to protect through the war: Russia, Iran, and Hezbollah were playing as pro-government forces, while the U.S., Saudi Arabia (and other Gulf states), Israel, ISIS, *Jabhat Fatḥ al-Shām*, nationalist jihadists, the Free Syrian Army, and Turkey were fighting, more or less, against Assad's government.[20] The result has been devastating for the people of Syria and has brought mass destruction to the country with some half a million people having reportedly been killed so far.[21]

The Shīʿa coalition involved in the Syrian war was centered around Iran, which had a clear political interest in taking sides with the Assad regime. Iran and Syria have been strategic allies since the Islamic revolution (despite having some conflicts of interest regarding Lebanon). In fact, their alliance has created one of the most enduring yet overlooked state relationships in the Middle East.[22] Iran needed Syria's support against the Baʿathist regime of Saddam during the 1980–8 war and afterward as a buffer against Israel, as an ally against U.S. interests in the Middle East, and as a base among Arab countries for its ongoing rivalry with Saudi Arabia for regional influence.[23] In return, the Assad family, coming from the minority Alawites, needed Iran's support as a powerful Shīʿa state in the region to maintain its rule over the majority Sunni population in Syria and deal with neighboring Sunni countries in the Arab world. With the civil war growing from different dimensions, the Syrian government relied more on Iran's support to maintain its grip over the country. Hezbollah's survival also depends on Iran as the militia gains its military equipment from Iran, which comes through Syria.[24] Iran, in return, relies on Hezbollah forces to influence the region without directly sending troops overseas. Hence, Iran, in its propaganda, calls this alliance between Iran, Syria, and Hezbollah the axis of resistance against the U.S. and Israel.[25]

The deep political interests of Iran and Hezbollah in their struggle to keep Assad in power in the current Syrian crisis aside, as implied from the above-mentioned saying of Ayatollah Khamenei, there has been a sectarian rationale for the Shīʿas to fight in Syria and Iraq: defending the holy sites of the Shīʿa. In other words, this religious factor created a "powerful justification" for the Islamic Republic's unbreakable alliance with the Syrian government.[26] In short, fighting the Salafīsts and getting martyred in Syria and Iraq became all the rage for the lovers of martyrdom among the devout Shīʿa in Iran and elsewhere. By surfing online forums and social media, one could easily see that for those *Basījīs* and *Hezbollahis* who missed the caravan of martyrdom in the eight-year war with Iraq, and for their younger counterparts who had not experienced the war, the opportunity for martyrdom in Syria and Iraq was a dream come true.

Briefly, the current state of bloody sectarian conflict in Syria and Iraq has its roots in the mayhem following the American-led invasion of Iraq in 2003 that resulted in the collapse of Saddam's regime. The de facto power vacuum in the country coupled with regional (Iran and Saudi Arabia, Turkey and Syria) and world-power (U.S. and Britain) conflicts of interest helped destabilize the country.[27] The Shīʿa majority population of Iraq, after several decades of Sunni rule, found themselves at the helm of the country. The new arrangement angered Sunni Islamists; and some discriminatory policies of the Shīʿī government of Nūri al-Māliki (2006–14) toward Sunnis added to the miseries of the Sunnis and paved the way for violent sectarian tensions.[28] This has resulted in numerous suicide-bombing attacks mostly against the Shīʿa population and especially Shīʿī pilgrims to the shrines of the Imams ʿAlī, Ḥusayn, Mūsā al-Kāẓim, Muhammad al-Jawād, ʿAlī al-Hādī, and Ḥasan al-ʿAskarī in Najaf, Karbalā, Baghdad, and Samarra. Regardless of the part that Iran's and Iraq's Shīʿī governments have played in the escalation of the recent sectarian violence in post-Saddam Iraq, the whole Shīʿa community in the region has since felt threatened by the rise of Sunni extremists (derogatorily called *takfīrīs* by the Shīʿa community).

The first major sectarian incident happened just three months after the fall of Saddam. Mohammad Bāqir al-Ḥakīm, a top Shīʿa cleric and the leader of the Supreme Council for Islamic Revolution in Iraq, was assassinated in Imam ʿAlī's shrine together with some eighty-four Shīʿa worshipers on August 29, 2003, by a massive car-bomb explosion allegedly planned by the al-Qaida of Iraq. Al-Ḥakīm then became arguably the most high-profile "martyr" in post-war Iraq, on a par with the late influential Shīʿa cleric and jurist, Muhammad Bāqir al-Sadr, who had been martyred by Saddam in 1980. Nevertheless, of all attacks against the Shīʿa of Iraq and their revered places, it was the destruction of the holy shrines of Imams ʿAlī al-Hādī and Ḥasan al-ʿAskarī in Samarra by two suicide bombers on February 22, 2006, that sparked widespread hatred among the Shīʿa worldwide toward the so-called Sunni *takfīrīs*. Ayatollah ʿAlī Sistani, the top Shīʿa jurist residing in Najaf, and Iran's Supreme Leader, Khamenei,[29] condemned the attack yet forbade their followers to launch retaliation attacks against Sunnis.[30] In fact, both Shīʿa and Sunni leading figures called for unity between Sunni and Shīʿa instead of more bloodshed. They blamed the Iraq occupiers (American troops) for failing to provide security in Iraq. Some also called the Samarra attack an American and Israeli conspiracy to ignite the flame of sectarian war in Muslim countries.[31] Thanks principally to Iran, the shrine was restored to its original form with a new shiny golden dome;[32] however, deep down in the minds of devout Shīʿītes, the damage had already been done, and it was not something they would forget or forgive. Since then, the anniversary of the attack has been commemorated every year in Iran and Iraq, and mournful followers of the Imams take the attack as an assault on the family of the Prophet.[33] The commemorations painfully remind them of the permanent demolition of the tombs of the Imams al-Ḥasan, al-Sajjād, al-Bāqir, and al-Sādiq located in historic Medina's al-Baqīʿ cemetery in 1926 by Saudi Wahhabis,[34] hence their nickname as "the oppressed Imams of al-Baqīʿ" (*al-a'immat maẓlūm al-baqīʿ*).[35]

As is always the case when the subject is related to the so-called "infallible Imams," the destruction of the Samarra shrine was an extremely shocking and emotional tragedy for the Shīʿītes. Despite the calls for unity and peace, some retaliation attacks against Sunni mosques in Iraq and angry demonstrations around the Shīʿa world occurred immediately following the Samarra incident.[36] From my understanding, the Samarra attack was a turning point in the awakening of broader segments of the Shīʿa community regarding the grave threat that Sunni extremists (*takfīrīs*) can pose to their holy sites and the urgent need for sacrifice to ensure that they are "kept away from harm and desecration" (*hatk-i ḥurmat-i muqaddasāt*).[37] A consequence of the Samarra attack has been a new wave of zealotry, which was reinforced with the escalation of the war in Syria, especially since 2013 with the growing threat of the Islamic State (ISIS) in Iraq and Syria. A growing number of volunteer martyrdom-seekers, organized by Iran, Iraq, and Hezbollah, aimed to protect Shīʿa holy shrines in Syria and Iraq from any threat and desecration with a special focus on protecting the shrine of Sayyida Zaynab in Damascus. They gradually became known as "the shrine defenders" (*mudāfiʿan-i ḥaram*).

While Shīʿa militia had been involved in the sectarian conflicts to counter the threats of their Sunni counterparts against the Shīʿa holy sites in post-Saddam Iraq and Syria (since 2011), the official formation of the guards of the shrine defenders was revealed in March 2013 after a series of attacks aimed at the graves of some of the respected Shīʿa and Sufi figures, including a car explosion outside the Sayyida Zaynab's shrine which had wounded several civilians.[38] There was later a more serious incident in which the then al-Qaida-affiliated al-Nusra Front successfully demolished the gravesite of Ḥujr ibn ʿAdī, a revered Shīʿa martyr and companion of the Prophet and Imam ʿAlī, on May 2, 2013 in Syria.[39] The footages of the destruction and desecration of his remains were widely shared in Shīʿīte circles on social media and, once again, sparked widespread contempt and angry reactions. Those attacks had justified the formation of an organized group of shrine defenders. Interestingly, on April 30, two days before the attack on Ḥujr ibn ʿAdī's grave, Hezbollah's Ḥasan Naṣrallāh spoke live on television to officially announce Hezbollah's involvement in the Syrian civil war. He rationalized this foreign intervention in terms of defending Lebanese citizens living close to Syria's border in the northeast corner of Lebanon. He then declared that the religious motive that forced Hezbollah to deploy armed forces to Syria was to defend the shrine of Sayyida Zaynab. He painted a real threat facing the shrine by saying, "[The armed groups] belonged to the *takfīrī* school of thought, they sent a clear message and they threatened, even on the Internet. They said that if we enter and control this area [where Zaynab's shrine is located], we will destroy this shrine."[40] So, Nasrallah's speech clearly revealed the presence of a full-fledged sectarian conflict camouflaged in a politically ignited civil war in Syria.

Starting in mid-2013, the news of Iran's direct military involvement in Syria broke out to the public when the IRGC gradually lost some of its commanders and fighters in Syria, and their bodies were returned to Iran hailed as "martyred shrine defenders." Since the beginning of the Syrian crisis, the Iranian public was generally against their country's foreign military adventure in support of Assad; hence, Iran wanted only to showcase its advisory role for the Syrian army. But with a rising number of martyrs coming back to Iran from Syria, there was no point in hiding the truth on Iran's actual military presence outside its borders. However, the main combat roles were done by Hezbollah's forces and other Iran-led Shīʿa militia.[41] In addition, a great number of the Iranian-trained fighters were actually Afghan refugees in Iran.[42] For the Islamic Republic's leaders, losing Assad meant Salafīsts would capture Syria, which would endanger the holy sites in Syria and cause national security problems for Iran, Iraq, and Lebanon.[43] So, Iran was ready to do anything to protect its strategic and long-lasting ally from losing ground to the armed opposition forces. Iran's actions (with the help of Hezbollah) to save Assad eventually proved to be effective. By mid-2014, the Syrian government collected itself and regained some of its lost regions from opposition forces.[44] However, because in late 2014 ISIS ascended as a ruthless force to be reckoned with, Iran needed external support to save the Syrian government so it turned to Russia. With Russia's sustained airstrikes against ISIS and the opposition forces, the Syrian government backed by Iran, Hezbollah and their organized Shīʿī militia were gradually able to gain victory, though it was very costly with thousands of casualties from Iran and its allies.[45]

Domestically, to reduce the backlash over the rising numbers of the Iranian casualties, Islamic Republic's leaders, as did Hezbollah, highlighted a sectarian rationale for the necessity of Iran's direct activities in support of the Assad's regime to fight against the *takfīrī* groups in the region.[46] The martyrs were officially declared heroes as they sacrificed themselves for the holiest cause possible, that is, guarding and protecting the sanctuaries of the holy Prophet's family.[47] Moreover, the Iranian martyrs in Syria have been praised in the same way as the legendary martyrs of the so-called eight-year holy defense. Khamenei even glorified martyred shrine defenders by claiming that if it had not been for their sacrifice and martyrdom, Iran would have fought Salafīsts and ISIS in its own cities and in the streets of Tehran.[48] With the same rationale, Major General Qasem Soleimani, then Iran's top commander involved in Syria and Iraq and the man behind the shrine-defenders' movement, villainized ISIS to create a united Shī'a front against the Islamic State in Iraq and Syria:

> Swear to Allah, defending the shrine of Zaynab means defending the shrine of 'Alī in Najaf. Swear to Allah if Syria were collapsed by the hands of these [ISIS and other Salafīs], they would destroy all the Shī'a holy places, as they blew [the] Samarra [shrine] by a bomb. Defending the Zaynab's shrine also means defending the shrine of Imam Rida in Iran; all of those are interconnected.[49]

The Iranian public directly engaged with the Syrian crisis when the bodies of "martyred shrine defenders" (*shahīdān-i mudāfi'-ī ḥaram*) were returned to the country for public and televised funeral services. The funeral processions attracted large crowds, much like the martyrs of the war with Iraq. The memorials and the buzz around them in the state-run media worked very effectively as a propaganda tool to justify the IRGC's involvement in Syria. The funerals were also seen as a recruiting platform for martyrdom-ready volunteers to join the so-called "jihad against the enemies of *Ahlul-Bayt*." While Iran has "geostrategic and ideological" motives and reasons "to protect its ally in Damascus and project power within Syria, Iraq, and across the Middle East," highlighting the religious goals for the military intervention and riding on the wave of public zeal and enthusiasm for sacrificing for the sake of the family of the Prophet have proved to be a winning recipe.[50] Iranian military officials called their presence in Syria "defending the pure Islam."[51] The IRGC openly invited members of the *Basīj* and those religiously minded youth to join the Shī'a forces in Syria. For example, in 2015 as the Syrian government was losing ground to the then mighty ISIS and other opposition forces, Rahim Nowi-Aghdam, an IRGC major general urged people to join the "religious" war: "If you do not volunteer to fight in Iraq and Syria, I will go myself, and I will martyr myself in defence of Sayyida Zeynab or the Shī'a shrines in Iraq."[52] Simply by surfing the Internet and reading online comments one could see that genuine enthusiasm for becoming a shrine-defender martyr has been very high. Reportedly, there were many Iranian volunteers ready for martyrdom in Syria who registered in mosques and *Basīj* offices throughout the country or online through dedicated recruiting websites.

As a result, officials asked those who would like to volunteer for the "jihad in Syria" to financially support the cause instead.[53]

Ayatollah Khamenei, in particular, has played a very influential role in promoting the idea of fighting Salafism and seeking martyrdom for defending the Shīʿa shrines. He has led the praise for those who laid down their lives for that cause.[54] For instance, in a meeting with several families of martyred shrine defenders in October 2016, Khamenei pointed to the "exceptional characteristics" of the new martyrs. First, he praised the "invaluable trait" of the martyrs for their determination to defend the sanctuary of *Ahlul-Bayt*, something that he believed should be cultivated inside every believer. He then proudly quoted remarks of a martyr's mother toward Zaynab in a complimentary way: "I gave my Muhammad Ḥusayn [her son's name] to you, O' Zaynab!" Khamenei then went on to describe the newly found joy of martyrdom-lovers and their impatience to get to Syria for a chance at martyrdom:

> Another point that exists in them [martyred shrine defenders] is their enthusiasm for martyrdom. After the end of the imposed war [with Iraq], we – who were in the middle of the arena – had the feeling that that vast multi-lane road, which was open to us, had been closed: the road to martyrdom. It was a door that had been closed. Those who loved jihad and martyrdom in the way of God felt low in spirit. Most of your youth did not see that era, but they had the same enthusiasm which made them engage in jihad. In the present time too, youth write letters to me. Of course, I do not answer them. Youth from throughout the country write letters begging me to let them go. They think that I am the one that should give them blessing to go or to intervene. They say, "let me go to Syria for jihad!". This is enthusiasm for martyrdom which is very important. If a nation or a group of people has the capability to forgo power and life, that group of people will be invincible.[55]

Much like the Iran–Iraq war period, there have been extensive state-sponsored campaigns to cultivate the culture of martyrdom (particularly among the youth) and depict the Syrian conflict as a genuine holy jihad. Many television programs such as a TV show called *mulāzimān-i ḥaram* ("Shrine Companions"), which was a documentary program for introducing the martyrs to the public, and other cultural products have been produced and dedicated to the subject of shrine defenders. One interesting case was a music video, which was broadcast on national television and spread on social media targeting young students. As the text of this song follows, it is dedicated to the teenage son of one of the martyred shrine defenders. The song sends a powerful and epic message and depicts children who volunteer to console the son (for the loss of his father) by pledging to continue and finish his father's task in defending the shrine and destroying the enemies of *Ahlul-Bayt*:

> Dedicated to Amir Ḥusayn (son of Martyr Taqī Arghawānī): Since childhood, I have been the servant of his dignified clan. I am a defender of the holy shrine like Ḥabīb ibn Maẓāhir.[56] With the intention to preserve the sanctum of the shrine. I have risen marching beside the lovers of Imam Ḥusayn. If the sanctity of the shrine is severed; or if the road to Karbalā is barred. I will strike the usurper of Syria and Iraq; such that their existence is annihilated. I have been summoned to safeguard the Shrine from *Shāh-i najaf* [Imam ʿAlī]. With the command of my leader [Ayatollah Khamenei], I am ready to take my life into my own hands. My goal is not just the liberation of Iraq and Syria. The journey is through Aleppo and the aim is toward Quds [Jerusalem]. I am not grieved by the separation from my loved ones and my country, with the command of Almighty and absolute conviction of my heart. I have a shroud on my body. Escaping from the cage does not require wings, I have wings of LOVE to fly. My lips chant "O' Zaynab!" My heart is free from fear. I desire nothing but the *zīyārat* [pilgrimage] of Imam Ḥusayn, son of Fāṭimah. Lord forbids that I get separated from this door [of *Ahlul-Bayt*]. I don't have an end without serving at this door. Red lines encircling the shrine are with my blood. I am like a lake, my death is the same as my calmness. I will go walking from Mashhad of Imam Riḍā to Syria. My restlessness resembles that of the pigeons of the shrine of Imam Riḍā.[57]

In some ways, one could argue that the martyred shrine defenders brought more sympathy among the religious population in Iran than previous martyrs in modern Iran. The Iran–Iraq war drew many concerns, especially after Iran repelled the Iraqi forces from most of its territories in 1982. Liberals and like-minded political activists such as Iran's Freedom Movement (*nihḍat-i āzādī-i īrān*) had issues with the continuation of the war, thinking that it would hurt Iran domestically and internationally.[58] Moreover, ultra-Shīʿa traditionalists fundamentally questioned the legitimacy of waging war in the absence of the twelfth Imam, as they already had problems with Khomeini's idea of an Islamic revolution and his theory of *wilāyat-i faqīh*. For them, martyrs of the war at best were not comparable with the martyrs of the formative period of Shīʿīsm, and at worst, they wasted their lives for the political ambitions of the Islamic Republic's leaders.[59] In the case of the martyred shrine defenders, while liberal minds and opposition groups have relatively negative views of Iran's military adventures in Syria and Iraq, the ruling pro-*wilāyat-i faqīh* faction of the Islamic Republic has enjoyed the unlikely ally of some usually reluctant ultra-traditionalists like Ayatollah Wahīd Khurāsanī (residing in Qum). The point of convergence comes from the ultra-traditionalists' firm and uncompromised sectarian beliefs and their abhorrence of Salafīsts and Wahhabis as "the sworn enemies of the Prophet's family"; hence, their support and readiness for "martyrdom" in the way of defending the shrines from what they count as the ill intention of the armed Salafīsts in the region. For example, on May 15, 2013, following the destruction of Ḥujr ibn 'Adī's grave, Ayatollah Khurāsanī in a lecture for his students denounced the attack and called the Salafīsts and Wahhabis involved in Syria and Iraq "atheist" (*mulhid*) and "unbeliever" (*kāfir*).[60]

Regionally, in order to effectively mobilize Shīʿa fighters to join the Iran-led shrine-defenders' movement, the Islamic Republic needed the consent of the senior Shīʿa clerics in the region. Therefore, as the most prominent jurist outside Iran, the position of the Najaf-based Ayatollah 'Alī Sistani (a rather quietist figure with minimal involvement in politics) regarding the conflicts in Iraq and Syria became so important for the success of the movement. While he has been reluctant to issue a written fatwa for the Iraqi Shīʿītes to fight against the Salafīsts in Syria, with the rapid advance of ISIS in Iraq in 2014, Sistani called for the Iraqis to defend the holy shrines (though he still did not issue a written fatwa; rather, his representative announced the Ayatollah's views on the fight with ISIS).[61] It was also reported that Sistani's son joined a group of volunteers defending the shrine of Samarra in Iraq.[62] Sistani's fatwa proved to be decisive in the formation of organized Shīʿa fighters and the eventual defeat of ISIS in Iraq.[63] Before the spoken fatwa by Sistani calling the fight against ISIS and other Salafī groups in Iraq, the Iran-organized campaign of shrine defending campaign was so desperate to bring the Iraqi Shīʿia population on board that it tried to undermine the importance of Ayatollah Sistani and other Iraqi senior clerics with regard to the fight against Salafīsts in Syria and Iraq. So, the Popular Committee for the Mobilization to Defend Sayyida Zaynab (*Lijna al-taʿbi'at al-shaʿbiyah li-difaʿ an al-sayyida zaynab*) issued a long statement in December 2013 making an argument that the ruling of the *walī-i faqīh* in Iran is sufficient and binding for all Shīʿa Muslims (regardless of which jurist they follow); hence, they all (if capable) must participate in the fight against the Salafīsts and the defense of the shrines:

> It is obvious that the goal of going to Syria is to defend the Shīʿītes and the sect of [*Ahlul-Bayt*] and Islamic shrines and the resistance because the *takfīrī* groups in Syria have been targeting our sect and our shrines in a clear and direct way. We also confirm that our goal is not just restricted to Syria but also extends to our presence in Iraq, especially in Najaf. And we are going to defend and fight assailants who are coming to fight us, just like the prophet came out of Medina

> to face the *mushrikīn* [idolaters] when he was informed that they were heading to Medina to destroy Islam. Thus, this is a defensive war and defensive wars do not require permission from anyone . . . Despite the issue not requiring anyone's permission, [the jihad in Syria] has been overseen by a legitimate ruler who is the *walī-i faqīh* [Ayatollah Khamenei] . . . Based on this, there is no doubt about the legitimacy of the figures who are abiding by the [leadership of absolute] *wilāyat-i faqīh*. There is a dispute that some are bringing up, which is that some religious figures are saying: "I do not see any interest in going [to war]." Regarding these statements, they do not harm the legitimacy of those who go to fight under the emblem of obligatory interest [duty to go to war] . . . and this is something *walī-i faqīh* supports and is convinced about. Not seeing the interest [in going] and labeling going as illegitimate activity are two different matters. The higher religious figures support the leadership of *walī-i faqīh* and acknowledge [his] capability. [This is] why there is no doubt about the legitimacy of going to fight and fighting *takfīrī* groups to defend the Shīʿītes of Syria and (Sayyida) Zaynab and also to defend ourselves and our existence in Iraq, because the *takfīrīs* are targeting the existence of the sect and its followers.[64]

The Shīʿī Symbolism of Shrine Defenders

As discussed above, the term "shrine defenders" refers to some groups of Shīʿa fighters organized mostly by Iran, Iraq, and Hezbollah to defend their geopolitical interests in the war-affected zones of Syria and Iraq. However, the term "shrine defenders" exposed a deeper religious layer in the conflict which needs to be delineated here to make better sense of what has made this new development in the concept of martyrdom unique and what connection it has had with messianism. We know that it was the Sayyida Zaynab's shrine that symbolically mattered the most for the shrine defenders.[65] This was evident from the primary chant that shrine defenders used and was written on their headbands: "*Labbayk yā Zaynab*" ("At your service, O' Zaynab"). This chant was also the theme for a few propaganda songs which Hezbollah created to highlight its role in defending the shrines.[66] Moreover, on social media (such as Facebook), *Labbayk yā Zaynab* was like a banner for identifying those pages in favor of the shrine defenders. A simple search for this term on Facebook brings many pages created with the title of *Labbayk yā Zaynab*.

Besides the fact that Zaynab's shrine was at the center of a vicious civil war and has been under threat from Salafī fighters, there is something in the figure of

Zaynab and her significance in the Shīʿī concept of martyrdom that has put her shrine at the forefront of the shrine-defenders' agenda. First of all, females among the family of the Prophet traditionally draw extreme emotion from devout Shīʿa as they are thought to be the embodiment of the suffering of *Ahlul-Bayt*; in particular, Fāṭimat al-Zahrā, the daughter of the Prophet and a highly important figure in Shīʿīsm ("mistress of womankind of the universe," *sayyidat nisāʾ al-ʿālamīn*),[67] is at the center of lamentations for the sufferings of the Imams.[68] Zaynab, Fāṭimah's daughter, inherited her mother's nature as the receiver of all the sorrows of *Ahlul-Bayt*. She had to suffer from the loss/martyrdom of her grandfather (Muhammad), her father (ʿAlī), her mother (Fāṭimah), her brother (Ḥasan), and above all, the unbearable sorrow and grief of the martyrdom of her brother, Ḥusayn, the last remaining member of the "People of the Cloak," along with her children and nephews and other martyrs of Karbalā.[69] Zaynab has become a cornerstone of the concept of martyrdom and the tragedy of Āshūrā in Twelver Shīʿīsm. As Syed Akbar Hyder has written in his extensive study of Zaynab's position in Twelver Shīʿīsm, "Ḥusayn and ʿAbbās are the masculine faces of martyrdom; Zaynab is its feminine face."[70] In Karbalā, Zaynab was at the center of Ḥusayn's harem,[71] the chief witness of Imam Ḥusayn's ordeal and martyrdom. A much-recited salutatory prayer to Zaynab (which is part of the liturgy used in pilgrimages to her shrine) best describes the suffering of Zaynab in Karbalā and then as a captive of Yazīd:

> Peace be upon you, O' the representative of the infallible Imam. Peace and Allāh's mercy and blessings be upon you, O' you who were tested through patience against misfortunes, like that of al-Ḥusayn the oppressed. Peace be upon you who are far away from your home. Peace be upon you who wandered as captives in cities. Peace be upon you when you were bewildered in that ruined place in Syria. Peace be upon you when you were bewildered as you stood by the (severed) body of the master of martyrs and called at your grandfather; the Messenger of Allāh, may Allāh bless him and his family, saying, "O' Muhammad! May the angels in heaven bless you! This is Ḥusayn under the open sky! His turban and his clothes are stripped! His limbs are severed! And your daughters are taken captives! Complaining (about this) is only to Allāh."[72]

Here comes the prominence of another mythical figure in Twelver Shīʿīsm: Ḥusayn and Zaynab's half-brother, ʿAbbās ibn ʿAlī, himself the greatest martyr of Karbalā after Ḥusayn and the standard-bearer of his army. ʿAbbās is also the epitome of loyalty as he always put Ḥusayn and Zaynab and their children ahead of himself. Moreover, ʿAbbās is a symbol of *ghīrah* (the sense of protectiveness a Muslim man should show toward his female relatives) as in the traditional storytelling of

Karbalā, he was the one on whom the women in Ḥusayn's camp, especially Zaynab and the daughters of Ḥusayn, relied for protection and help. 'Abbās was the protector of the harem, and his martyrdom in the afternoon of Āshūrā was felt as the fatal blow to Imam Ḥusayn's camp and the harbinger of misery and captivity for the women of Karbalā. 'Abbās was such a towering figure for the *Ahlul-Bayt* in Karbalā that, after the martyrdom of 'Abbās, it is said that people heard Ḥusayn whispering "now my back has broken, and my options are few."[73]

In the above-mentioned salutatory prayer, the faithful recite Zaynab's heartfelt words to 'Abbās after the day of Āshūrā (while she was captive) which best depict the prominent position of 'Abbās as the protector of the harem of the *Ahlul-Bayt*: "Peace be upon her [Zaynab] who had to ride a saddleless camel and then called on her brother Abul-Faḍl ('Abbās), saying, 'O' brother! O' Abal-Faḍl! It was you who helped me ride on a camel when I left Medina.'"[74] Hence, there is a perpetual sense of guilt and shame among devout Shī'a, similar to that of the *Tawwābūn*, that Zaynab, who had been taken care of with utmost respect by 'Abbās and other youth of the Prophet's clan (*Banī hāshim*), had to wander from Karbalā to Yazīd's court in Damascus as a prisoner and in a pitiful state since the community of the Shī'a failed to support the family of the Prophet.

The shrine defenders felt the obligation to undertake the daunting task of filling the shoes of 'Abbās in protecting the harem of the *Ahlul-Bayt*, especially the shrine of Sayyida Zaynab, who suffered the most during the course of events since the day of Āshūrā. Hence, chants like "*Lan tusba Zaynab marratayn*" ("Zaynab will not be captive twice"), "*kunnā 'Abbāsuki yā Zaynab*" ("O Zaynab, we are all your 'Abbās") appeared on social media, blogs, and in songs and music videos created by pro-shrine defenders.[75] With all this, it is no coincidence that one of the main Twelver Shī'a militias involved in the defense of Sayyida Zaynab's shrine is named after 'Abbās: *Liwa Abū al-Faḍl al-'Abbās* ("al-'Abbās brigade"). The brigade was formed in 2012 by predominantly Iraqi Shī'īte shrine defenders.

However, the Quds Force primarily organized the brigade, an elite branch of the IRGC that major general Qasem Soleimani then led.[76]

Finally, Zaynab is seen in Twelver Shī'īsm as the second Fāṭimat al-Zahrā.[77] Given the fact that the exact burial place of Fāṭimah is a mystery, the pilgrimage to her daughter (Zaynab)'s shrine as well as the shrine of her descendant Fāṭimat bint Mūsā (daughter of the seventh Imam, Mūsā al-Kāẓim) in Qum would substitute as the pilgrimage to the shrine of Fāṭimah.[78] This adds to the symbolic importance of protecting the shrine of Zaynab, so martyred shrine defenders see themselves as those who sacrifice themselves for Fāṭimat al-Zahrā, which is one of the greatest honors in Twelver Shī'īsm.

6

Shrine Defenders: A New Beginning

The Sectarian Factor

With the practical defeat of ISIS in 2017 and the later death of the group's leader Abu Bakr al-Baghdadi in October 2019, things in Syria and Iraq started to normalize, with less violence and thus, fewer new martyrs. The only official statistics on the number of martyred shrine defenders are from March 2017. The head of Iran's Foundation of Martyrs and Veterans Affairs counted 2,100 martyrs without clarifying whether that number was only for Iranian martyrs or if they had considered other nationalities as well.[1] Iran's leaders and state media crafted a sacred image of the Shīʿa fighters and martyrs and their mission in Syria and Iraq. They only allowed a highly controlled and engineered flow of information regarding the Syrian crisis, which favored the ideological orientation and geopolitical interests of the Islamic Republic and Hezbollah in the region. For the most part, the government's approach worked well with the base supporters of the revolution and the government. However, Iran's military involvement in the Syrian civil war and the propaganda around the shrine defenders also fueled a backlash among Sunni states and attracted its share of domestic criticism from some sectors of the public, as well as opposition groups outside the country.[2]

As discussed earlier, initially Iran was cautious not to publicly disclose its presence in Syria during the first years of the civil war for fear of public backlash. Part of the problem was that Iran's campaign in Iraq and Syria was not about defending the country's borders from a foreign enemy. So, the first waves of martyred shrine defenders were returned home and buried secretly, without any public display. The new martyrdoms that were no longer a part of the theology of defensive jihad (as was largely the case with the Iran–Iraq war in the 1980s) thus needed a convincing and legitimate justification. Thanks to the rise of ISIS, that justification was achieved by depicting the image of the shrine defenders as selfless heroes in the fight against satanic forces to protect the legacy of true Islam.

Moreover, the state's reasoning that taking the fight against ISIS in Syria instead of letting them advance into the country was the winning card that the Islamic Republic's leaders played well in depicting the Syrian crisis as a major threat for Iran and the rest of the region. Consequently, the religious public rallied behind the Islamic Republic's Syrian campaign. A 2019 public opinion study by the University of Maryland, for instance, showed 61 percent of Iranians supported keeping Iran's military presence in Syria.[3] However, once there was no more viable threat of ISIS, the public and dissidents had reasons to question the Islamic Republic's role in the Syrian civil war. The main criticism has been Iran's ongoing military and financial support of the Assad government and Hezbollah and Iran's other proxies in the region where those resources were most needed domestically to mitigate Iran's weakened economy due to the U.S.-implemented sanctions on the country. The open public opposition to Iran's ongoing involvement in Syria and its support of the so-called axis of resistance in the region emerged during the series of unprecedently deadly protests that have occurred periodically since 2017. In particular, during the November 2019 uprising that started because of the sharp hike in petrol prices but quickly turned anti-regime (with allegedly 1,500 protestors being killed), some chants directly targeted Iran's foreign policy and its support of Assad, Hezbollah, and Hamas.[4] Among the chants, in particular, "Leave Syria alone, think about us instead," became popular on the streets and social media.[5]

Regionally, Iran's response to the Syrian crisis by putting its weight behind Assad's regime also hurt its (and Hezbollah's) reputation, particularly among Sunni Arab countries. For decades, the Islamic Republic had tried to export the Islamic Revolution to other Muslim countries in the region and become a model for them to follow by downplaying its Persian and Shīʿī identity. As Thomas Juneau put it, the Islamic Republic aimed (though not fully successfully) to "position itself as a leader among Muslim nations, as the vanguard of resistance against American and Israeli policies."[6] Syria and Hezbollah had played a great role in Iran's goal of becoming the champion of Palestinian rights in the fight against Israel. The perceived victory of Hezbollah (with Iran's support) in 2006's 33-day war with Israel was the high point that brought the popularity of Hezbollah among Sunni Arab countries to an all-time high. However, the Syrian crisis severely damaged the image of anti-imperialism/-Zionism associated with the alliance of Iran–Syria–Hezbollah because of their part in brutally cracking down on peaceful demonstrations and being responsible for the blood of civilians. At the beginning of the crisis, Iran's leaders had to choose between two unfavorable paths: to either stick with the Syrian government despite the apparent vicious mistreatments of its people that could further isolate Iran and

Hezbollah in the region or to support the popular movement that had stemmed from the Arab spring.[7] They chose the former and were willing to pay the price. Iran's decision to stick with the Syrian government despite its brutality in cracking down on initially peaceful protests in 2011 was due to the geopolitical importance of the Iran–Syria–Hezbollah alliance that the Islamic Republic could not afford to lose. However, as the crisis unfolded and Iran and Hezbollah officially got involved in the conflict to support Assad, so did Saudi Arabia and other Sunni Arab states engaged in the war by supporting Sunni Salafī fighters in Syria. Therefore, the war in Syria quickly turned into a full-fledged and multidimensional sectarian conflict that would linger for years to come.[8]

Initially, the Islamic Republic's leaders were very concerned about the transformation of the Syrian civil war into a large-scale sectarian conflict because, for three decades, they had rooted for the Muslim unity and tried to export their revolutionary ideology.[9] But as the Islamic Republic's aspirations to be a model and leader for the rest of Muslims beyond sectarian boundaries became unattainable with the way the Syrian crisis unfolded, the next best bet was to focus on what was in the DNA of the Islamic revolution, that was a Shīʿī movement with messianic tendencies. With the Syrian crisis turning into a sectarian conflict, the Islamic Republic gained the opportunity to be unapologetically and openly true to itself and implement those Shīʿī messianic ideas the revolution was looking after. So, while the Islamic Republic to a large extent lost the trust of the Sunni audience with the Syrian crisis, it gained the recognition of the Shīʿa population in the region.[10] That is why resorting to Shīʿī symbolism in the fight against ISIS under the banner of shrine defenders became a crucial strategy for Iran. It was hard to justify Bashar al-Assad's brutal crackdown on his people's peaceful protests, so it was a strategic move for Iran to channel the Shīʿa population's attention to the religious and sectarian aspects of the conflict and to highlight the need for a decisive Shīʿī campaign to take down the rising threat of militant Salafism.

Eventually, the Islamic Republic found the sectarian nature of the Syrian crisis to be a sort of blessing both domestically and regionally. Iran used the Syrian war to flex its muscles, confront its archrival Saudi Arabia, and demonstrate itself as the defining force within the Muslim world. The sectarian conflict also gave Iran the much-needed opportunity to organize transnational Shīʿa forces from countries like Lebanon, Iraq, Afghanistan, Pakistan.[11] So, Iran's open involvement in the war with the Sunni Salafīsts reinforced its status as the leader of the Shīʿa world. Moreover, it proved Iran's abilities in mobilizing, deploying, and sustaining organized Shīʿa fighters for an extended period of active war. According to some estimates, by 2017 between 30,000 and 60,000 foreign Shīʿa fighters were deployed in Syria.[12] They all were organized by the IRGC's Quds Force, then headed by Qasem Soleimani.

The war in Syria then let Iran put its messianic agenda on display. So, in 2016 and at the peak of the shrine-defenders' movement, Major General Mohammad ʿAlī Jafari, the then head of the IRGC, proudly claimed that Iran had organized an army of 200,000 Shīʿa fighters who could be the backbone of the army of Al-Mahdī: "The current developments in the region, the formation of Daesh [ISIS] and Takfiri groups, and the events that occurred in the past years are paving the ground for the emergence of Imam Mahdi, and you can now see the positive results in the readiness of nearly 200,000 young armed in Syria, Iraq, Afghanistan, Pakistan and Yemen."[13] This sort of Shīʿī political messianism already had been brought to national and international attention by Iran's former president, Mahmoud Ahmadinejad. In his controversial United Nations speeches and other international presences, Ahmadinejad showed no hesitation in explicitly expressing his belief that the coming of al-Mahdī is imminent and the idea that he "will lead the world to justice and absolute peace."[14] As the then president of the Islamic Republic, he considered himself being supported by the Hidden Imam and wanted to be seen as his spokesperson and a herald of the just world to come.[15] While the Ahmadinejad phenomenon raised both domestic and international controversies and speculations about radical messianic beliefs and behaviors, it was with the Syrian crisis and the creation of the shrine-defenders' movement that the Islamic Republic actually got a chance to fully materialize the messianic promises that had been at the core of the 1979 Islamic revolution.

The Imagined Nation of Heroes

The shrine-defenders movement affected Iran's religious public sphere almost unprecedentedly. The movement has produced many instant proclaimed heroes who died fighting against the jihadi Salafīsts. Perhaps, the most iconic martyr who became an overnight face of the shrine defenders was a 25-year-old father and shrine defender named Mohsen Hojaji, an IRGC officer, who had been sent as a military advisor to Syria. In a surprise attack on August 7, 2017, he was captured by ISIS forces and was decapitated two days later. ISIS released the video of his capture, but a still image extracted from the video got the most attention in Iran and went viral on social media. The photo (see Figure 6.1) showing Hojaji being escorted by an ISIS fighter holding a knife in one hand against a background of fire and smoke instantly became iconic. As Shirin Saeidi

Figure 6.1 Mohsen Hojaji being escorted moments before decapitation by ISIS fighters.

analyzed the deeper meaning behind the image, "a physical reaction to the brutal death that awaits him is overshadowed by Hojaji's demureness, expressed with a gaze that struggles not to blend into the scary space that his body occupies."[16] Though Saeidi sees this photo as a challenge to the ideological ideals of both ISIS and the Islamic Republic, because Hojaji "is not showing the terror his captors must have hoped to convey, and he lacks the certainty the Islamic Republic sought to highlight by extracting a photograph of the moment."[17] However, the way this photo and its artistic adaptations were seen and interpreted by the pro-shrine defenders in Iran showed exactly the characteristics of the new martyrdom paradigm discussed earlier: martyrs who were super-confident fighters with a godly mission and refused to be seen as defeated. The *Al-Monitor* report on the incident described the photo and the statement of Hojaji's wife, which was widely shared among pro-shrine defenders' circles in Iran:

> While it is often the more gruesome IS videos that go viral, it was Hojaji's picture the moment he was captured that took off. The picture is particularly haunting and looks like something out of a film. Hojaji, dressed in military fatigues, is held by an IS fighter with a knife in his hand. In the background, black smoke rises from the overtaken camp. Many who saw it drew comparisons between the expressions of Hojaji and his captor. Hojaji, who likely knew his death was imminent, seems resigned to his fate. The IS fighter, with blood running down his cheeks, appears almost anxious. Zahra Abbasi, Hojaji's wife, told the Iranian press, "Look into my husband's eyes. There is no fear in these eyes. It is all bravery, courage. He is like a mountain."[18]

Figure 6.2 The adaptation of Hojaji's capture painted by Hassan Rouholamin. It shows the headless Ḥusayn and his sister Sayyidah Zaynab greeting Hojaji as he is being escorted by ISIS fighters (depicted as Yazid's soldiers) to be beheaded shortly.

Hojaji's martyrdom, thanks to the powerful photo of him before decapitation, was arguably one of the most dramatic instances of martyrdom in the shrine-defenders movement as it had parallels to the martyrdom of Imam Ḥusayn, the master of martyrs. The gaze that his wife pointed at, the dramatic background, the appearance of Hojaji's captor, and the fact that he was brutally beheaded made the image central to the Islamic Republic's propaganda in legitimizing Iran's involvement in the Syrian war. In an adaptation of the photo, the scene's sacred Shīʿī imagery was highlighted by depicting shrine defenders standing on the right side of history in the camp of Ḥusayn fighting against the Yazid's soldiers (see Figure 6.2). Consequently, Hojaji's capture and beheading brought the attention of the Iranian public to the news of the Syrian war and provided a major internal boost for the legitimacy of Iran's military involvement in Syria. So, since 2019, August 9th has been named the national day to recognize martyred shrine defenders in Iran's official calendar. The news of his martyrdom quickly spread on social media, and all sorts of eulogies were poured on him from different sectors of Iranian society (see Figure 6.3). Most notably, Iran's Supreme Leader, during his visit to the family of Hojaji on October 3, 2017, proudly called him the spokesperson for all innocent martyrs and cemented his position as one of the defining figures of the shrine-defenders movement:

> Today, Hojaji's name has become an outstanding, brilliant and prominent name throughout the country. This is because of the endeavors of your youth and his

Figure 6.3 Mourners attended the funeral procession of Mohsen Hojaji at Imam Hossein Square in the capital Tehran on September 27, 2017. (Photo by Fatemeh Bahrami/Anadolu Agency/Getty Images)

> innocent martyrdom. Of course, all our martyrs are dear and innocent. As well as your martyr—our martyr—there are other martyrs who were martyred in the same manner. The enemy beheaded them and delivered mortal blows to them while they were alive. We have such martyrs. All of them enjoy an exalted position. All of them are dear to Allah the Exalted. However, when a group of people enter somewhere, one of them speaks as their representative and as their spokesperson. This martyred Mohsen became the representative of all these innocent martyrs. In fact, he became their spokesperson. All the martyrs from Iran, Afghanistan, Iraq and other places who were martyred in the front of fighting against *takfīrī* thugs and the puppets of the U.S. and England are in fact embodied by and reflected in this youth. He became their representative. He became the symbol of innocent martyrdom. He became a symbol. God turned your child, your son and your youth into a symbol of innocent and courageous martyrdom.[19]

While the Islamic Republic's leaders have hailed Hojaji and all other martyrs of the shrine defenders as exemplary heroes, undoubtedly the standout proclaimed hero of the movement and its towering figure was the assassinated Major General Qasem Soleimani. As the commander of Iran's Quds Force that specialized in unconventional warfare and military intelligence, Soleimani was one of the most powerful, influential, and enigmatic leaders of the IRGC. He had been credited by Iran's state media and foreign observers as the military brain behind IRGC's extraterritorial operations since the end of the Iran–Iraq war,[20] and the "guardian of Iran's regional interests."[21] Soleimani directly cooperated with Bashar al-Assad's regime as they struggled to survive during the early stages of the Syrian civil war. He was also a key figure and coordinator of the coalition of Shīʿa fighters against ISIS in Iraq and Syria since 2014 and helped the creation of Iraq's *al-Ḥashd ash-Shaʿbī* ("the Popular Mobilization Forces"), a Shīʿa militia organization that was modeled on Iran's *Basīj* force to fight against the Islamic State in Iraq and the Levant.[22] Particularly after the de facto defeat of ISIS in 2017, Soleimani enjoyed a superstar and celebrity status and became a national champion for many sectors of Iranian society.[23] So, when it comes to the discussion of Shīʿa shrine defenders, Soleimani's name always pops up as the architect of the movement. The title of "shrine defenders" was also coined by Soleimani himself, a clever naming to inspire zeal among Shīʿa fighters and draw the sympathy and support of the broader community of the Shīʿa towards Iran and its proxies' military adventures in Syria and Iraq. In a recorded speech, Soleimani described his rationale for choosing the title "shrine defenders":

Figure 6.4 A portrait of slain Iranian military commander Qasem Soleimani is pictured on the main road leading to the airport in the Lebanese capital Beirut on January 11, 2020. The poster reads: "master of the martyrs (*sayyid al-shuhadā*) of the Axis of Resistance." (Photo by Joseph Eid/AFP via Getty Images)

> When I wanted to name this, at the beginning of the Syrian crisis, I was thinking a lot about what name we should pick to attract people from the Islamic world to join us to defend the shrine. I thought the most attractive name that could be put on this new jihadi movement was the title of "shrine defenders."[24]

When on 3 January, 2020, Qasem Soleimani was assassinated along with Abu Mahdi al-Muhandis, the deputy chief of the Popular Mobilization Forces, by a targeted U.S. drone strike, Soleimani's celebrated and heroic position in the shrine-defenders movement and his perceived contribution in the defeat of the ISIS effectively turned him into the highest-profile martyr after the Iran–Iraq war. In the words of Khamenei, in a message following his martyrdom, Soleimani was counted the best that Ayatollah Khomeini's Islamic revolution could offer.[25] Moreover, already being called a "living martyr" by Khamenei before his assassination, Soleimani has become the definition of martyrdom for his supporters. He is even called the "master of the martyrs" (*sayyid al-shuhadā*) of the Axis of Resistance (the Iran-led Shī'a coalition in the Middle East) (see Figure 6.4).[26] To get an idea of how deeply the Iranian public (from various

Figure 6.5 Coffins of Iranian Major General Qassem Soleimani and others, who were killed in Iraq by a U.S. drone strike, are carried on a truck surrounded by mourners during a funeral procession on January 6, 2020, in Tehran, Iran. (Photo by Majid Saeedi/Getty Images)

religious and political orientations) had felt about Soleimani and come on board with the government's military adventure in Syria, one had to observe the massive crowds of mourners during funeral processions in various cities in Iraq and Iran for the martyrs Soleimani and al-Muhandis. In Iran, the scale of Soleimani's funeral processions has been unprecedented since the funeral of Khomeini, the founder of the Islamic Republic, in 1989 (see Figure 6.5). The mourning crowds were so huge that the burial procession of Soleimani in the southern Iranian city of Kerman (Soleimani's birthplace) caused a stampede killing fifty-six and injuring more than two hundred.[27] Moreover, since his martyrdom, Soleimani has become the subject of multiple high-volume hagiographies, children's books, national TV programs, unprecedented compared to other martyrs of the revolution and the Islamic Republic.

Regionally, the martyrdoms of Soleimani and al-Muhandis created uncertainty and doubts about the future of the shrine-defenders movement and Iran's ability to retain its direct influence through its proxies in Iraq and Syria.[28] As his most trusted commander of the IRGC, Soleimani's martyrdom was also a severe blow to Iran's Supreme Leader and the shrine-defenders movement in general. At the same time, Soleimani's martyrdom cemented his status as a towering icon of the Shīʿī jihad and evoked apocalyptic aspirations that fit the characteristics of the new martyrdom paradigm. In his speech for the first anniversary of the assassination of Soleimani on December 16, 2020, Khamenei called Soleimani "the champion of the Iranian nation and of the Islamic *Ummah*."[29] Moreover, posthumously, Soleimani has become the face of the Islamic Republic's anti-Western propaganda. For instance, on the first anniversary of his martyrdom, an animated short video with an apocalyptic message was broadcast by the state-sponsored Mehr News Agency focusing on the power of the Iranian-led Shīʿī axis of resistance and its heroes who execute the promised "hard revenge" against the United States for the killing of Soleimani. The animation, showing the photos of Soleimani and al-Muhandis and the flags of the IRGC and Lebanon's Hezbollah, starts with the voice of Hossein Salami, the commander-in-chief of the IRGC, speaking during the funeral procession of Soleimani in Tehran: "We will take revenge, hard, firm, remorseful, decisive, and final."[30] The animation then shows the IRGC commanders turning into eagles attacking the Ayn al-Asad, the U.S. airbase in Iraq. An Arabic epic song played in the background reads:

> We make a pact with friends near and far; we swear on the blood of Soleimani. From his determination, the resistance front becomes stronger. And we will

> destroy the great devil. A massive attack awaits the false front. We swear on the blood of Soleimani, we will destroy your authority. And the world will witness your humiliation. And your coffins will be sent in a row. We swear on the blood of Soleimani, Soleimani's soul will destroy you. And it will destroy your comfort. And you will suffer a dark death. We swear on the blood of Soleimani, Soleimani's soul will destroy you. And it will destroy your comfort. And you will suffer a dark death.[31]

The video ends with depicting an eagle grabbing a U.S. soldier and dropping him dead in the middle of former President Donald Trump's speech in front of the U.S. Congress. In the final scene, a quote from Khamenei appears on the screen, reading: "Harsh revenge awaits the criminals whose hands are stained with the blood of Soleimani and other martyrs."

While the relative stability in the Syrian political landscape in favor of the Syrian government wound down the shrine-defenders movement, its effect on the Shi'a community in the region, Iran in particular, is lingering. The phenomenon of shrine defenders, while polarizing, has dominated the martyrdom paradigm in Iran and changed its perception. A good representative of this change in Iranian society is the painting (see Figure 6.6) which was unveiled for the so-called "Sacred Defense Week" (the annual commemoration of the Iran–Iraq war at the end of September) on a giant billboard (the largest in Iran) in Tehran's Valiasr Square. The painting shows a quote from Qasem Soleimani saying, "We are the nation of martyrdom." It also portraits several martyrs, including Mohsen Hojaji, Majid Shahriari (an assassinated nuclear scientist), and Soleimani (the biggest one). The point here is that the painting for the commemoration of the Iran–Iraq war has no single portrait of a martyr from

Figure 6.6 A billboard painting installed in Tehran that reads, "We are the nation of martyrdom." Source: http://www.owjmedia.org/.

the war period. It symbolizes a change in the perception of heroes; a departure from the past generation of national heroes and martyrs of the so-called imposed war who fought tooth and nail to defend their frontiers and resembled those martyrs of Karbalā to the new generation of martyrs of the proud and proactive nation that aggressively has expanded jihad in new frontiers. It shows the new paradigm of martyrdom that values dying not from a defensive and weak position but with a messianic mindset to change their surrounding world. In other words, and according to the terminology of the shrine-defenders movement, the new martyrdom paradigm is not about dying oppressed while being in the camp of Ḥusayn, rather it is all about dying in the camp of Al-Mahdī, taking revenge against those who oppressed Ḥusayn.

A part of the shifting martyrdom paradigm in contemporary Iran, affected by the shrine-defenders movement, has been the response to the Covid-19 pandemic that hit the country hard grom early 2020. In the above-mentioned painting (see Figure 6.6), there is a portrait of a medical professional who seemingly died as a martyr while doing her job of caring for Covid-19 patients. Dead doctors and health-care workers being called "martyrs" is not something new. As we saw earlier, the definition of martyrdom expanded to cover many kinds of death other than dying on the battlefield. However, the interesting point here is how the concept of shrine defenders has affected the vocabulary and the imagination of a nation gripped by the pandemic. In line with the martyred shrined defenders being remembered and respected as selfless heroes who died to defend the Shīʿī shrines and the frontiers from the rising threat of Salafī fighters, the fight against Coronavirus has been described in terms of the sacred defense of the health of society. So, similar to the term "martyred shrine defenders," the dead health-care workers in the fight against Covid-19 have been widely called "martyred health defenders" (*shuhadāy-i mudāfiʿ-i salāmat*). Accordingly, doctors and nurses are described by terms like "selfless soldiers," who are fighting in an unequal war against Coronavirus. Drawing similarities between doctors who fight against Covid-19 and the martyrs of the Iran–Iraq war and the shrine defenders is seen in state-run media and has been discussed by state officials. Saeed Namaki, the then Iranian health minister, in his message for the 2020 Sacred Defense Week, connected the Iranian soldiers' sacrifice in the Iran–Iraq war to those of the shrine defenders and health-care personnel. He wrote:

> This year's commemoration [of the war] has two differences [compared to the previous years]. First, Major General Qasem Soleimani ... joined his martyred

friends [who died in the war] and the master of the martyrs [Imam Ḥusayn]. Second, this year, Iran is grappling with the [corona] virus like the rest of the world. For months, the health defenders with similar love and dedication of the defenders of our frontiers during the sacred defense, have thrown themselves into this calamity to defend the health of their compatriots, and in this path, some of our dears have joined the ranks of martyrs . . . In the past few days, the empathy and harmony of the Iranian nation with the efforts of all shrine defenders and health defenders created epic scenes even more beautiful than the days of the sacred defense.[32]

Many posters and street billboards that have been created since the Covid-19 pandemic in recognition of the efforts of the health-care personnel show them side-by-side with soldiers of the Iran–Iraq war or shrine defenders as two sides of the same coin, implying that hospitals are the new frontline of jihad (see Figure 6.7). Qasem Soleimani, as the symbol of martyred shrine defenders, has also been included in some of those artworks as the symbol of selfless defence. For example, a picture of Soleimani (see Figure 6.8) is displayed as part of the *Haft-Sīn* (the traditional table setting of Nowruz that incorporates seven items that start with the Persian letter 'س', pronounced like 's' in English), while doctors

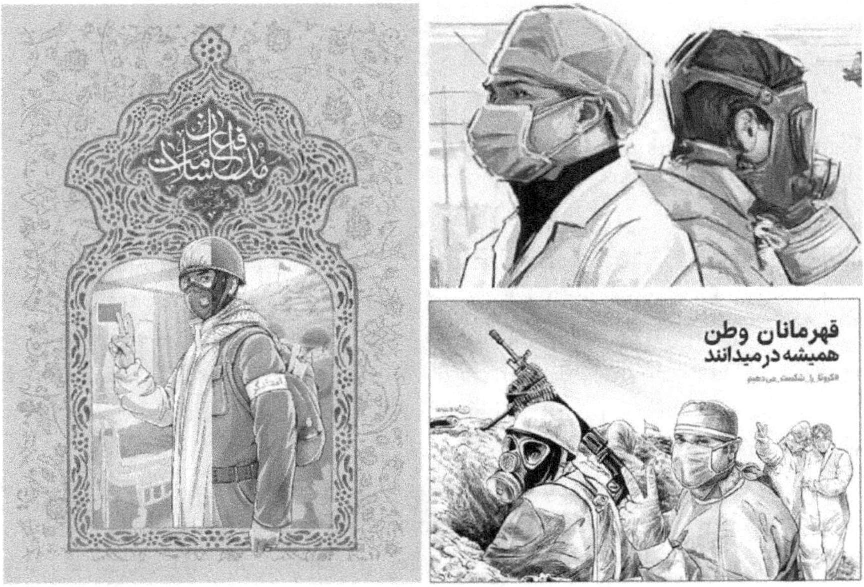

Figure 6.7 Artworks showing doctors during the Covid-19 pandemic like soldiers of the Iran–Iraq war, having the same goal on a different battlefield. Source: http://www.asr-entezar.ir/archives/63948; https://www.yjc.ir/00UUmm; https://tn.ai/2269538.

Figure 6.8 Celebration of Nowruz with Qasem Soleimani depicted as an element of the *Haft-Sīn* table. Source: https://www.borna.news/fa/tiny/news-979037.

and Iranian soldiers are depicted sitting beside each other celebrating Nowruz. In this case, Soleimani, sanitizer, *silāh* (rifle), *sabzeh* (wheat grown in a dish), *sajjādih* (prayer mat), *sīr* (garlic), and *sīb* (apple) form the seven elements of the *Haft-Sīn*.[33] They combined Persian traditions with Islamic as well as jihadi values, something that the Islamic Republic has been actively tried to institutionalize within Iranian society.

All this shows how the culture of martyrdom has been aggressively institutionalized in the Islamic Republic and has become part of the religious public's mindset. So, defending tradition and the way of the Imams, particularly the commemoration of Ḥusayn, martyrdom is always the answer, and even the deadly pandemic can only be understood through that concept. While Iran's Covid-19 cases hit a new record,[34] just ahead of the 2021 month of Muḥarram, public indoor gatherings for the commemoration of Āshūrā never stopped. Instead, some ultra-traditional religious preachers encouraged people to stick to the practice despite the obvious fatal dangers associated with those packed events during the pandemic. For instance, a video of a speech given by an ultra-traditionalist cleric and an instructor at the Isfahan religious seminary was widely distributed online. The cleric urged the Shīʿi believers not to abandon the Muḥarram events for fear of Covid-19. He argued that those who died from the infection due to participation in the public mourning for Imam Ḥusayn would be among the martyred shrine defenders. In his view, the martyred shrine defenders also knew they would probably die, but they never hesitated and rushed to the defense of the shrines. Similarly, those committed to keeping the Āshūrā tradition alive and raising the flag of Ḥusayn understand that they might be infected and die, but they should continue to do so because the "shrine" is where there is a mourning flag of Ḥusayn. If the mourners contract the coronavirus in those places and die of it, they will be martyred shrine defenders.[35]

7

From Karbalā to Damascus

The shrine defenders mark the transition (or the full circle) from the original Shīʿī understanding of martyrdom in terms of tragedy, oppression, and the usurpation of the Twelve Imams' rights. In the eyes of the Shīʿa, no other martyrdom, even that of Alī, the first Imam, can compare to what happened on the day of Āshūrā. Thus, the traditional martyrdom paradigm in Shīʿīsm has long been dominated by Karbalā narratives. However, the tragedy symbolizing the betrayal of and enmity toward the Prophet's immediate family (shortly after his death) also emerged from heroic stories and myths about seventy-two (or more) of Ḥusayn's ultra-devoted family members and followers. Based on the written martyrologies, they competed with each other to be the first to shed their blood in defense of the last remaining grandson of the Prophet, the son of ʿAlī and Fāṭimah. They become exemplary heroes of the Shīʿa for their ultimate faithfulness to their Imam while others failed shamefully. In short, the tragedy of Āshūrā and its tales of heroism turned out to be a massive shock and a wake-up call for those Muslims who had sympathized with ʿAlī as the perceived rightful successor to the Prophet. Ḥusayn's martyrdom became a defining moment in Islamic history that separated the Shīʿa of ʿAlī from the rest of the Muslim world that later became identified as Sunni.

The shock of Ḥusayn's martyrdom reverberated for decades after Āshūrā and, as briefly reviewed in Chapter 1, it fueled several Shīʿī-branded revolts against the Umayyads and the Abbasid rules, with varying degrees of success and intention. However, with not enough fighters or resources and a lack of unifying leaders, the Shīʿī rebels had no realistic chance of lasting victory. In retrospect and from the point of view and perception of the contemporary community of the Shīʿa, with every revolt during the formative period of Twelver Shīʿīsm came the disappointing reality of defeat and the ever-growing sense of being oppressed and victimized by the fruits of the so-called unholy coalition of the *saqīfah*[1] that allegedly deviated Islam from its essence and deprived Muslims of being led by "the divinely guided Imams." It is the common understanding of today's Shīʿa Muslims that the Imams, while being the heads of the Prophet's family and divinely chosen successors to the Prophet, neither engaged in direct confrontation with Sunni caliphs nor called their followers to rebellion after the events of Āshūrā. There is no strong tradition suggesting that they explicitly approved any of the Shīʿī revolts. But, in some cases, like the *martyrs of Fakhkh*, the Imams endorsed the fallen rebels as virtuous martyrs. Instead of avenging Ḥusayn to the point of dying on that path, the Imams highlighted the tragic side of Āshūrā. They promoted the culture of mourning the Ḥusayn's martyrdom and the practice of cursing his killers by reciting liturgical texts like the *zīyārat āshūrā*.

The practical silence of the Imams when it came to military campaigns against the Sunni caliphate system became a major factor that later made Twelver Shīʿīsm a quietist tradition for most of the medieval period until the modern era. With the growing importance of *taqīya* and quietism in the formative period of Twelver Shīʿīsm, particularly after the disappearance of the Twelfth Imam, the martyrdom of Imam Ḥusayn remained mainly a tragedy that should be passively mourned rather than celebrated or seen as an inspiration for political rebellion. Hence, the dominant narrative of Ḥusayn's martyrdom depicted Ḥusayn's fate as a divinely planned scenario that has been part of the creation story since the beginning of time. Ḥusayn was the "great sacrifice" that was foretold to all prophets, and they all wept for the cruelty that would occur.[2] The martyrdom of Ḥusayn, then, was seen primarily as the source of intercession, and weeping for him became associated with miracles and a sign of eternal redemption. Āshūrā was the darkest scene in the history of creation—the climax of oppression, injustice, cruelty, and inhumanity. However, all those tragic aspects of martyrdom had been balanced by an eschatological hope of justice in this world before the judgment day: a redeemer from a descendant of Ḥusayn would rise to rescue humanity, fix all wrongdoing, and avenge the blood of the great sacrifice (Ḥusayn). The idea of al-Mahdī's triumphant return at the end of time was the divine promise that made the pain of Ḥusayn's martyrdom bearable for the faithful followers of the Imams.

While the process of repoliticization of Twelver Shīʿīsm after the period of the Imams was gradual, as I have discussed in earlier chapters, it was the twentieth century that saw a big push in that direction and made the tradition politically conscious again. Within around fifteen years, and by the 1979 Islamic revolution, an entire generation of students of Iran's traditional Shīʿī seminaries was politicized. Following the revolution, the Islamic Republic's leaders valued cultivating the culture of martyrdom among the youth. It became clear that the martyrdom-seeking culture was a driving force and a key factor in the revolution's success that later inspired Iran's massive *Basīj* volunteer forces to push the technologically superior Iraqi troops out of Iran's territory. Martyrs of the revolution and the war were praised as national heroes who sacrificed everything for the sake of the revolution and the Islamic government under the leadership of the charismatic Khomeini. Their martyrdoms were linked to the martyrdom of Ḥusayn as the ultimate model for martyrs. The newly established Islamic government desperately needed those acts of heroism and sacrifice to ensure its survival; hence, the need to constantly refuel the nation with the emotional "commemoration of Ḥusayn" (*shūr-i Ḥusayni*). So, Khomeini repeatedly said that Islam survived because of Āshūrā and the annual commemoration of Ḥusayn's martyrdom. He demanded that public commemorations be observed for inspiration because as the martyrdom of exemplary martyrs saved Islam, so too does the Islamic government need the blood of martyrs to guarantee its success:

> This religion is alive, thanks to traditional ways of remembrance and commemorating the martyrs of Karbala. Do not let the devils instill into you that we have staged a revolution and should now talk about the issues of the revolution and that the questions of the past should be forgotten. Never. We should keep the Islamic traditions and these blessed Islamic processions to commemorate Āshūrā in the months of Muharram and Safar.[3] We should emphatically call for greater attention to the event. It is Muharram and Safar that have kept Islam alive. It was the selflessness of the *sayyid al-shuhadā* [Imam Ḥusayn] (may God's peace be upon him) that has kept Islam alive for us. Keep Āshūrā alive in its former traditional frame.[4]

Despite the eventual success of the revolution and the Islamic Republic, however, Khomeini had faced internal opposition from ultra-traditionalists among his peers in religious seminaries when he started his extreme political activism against the Shah of Iran in the 1960s. That was due to the deeply embedded culture of *taqīya* and pietistic and eschatological readings of the martyrdom of Ḥusayn that for centuries had been the norm among top Shīʿī jurists. Even with the Islamic Republic well in place, the now minority apolitical traditionalists still kept their distance from the politics of the government. The ultra-traditionalists either voiced their objections to the *wilāyat-i faqīh*-based government and were repressed as a result[5] or, following their quietist approach, got along with the Islamic Republic without being involved in politics, as their predecessors did with secular governments before the revolution.

Doctrinally speaking, the ultra-traditionalists particularly take the lack of political activism in the life of the Imams after *Āshūrā* (i.e., successors of Ḥusayn) as a blueprint on how the community of the Shīʿa should be until the awaited Imam Mahdi returns at the end of time to lead his promised world revolution. For them, jihad and martyrdom are not applicable to the present time when the infallible Imam is not available to guide the Muslim community. The most active and organized group within the camp of contemporary ultra-traditionalists was the now-defunct Association of *Hujjatīyeh-Mahdavīyeh*, founded in 1953 by Mahmoud Halabi (d. 1996), a charismatic traditionalist cleric. The *Hujjatiyeh* was initially created to "train cadres for the 'scientific defense' of Shīʿīte Islam in the face of the *Baha'ī* theological challenge."[6] In addition, according to its constitution, the *Hujjatīyeh* "wanted to cultivate and nurture people who would be both highly trained in the modern sciences and well-grounded in their religious tradition and culture."[7] Halabi, in his public lectures, vehemently insisted that the priority of the Shi'a must be in defense of the Imam of the time (i.e., the hidden twelfth Imam). In Halabi's understanding, jihad was not necessarily equal to going to war against the enemy of God, but rather, it was doing what the Imam expected from the Shiʿa. He maintained that the Imams determined the duty of the Shīʿa just in waiting for the return of Imam Mahdi, endeavoring to promote the cause of the Imam and rectifying the minds of the believers from doubts and obscurities to prepare them to accept the rule of the Imam at the end of time.[8] Not surprisingly, this put the *Hujjatīyeh* at odds with the action-minded revolutionaries.[9] Following Khomeini's public speech on August 12, 1983, where he publically criticized the beliefs associated with the group, the *Hujjatīyeh* was disbanded.[10]

The *Hujjatīyeh* was the systematic and modern response of the ultra-traditionalists to the then growing extremist and militaristic interpretation of Twelver Shīʿīsm in late-twentieth-century Iran. Having a ritualistic and *ḥadīth*-oriented mindset, the ultra-traditionalists associated with or close to the *Hujjatīyeh* favored pietistic cultural activism over political activism aiming to transform the society by acquiring political power. They ultimately failed to popularize their ideas, giving in to the over-the-moon, clerical-led revolutionaries who had risen to topple the pro-Western Pahlavi dynasty and establish an Islamic government with the then-popular mottos of independence and Islamic social justice. While the *Hujjatīyeh* organization ceased to exist, its doctrinal values remained alive and developed in a growing niche of highly religious and educated traditionalists. So, the Hujjatīyeh has had its share of influence on the religious culture of the Islamic Republic. The *Hujjatīyeh*, at its core, was a messianic ideology. As such, the organization's legacy and several doctrinally affiliated cultural and educational institutions, like the Alavi school, that trained many high-ranking Islamic Republic officials, in addition to some highly respected top jurists—like the ultra-traditionalist Ayatollah Wahīd Khurāsanī, who has a large following—have been influential in cultivating messianic tendencies. This has increased attention to the Hidden Imam and the idea of *intiẓār*, which, as discussed, had been overshadowed in the formative periods of the revolution and the Islamic Republic. This renewed attention to Imam al-Mahdī and his promised apocalyptic cause resulted in a paradigm shift in the understanding of martyrdom that emerged with the shrine-defenders' movement.

As the Islamic Republic and its proxies evolved, got stronger, and turned into regional powers, so did the understating of martyrdom and martyrdom-seeking among Twelver Shīʿītes develop to a whole new level, which peaked during the Syrian crisis and the war on ISIS. So, the martyred shrine defenders went beyond national heroes and acted as the protectors of the legacy of the Prophet's family. The state media presented victims of the Iran–Iraq war as wronged martyrs as they were in a weaker position, fighting against a militarily and technically better-equipped enemy backed by Western powers.[11] That, of course, has been a source of pride and propaganda for the revolution and government leaders, who saw it as a modern example of the victory of blood over the sword, as was the case with the story of Āshūrā. The shrine defenders, on the contrary, have had mostly the upper hand in their fight against the Sunni Salafīs and their supporters, as the Islamic Republic, with the support of its proxies, had turned into a regional power. That mentality of fighting and commanding from a position of power gave the implicit impression of being practically in the position of the awaited al-Mahdī and doing what he promised to do at the end of time, that is, avenging the blood of Ḥusayn and other wronged martyrs of the Shīʿa. In other words, new martyrs saw themselves dying in the closest circumstances to that of the promised period of al-Mahdī's reappearance and the final confrontation of good versus bad. That has been a big deal for devout shrine defenders, as dying in the path of avenging the blood of Ḥusayn is one of the greatest honors that a Shīʿa can achieve. For centuries, believers could only wish for it (without an actual opportunity to do so). That wish is embedded in the *zīyārat ʿāshūrā*, which is a highly treasured salutatory prayer that a pious Shīʿa regularly recites: "May my father and mother be sacrificed for you [Ḥusayn]. Surely, my sorrow for you is great, and I pray to Allah who has honored your status and has also honored me through you that He grant me the opportunity to seek your revenge with the victorious Imam [al-Mahdī] from the family of Muhammad."[12] Shrine defenders could then proudly see this prayer as getting fulfilled.

In a sense, and from a sectarian point of view, the significance and value of the sacrifices made by martyred shrine defenders lie in the fact that they died for a uniquely global Shīʿī cause to end an age-old assault on the tradition of the Prophet and *Ahlul-Bayt*, now represented in Zaynab. The Iran-led shrine defenders movement can be described as a three-fold phenomenon. First, it was shaped by the Shīʿī reading of the messianic prophecies related to the return of al-Mahdī. Second, it is emotionally fueled with the tragic tales of Zaynab and Ḥusayn and, to a broader extent, Fāṭimah as the symbol of sorrow and the oppressed soul of the tradition. Last, the leadership ties to the messianic nature of the movement. The shrine defenders march behind Iran's Supreme Leader, a descendant of the Prophet acting as the deputy of the Hidden Imam, thanks to his position as the *walī-i faqīh*. They respect him just short of the twelve infallible Imams and affectionately call him *āqā* (master). To understand how those three factors have come together and formed the new martyrdom paradigm in Twelver Shīʿīsm, look at this English translation of a lamentation performed by a large group of the shrine defenders in the presence of Iran's Supreme Leader, Ayatollah ʿAlī Khamenei. This is from 2016 at the peak of the shrine defenders movement:

> Ḥusayn, my master. Are you watching the magnificent unity of the followers of Ḥusayn? Are you watching the huge force of the followers of Ḥusayn at Arbaʿīn? We will install the flag of Ḥusayn all over the world. We will finish of the last of the Yazīd [ISIS] from the earth. We will walk on foot while wearing a black suit. That black suit will be our coffin suit. O' Leader Ḥusayni [Ayatollah Khamenei]! We are waiting for your signal. Ḥusayn, my master. (Remember everyone who was martyred to guard the shrine of Zaynab.) For a moment watch me, watch my lamentation for Ḥusayn. See tears overflowing for Ḥusayn and wetting the face, I am your servant. My heart is restless, but I am patient. How many martyred are coming home from Syria. I should also go, let my head be chopped off. I will not allow that bastard [ISIS] to come near the shrine of Zaynab. One day will come my last breath. I am a mother and I love my child. But I offer my youth to Lady Zaynab. Please accept my gift so he becomes a defender of your shrine. Ḥusayn, my master.[13]

To sum up the above discussion, the phenomenon of shrine defenders thus exhibits a shift in the contemporary Twelver Shīʿī worldview. In other words, fighting and dying for the protection of the Shīʿa shrines and sacred places in Iraq and Syria symbolized a new era, a kind of transition from the practice of passive *intiẓār* to pragmatic messianism. Twelver Shīʿīsm has always been understood as an idealistic ideology advocating an authentic Islamic government under a just ruler appointed by God, something that never happened after the Prophet. Even ʿAlī's almost four-year caliphate was not ideal, as his political authority was constantly challenged and weakened by rival factions. Shīʿī messianism envisioned al-Mahdī as the promised savior who would finally turn that idealism into a reality with his world revolution at the end of time, making right everything that has gone wrong. So, *intiẓār* and passively waiting for al-Mahdī's return had long been the dominant paradigm in Twelver Shīʿīsm. The Islamic revolution of 1979, under the leadership of the charismatic Khomeini, was a turning point, a step in the direction of making that idealism a reality by hastening the return of al-Mahdī through simulating the presence of the Imams, though Khomeini never implied that. The formative period of the Islamic Republic was all about survival and presenting a viable model of the Islamic government to the Muslim world. Therefore, the martyrs of the war with Iraq died in the circumstances closest to the martyrs of Karbalā; they held on to their Islamic ideals under the rule of their Imam Ḥusayn-like leader. But practically, the revolution was a call for an active *intiẓār*, and that became more pronounced in later years because of the increased public attention to al-Mahdī. Khomeini defined *intiẓār* as preparing for the power of Islam; for him, *intiẓār* was the effort to spread the power of Islam throughout the world.[14] So, Khomeini saw the active *intiẓār* as standing up against injustice.[15] He perceived the revolution as part of *intiẓār* and wanted to establish divine justice in the country and the rest of the Muslim world by exporting the values of the revolution.[16]

In my understanding, as the years have passed, there appeared to be a sort of identity crisis for Iran's Shīʿī ruling establishment. The successful transition from the revolution to the firmly established Islamic Republic (with considerable political power and regional influence), and the full implementation of the theory of *wilāyat-i faqīh*, made waiting for the return of the promised al-Mahdī less necessary, as the *walī-i faqīh* practically acquired the same authority and mentality as the infallible Imam. This is not to say that the devout adherents of the *wilāyat-i faqīh* think they are leaving the age of *intiẓār* behind; rather, I am referring to the mentality that comes with this change. In other words, Khamenei, being the current ruling jurist, practically assumed the al-Mahdī-like position of leading his army in a jihad against what he describes as the satanic forces (orchestrated by the United States) that aim to stop the awakened Islamic *Ummah*.[17] This is where the Iran-led Shīʿa coalition's decisive, successful involvement in the sectarian regional conflict in Iraq and Syria (leading to the de facto defeat of ISIS and their fellow Salafī jihadists) became so important as a turning point. Here, I have to emphasize the point I made earlier: While the Iranian Shīʿa fighters and martyrs of the eight-year war with Iraq exemplified those who fought and martyred alongside Ḥusayn in Karbalā, the shrine defenders saw themselves more like the soldiers of al-Mahdī.[18] They acted from a position of power and assumed the same kind of responsibility that al-Mahdī is supposed to have with his promised return, that is, avenging the blood of Ḥusayn, restoring the Prophet and the Imams' legacy, and making right what has gone wrong. Having said that, martyrdom in Twelver Shīʿīsm is now fully understandable in terms of sacrifice for the sake of the already ongoing de facto cosmic battle between the party of God (*hizbullāh*) and the forces of "Satan."

Appendix: Martyrdom in Classical Islam

Martyrdom in Sunni Traditions

Moving from the Qur'an to the post-Qur'anic *ḥadīth* literature, we see a huge difference in how martyrdom is presented. The Qur'an does not explicitly recognize martyrdom in a particular fashion and frequently speaks vaguely regarding the martyrs' rewards and position compared to the rewards of other believers. On the contrary, the vast corpus of *ḥadīth* literature and Qur'anic exegesis (*tafsīr*) present the concept of martyrdom, in varying degrees, as the best way of leaving this world, and priceless honor. In *ḥadīth* collections, martyrdom has been delineated in great detail: forms of martyrdom, its conditions, the status of martyrs in this world and the world to come, and exclusive rewards for true martyrs. We also see the concept of martyrdom being expanded for pious Muslims to include normal (non-violent) ways of dying, virtually opening the door for anyone to be honored by martyrdom. In her examination of Sunni *ḥadīth* narrations on martyrdom, Roberta Denaro has divided them into two broad categories of Definition and Narration.[1] According to this classification, the first group of martyrdom traditions defines the concept of martyrdom and explains different kinds of martyrs. The second group depicts desirable accounts of martyrs' conditions after death, their special status, rewards, and visions (mostly for battlefield martyrs). In this section, I will examine how Sunni traditions define and describe martyrdom.

The first thing that comes to mind in comparing the literal text of the Qur'an and the *ḥadīth* literature is that, in the latter, the words *shahīd* and *shahādah* are used unambiguously for "martyr" and "martyrdom," respectively (in cases where their literal meaning as "witness" is not meant). As a result, many exegetes have read the Qur'an with this mindset; they interpreted verses of the Qur'an that include the term *shuhadā* as a direct reference to the concept of martyrdom. Moreover, looking at the different *ḥadīths* on martyrdom reveals how time and place shaped the tone of *ḥadīths* regarding the definition and boundaries of martyrdom. For example, during the peak of Muslim conquests in the seventh and eighth centuries and in the frontiers (particularly in Syria where it was both the Umayyads' capital and close to the battleground with the Byzantine), typically those who documented *ḥadīths* were interested in the ideas of military jihad and in emphasizing the extraordinary rewards that await those who experience violent forms of martyrdom on the battlefield. On the other hand, in places where people were less loyal to the central government and its military agenda, or after the periods of the conquests and with the rise of Sufism beginning in the ninth century, we see more traditions that highlight the inner (esoteric) aspect of jihad, and a broader understanding of martyrdom, which goes beyond just the battlefield martyrs to include even those who die of a stomach disease, as an example. In the following discussion, I will look into these traditions in more detail.

Who is a Martyr?

The basic question for early Muslims was to find out who would get the prestigious title of "martyr." The default (and obvious) answer was one who was killed in the path of God, although with some qualifications. The earliest document available devoted to the subject was written by an eighth-century ascetic/warrior, Abdullāh ibn Mubārak (d. 797), who emigrated to Syria to be at the forefront of the war with the Byzantines. In his book, *Kitāb al-Jihad*, ibn Mubārak's great contribution lies in collecting and preserving many *ḥadīths* on jihad and martyrdom, which then reappeared in later *ḥadīth* works. His first major tradition on martyrdom (*ḥadīth* number 7) is about its classification and ranking of martyrs in comparison to each other (note that for ibn Mubārak, the default definition of "martyr" is one who is killed on the battlefield). In this category of traditions, the question is not just who is a martyr and who is not; rather, how martyrs fare in comparison to each other is also important for *ḥadīth* compilers:

> The slain [on the battlefield] are three men: [1] a believer who struggles in the path of God with himself and his wealth (possessions) and, when he faces the enemy, he fights with them until he is killed; he is a tested martyr (*shahīd*), is placed under God's throne among his camp, and the prophets are not above him in rank except for the level of prophecy. [2] A sinful believer who struggles in the path of God with himself and his wealth (possessions) and faces the enemy, fights with them until he is killed; he is cleared, his sins will be forgiven, the sword wipes away sins, and he will enter heaven from whatever gate he pleases (heaven has eight gates while hell has seven gates, some are worse than the others). [3] And a hypocrite who struggles in the path of God with himself and his wealth (possessions) and faces the enemy, fights with them until he is killed; he is in hell since the sword will not wipe away hypocrisy.[2]

In this case, the tradition suggests that the martyr is devoted to God's cause (not specified whether it is out of fear of God or love of God). It also implies that forgiveness would be a great motivation for being martyred, though not every sin will be forgiven, hypocrisy in particular. Another tradition puts martyrs into four different levels in rank. It demonstrates how prior sins and moral offenses have adverse effects on the level and value of martyrdom. Here again sin (there is no mention of the grave and unforgivable sins such as hypocrisy) will be forgiven, yet it affects the quality of martyrdom in accordance with the degree of the sin:

> A firm believer who meets the enemy and fights until he is killed; people will look at him in awe on the day of judgment . . . And a firm believer who becomes scared when he meets the enemy and somehow an arrow hits him and he dies; he is in the second level in rank. And a believer with a mixture of good deeds and misdeeds who, when he meets the enemy, fights for the sake of God until he is killed; he is in the third level in rank. And a believer who has harmed himself with his own excess, but when he meets the enemy fights for the sake of God until he is killed; he is in the fourth level.[3]

Other *ḥadīths* classify fighting martyrs from a different point of view: intention. In one instance narrated by ibn Mubārak, we read that angels came down to a group of soldiers slain in the path of God and separated them on the following basis: "This one fought for this world, and that one fought for gaining political power, and the other fought to be remembered, . . . and another fought for the sake of God, and he will be in heaven."[4] Hence, an important factor from the *ḥadīth*'s point of view is the critical importance of pure intention (*nīyyat al-khāliṣah*) as the absolute prerequisite for the acceptance of martyrdom. In another tradition, which appeared in later collections, God dismisses claims of martyrdom because of a lack of pure intention from the person dying like a martyr:

> The first of people against whom judgment will be pronounced on the day of resurrection will be a man who died a martyr. He will be brought and God will remind him of his favors and he will recognize them. [The Almighty] will say: "And what did you do about them?" He will say: "I fought for you until I died a martyr." He will say: "You have lied—you did but fight that it might be said [of you]: "He is courageous." And so it was said. Then he will be ordered to be dragged along on his face until he is cast into hell-fire.[5]

There is no dearth of traditions emphasizing the importance of having pure intentions in virtually every category of beliefs and practices, jihad and martyrdom particularly included. Hence, we should assume that the level of the would-be martyr's intention and his/her expectation of worldly returns determine rank among martyrs as well. In a tradition collected by ibn Mubārak, we read:

> Martyrs are three types: [1] a man leaves his home, loving martyrdom, yet loving to return [safe home as well]. He gets killed accidentally by an arrow, and God forgives all his sins with the first drop of his blood, and with every drop of his blood he elevates in rank. [2] Then a man leaves his home, loving martyrdom, yet loving to return [safe home as well]. He initiates fighting [in the path of God and gets killed]. He accompanies Abraham (peace be upon him) in the high-ranking. [3] Then a man leaves his home, loving martyrdom and not loving to return home as well [wishes to be killed]. He initiates fighting [in the path of God and gets killed]. He will be like a king in heaven, live wherever he wishes, be given whatever he asks for, and his intercession will be accepted for anyone he wishes.[6]

Courage in facing death is another factor for comparing martyrs. In his work, ibn Mubārak included traditions to highlight this point, too. In one tradition, the best martyrs are counted as "those who attack [the enemy] and never look back until they get killed. They will dwell in the best places of paradise; God smiles at them, and when God smiles at some people they will not be asked [for their actions on the day of judgment]."[7]

The place and situation of martyrdom seemingly are important as well. According to some *ḥadīths*, the rewards for those martyred at sea will be twice as many as those martyred at land.[8] Perhaps this was due to the fact that naval operations against the powerful Byzantine fleet became more and more important in the course of the conquests since the mid-seventh century.[9] Later on, in the sixth canonical *ḥadīth* collection, *Sunan ibn Mājah*, written in the ninth century, we read more details on the merit of fighting and dying at sea:

> The martyr at sea is like two martyrs on the ground, and the one who suffers seasickness is like one who gets drenched in his own blood on the ground. The time spent between one wave and the next is like a lifetime spent in obedience to Allāh. Allāh has appointed the angel of death to seize souls, except for the martyr at sea, for Allāh himself seizes their souls. He forgives the martyrs on the ground for all sins except debt, but (he forgives) the martyr at sea all his sins and his debt.[10]

Merits of Martyrs

Ibn Mubārak in a number of traditions touched on the issue of the merits of martyrs compared to the merits of other believers who die of natural causes. In one narration, the Prophet stops at the body of Musʿab ibn ʿUmayr, a martyr in the battle of Uḥud (625), and recites this verse: "There are men among the believers who honored their pledge to God: some of them have fulfilled it by death, and some are still waiting. They have not changed in the least" (33:23). Then he turns to the people: "Visit the martyrs' tombs and greet them since, by the one who has my soul in his hand, until the day of judgment, no one greets a martyr unless he responds to their greeting."[11] In another tradition, martyrs are among those mentioned in the following verse where God spares them from the terrifying events of the day of judgement: "The trumpet will be sounded, and everyone in the heavens and earth will fall down senseless except those whom God spares" (39:68). Accordingly, martyrs stand around God's throne while holding their swords.[12] Similarly, martyrs are labelled God's trustworthy agents in another *ḥadīth*.[13]

Special praise for martyrs in various traditions highlights their absolute desire for repeating martyrdom in the path of God several times. Ibn Mubārak narrated a *ḥadīth* from the Prophet saying: "No one who has entered paradise will desire to return to this world even if he should be given all that the world contains, except a martyr. For he will yearn that he should return to the world and be killed ten times on account of the dignity that he will experience by virtue of his martyrdom."[14] In later works, including *Ṣaḥīh al-Bukhāri*, we see even the Prophet's desire to get martyred several times: "By him in whose hands my life is! Were it not for some men who dislike to be left behind and for whom I do not have means of conveyance, I would not stay away [from any battle]. I would love to be martyred in God's cause and come to life and then get martyred and then come to life and then get martyred and then get resurrected and then get martyred."[15]

As for other merits of martyrs, ibn Mubārak included a couple of *ḥadīths* where the martyr receives unique favors. One tradition says that the martyr will pass the critical *al-ṣirāṭ* stage on the day of judgment with ease and as fast as the wind.[16] Martyrs also will not be accountable for their deeds and will not face torment (though the text of this *ḥadīth* specifically speaks of those who die, perhaps by any means, while serving and guarding Muslim frontiers (*fī al-ribāṭ*)).[17] Another *ḥadīth* similarly praises fighting and dying in the frontiers, declaring one day of fighting there in the path of God to be equivalent to the value of fasting and worshipping for a whole month. A Muslim dying in that situation would be exempt from the trial of the grave.[18] Moreover, it is said that martyrs will go straight to paradise where they have impressive and stunning palaces, and angels come to visit them in groups with gifts from God.[19]

Types of Martyrdom

While ibn Mubārak was concerned almost entirely with the military aspect of martyrdom in the path of God, later *ḥadīth* compilers mostly embraced other forms of martyrdom. Perhaps this was because the waves of conquests gradually came to an end and dying in the frontiers became more unlikely for the overwhelming majority of Muslims living in the vast territory under the control of the Umayyads and then the Abbasid Caliphates. These later *ḥadīth* collections include *al-Ṣiḥāḥ al-Ṣittah* (the authentic six *ḥadīth* books),[20] the most authoritative books of *ḥadīth* in Sunni Islam and second only to the Qur'an, written around the ninth century. The authors of these books were all from the eastern parts of the Muslim world, far from the war zones and the non-Muslims of Byzantium. Although military jihad and martyrdom materials are found extensively throughout these books, the striking difference between them and the earlier work of ibn Mubārak is their focus on non-combative forms of jihad and martyrdom. In other words, literally, the later *ḥadīth* compilers widened the definition of martyrdom simply as dying in the path of God in order to include more believers in this prestigious and sought-after category (examples will follow in this section). Apart from non-military martyrdom, what is also absent from ibn Mubārak's work is assigning the title of martyrdom to those believers killed violently away from the battlefield for reasons other than fighting with the enemy in the path of God. They include a believer who is killed while fighting to protect themselves, wealth, or family against injustice.[21]

Moreover, while ibn Mubārak cited only four traditions on martyrs who are not killed violently, later works maneuvered extensively on this category of martyrs (in my survey, I found at least twenty related traditions in *al-Ṣiḥāḥ al-Ṣittah*). This trend is more noticeable in a much later collection by the fifteenth-century Jalāl al-Dīn al-Suyūtī in his *Abwāb al-Sa'ādah fī Asbāb al-Shahādah* in which I found at least forty-four *ḥadīths* that consider various non-violent forms of dying either as martyrdom or its equal in terms of rewards. Typically, traditions in this category cited by ibn Mubārak and numerously by later *ḥadīth* compilers count up to seven types of martyrs dying from different causes. The following tradition is an example that provides the seven ways of dying that can make someone a martyr:

> The Prophet came to visit 'Abdullāh bin Thabit (when he was sick) and found him very close to death. The Prophet called out to him, but he did not respond; so the Messenger of Allāh said: "Truly, to Allāh we belong and truly, to him we shall

> return," and said: "We wanted you to live but we were overtaken by the decree of Allāh, O Abū Ar-Rabi'." The women screamed and wept, and ibn 'Atik started telling them to be quiet. The Messenger of Allāh said: "Leave them; when the inevitable comes, no one should weep." They said: "What is the inevitable, O Messenger of Allāh?" He said: "Death." his daughter said: "I had hoped that you would become a martyr, for you had prepared yourself for it." The Messenger of Allāh said: "Allāh, the mighty and sublime, has rewarded him according to his intention. What do you think martyrdom is?" They said: "Being killed for the sake of Allāh." The Messenger of Allāh said: "Martyrdom is of seven types besides being killed for the sake of Allāh. The one who dies of the plague is a martyr; the one who is crushed by a falling building is a martyr; the one who drowns is a martyr; the one who dies of pleurisy is a martyr; the one who is burned to death is a martyr, and the woman who dies in pregnancy is a martyr."[22]

In a few traditions cited by al-Suyūṭī, we see some other (non-violent) ways of joining the ranks of martyrs. They include dying far away from home in a foreign land,[23] dying while traveling,[24] dying due to fever,[25] dying on Friday,[26] dying of cold while performing the full body-washing ablution with cold water,[27] dying of lovesickness,[28] or, generally, dying in any way in the path of God.[29] The problem of dying accidentally while struggling in the path of God was particularly an issue for early Muslims; hence, traditions were made to address the problem. ibn Mubārak touched the issue by narrating a tradition regarding a companion named Ḥarīthah, who was fatally hit by a random arrow while watching the fight at the battle of Badr (624). His mother came to the Prophet to inquire if he was among the martyrs in paradise. The Prophet confirmed his place in heaven, hence his status as a martyr.[30] Later traditions also backed the idea that being killed inadvertently while serving in the path of God is nothing less than martyrdom: "He who goes forth in God's path and dies or is killed is a martyr, or has his neck broken by being thrown by his horse or by his camel, or is stung by a poisonous creature, or dies in his bed by any kind of death Allāh wishes is a martyr and will go to paradise."[31]

According to some later traditions, becoming a martyr does not even require dying. This is where wishful desires for martyrdom become important and put the zealous believer besides actual martyrs in rank and rewards. Many traditions demonstrate how a believer can achieve the same level of rewards as a martyr killed in the path of God. In one such tradition we read: "If anyone asks God for martyrdom sincerely, God will make him reach the ranks of martyrs even if he dies in his bed."[32] Rewards of martyrdom can also be achieved through certain rituals and prayers. In one instance, the Prophet is narrated saying: "Whoever performs *salat al-duha*, and fasts three days every month, and never foregoes the *salat al-witr* at any situation, will be rewarded like a martyr."[33] In another tradition, the Prophet said to his wife 'A'ishah: "Whoever recites 'Lord, bless me in death and in the stages after death' twenty-five times every day and passes away in his/her bed will be granted the reward of a martyr."[34] There are similar traditions according to which, by reciting a particular chapter of the Qur'an or specific prayers, one is guaranteed to get the reward of a martyr after death.[35]

In a number of *ḥadīths* we also see the idea of "living martyr," although those that name a particular person usually bear sectarian tones, like the following tradition ascribed to the Prophet: "Whoever would be pleased to look at a martyr walking upon the face of the earth, then let him look at Ṭalḥah bin 'Ubaydullāh."[36] Other traditions are not specific and speak about Muslims with certain virtuous traits that entitle them to be regarded as martyrs. According to a tradition, "the trustworthy, honest Muslim merchant will be with the martyrs on the day of resurrection."[37] In another tradition (though apparently a weak *ḥadīth*), the Prophet allegedly said: "Whoever adheres to my *sunnah* (tradition) when my *ummah* (the community of believers) is corrupt will have the reward of a martyr."[38] Similarly, "a Muslim who works hard for the well-being of his family while enjoining them toward God's orders and feeding them with halal food will be with martyrs in their ranks."[39] In this pattern, some traditions accord high status to the "*ulamā*" (religious scholars), putting them on a par with or even superior to martyrs. According to a tradition from the Prophet, "When a seeker of [religious] knowledge passes away, he/she will die as a martyr."[40] Likewise, a famous (but weak) tradition regarding the virtue of seeking knowledge states: "The ink of the scholar is more sacred than the blood of the martyr."[41]

In a number of traditions that list different kinds of martyrdom other than being killed in the path of God (like the ones mentioned above), we find a clear rationale behind such a broad understanding of martyrdom. In those traditions, the Prophet explains the reason to his followers in this way: "You think that martyrdom only comes about when one is killed in the cause of God. In that case, your martyrs would be few."[42] In other words, the rationale is to make martyrdom more inclusive and available to all believers regardless of temporal and geographical boundaries. However, I found one exception in a tradition from 'Umar ibn Khattab, the second Caliph, that is actually the opposite of the above argument.[43] In this tradition, he argues that counting those who are killed in the cause of God as martyrs would result in too many martyrs; rather, true martyrdom is to make one's soul accountable (implying that this is a rare and precious virtue).[44] The interesting thing about 'Umar's tradition is that it is narrated by ibn Mubārak where he was obsessed with military martyrdom throughout his work.

Rewards of Martyrdom

Swift admission to paradise as a reward for martyrdom is taken for granted in the *ḥadīth* literature, like the ones I mentioned before from ibn Mubārak's work. It is also particularly well discussed in *al-Ṣiḥāḥ al-Ṣittah*. In these *ḥadīth* sources, paradise is the obvious reward for martyrdom. It is depicted as a strong motivation for early Muslims to participate in jihad against non-believers, such as in the following narration in *Sahih al-Bukhāri*: "On the day of the battle of Badr, a man came to the Prophet and said, 'Can you tell me where I will be if I get martyred?' The Prophet replied, 'In paradise.' The man threw away some dates he was carrying in his hand, and fought until he was martyred."[45] Since martyrs go directly to heaven and they are in a state of purity by virtue of their martyrdom, they do not need to be ritually cleansed. This, in part, comes from a number of traditions such as this one in *Sunan Abī-Dawud* that narrates the Prophet's behavior with the bodies of martyrs: "The martyrs of Uḥud were not washed, and they were buried with their blood. No prayer was offered over them."[46]

The sexual appeal of martyrdom is another theme that is seen as part of the exceptional reward package for martyrs.[47] There are very vivid depictions of sexual pleasures in heaven both in the Qur'an and the *ḥadīth* literature. Martyrs, in particular, are expected to enjoy this kind of delight to the full. Moreover, the whole process of violent and painful death actually turns sweet for martyrs according to a number of traditions such as this one: "The martyr does not feel the pain of being killed, except as any one of you feels a pinch."[48] Upon their death, martyrs also encounter heavenly wives who have been eagerly waiting for their (soon-to-be) martyred mates, right at the place of their martyrdom: "The earth does not dry of the blood of the martyr until his two wives rush to him like two wet nurses who lost their young ones in a stretch of barren land, and in the hand of each one of them will be a *hullah* that is better than this world and everything in it."[49] In another tradition we read that, in paradise, the martyr will marry his wives "from among the wide-eyed *hūrīs*."[50] Moreover, there are traditions about visions of the would-be martyrs prior to their deaths and their encounters with the *hūrīs*.[51]

Finally, another important aspect of martyrdom in the *ḥadīth* literature is the question of forgiveness, both for the martyrs and other believers. According to the Qur'an and traditions, the sins of martyrs are always forgiven. However, there is an exception to this rule, and that is debt, which cannot be wiped out through martyrdom: "All the sins of a martyr are forgiven except debt."[52] Debt is, in fact, such a serious matter that martyrs with outstanding debt not only lose forgiveness but also end up in hell as the following tradition explicitly states it: "On the day (of the battle) of Khaybar, some companions of the Prophet came and remarked: 'So-and-so is a martyr and so-and-so is a martyr.' When they came to a man about whom they said: 'So-and-so is a martyr,' the Prophet declared, 'No. I have seen him in hell for a mantle (or cloak) which he has stolen.'"[53] On the other hand, traditions maintain that those without debt who pay alms are true martyrs and can expect forgiveness for their sins.[54] They even enjoy the prestigious power of intercession and will be granted the right to "intercede for seventy of their relatives."[55]

Martyrdom in Sunni *tafsīrs*

Drawing on the traditions mentioned earlier, Qur'anic exegetes have read many verses containing the word *shahīd* (and its variations) and those related to dying for God with the concept of martyrdom in mind. Generally speaking, in such verses, we see one or more martyrdom tradition that links those verses to the notion of martyrdom. In this section, I will examine Sunni *tafsīrs* to understand their usage of martyrdom in various related verses.[56]

For Muslim exegetes, the most apparent verses referring to martyrdom are those that explicitly praise dying in the path of God with phrases like *qutilu* (or *yuqtal*) *fī sabīl-i allāh*. The most-cited verses here are 3:169–71 (as mentioned before) as well as 2:153–4: "O you who believe, seek help through steadfastness and prayer, for God is with the steadfast. Do not say that those who are killed in God's cause [*man yuqtal fī sabīl-i allāh*] are dead; they are alive, though you do not realize it." One of the earliest Sunni *tafsīr* was written by the eighth-century Muqātil ibn Sulaymān. Under 2:153–4, he uses the term *shahīd* to describe *man yuqtal fī sabīl-i allāh* ("those killed in the path of God"). Muqātil says that the verses were revealed after the battle of Badr, where fourteen Muslims lost their lives;[57] the purpose behind them was to reassure Muslims that their fallen peers were not actually dead; rather, they were alive and well received by God (a kind of psychological boost to keep Muslims steadfast in their belief and mission, I would say). Under 3:169–71, Muqātil narrates a revelation regarding a dialogue between God and the martyrs of Badr in which they ask God to send them back to the world in order to fight for God and be killed one more time and to let their fellow Muslims know how pleasing their heavenly position is so that they can also be encouraged to rush for martyrdom; in response, God reveals verses 3:169–71.[58]

Abū Ja'far Muhammad ibn Jarīr al-Ṭabarī, a prominent historian and exegete of the Qur'an in the ninth and early tenth centuries, uses the same tradition[59] (mentioned above) in his *tafsīr* to describe the enviable position of martyrs after death.[60] Under his discussion of verse 2:154, he also raises the issue of whether martyrs receive this favor of being alive and well provided for by God because of their martyrdom, or whether every true believer should expect such an ending. al-Ṭabarī accepts that there are some *ḥadīths* from the Prophet indicating that the graves of believers will open to the doors of heaven and the graves of unbelievers will open to the gates of hell; and that both groups will be alive after death in *al-barzakh*, though one in happiness, another in misery.[61] However, pointing to verses 3:169–170, al-Ṭabarī argues that what is exclusive to martyrs is that they will be provided with all the foods and drinks of heaven while other believers do not enjoy the pleasure before the resurrection.[62]

Ahmad ibn Muhammad al-Tha'labī, the renowned eleventh-century exegete, in his *al-Kashf wa al-bayān 'an tafsīr al-Qur'ān*, mentions the tradition that only martyrs yearn to return to this world in order to get martyred again and again as they know how blissful martyrdom is.[63] al-Tha'labī under 2:154 also narrates a tradition from the Prophet that the martyr's first drop of blood has six consequences for the martyr: "It will atone all his sins; he will see his place in heaven; he will marry maidens with large and dark eyes; he will have no fear of the great terror [on the day of judgment] and torments of the grave; and he will be honored with the honor of *iman* [faith]."[64] Abū 'Abdullāh Al-Qurtubī, the great thirteenth-century exegete, in his *Al-Jāmi' li Ahkām al-Qur'ān*, cites a similar tradition under 3:169–70 regarding five advantages of martyrs over prophets. Accordingly, while the angel of death takes the soul of every prophet, God himself does the job for martyrs; all prophets were ritually washed upon death, whereas martyrs do not need that ritual washing (*ghusl*) after martyrdom; while prophets needed burial shrouds, martyrs are buried with their clothes; prophets are not called "martyrs" after death; and finally, prophets can only intercede on the day of judgment while martyrs can do that all the time before the last day.[65]

The well-known twelfth-century theologian, Muhammad ibn 'Umar Fakhr al-Dīn al-Rāzī, in his *Tafsīr al-kabīr*, raises several points regarding 3:169–70.[66]

First, he sees the verses as a response to those so-called hypocrites who discouraged Muslims from joining jihad in the path of God so that they could live longer and accumulate a fortune and have a pleasant worldly life. So, according to him, the Qur'an here argues that, even though by refusing to participate in jihad one can achieve happiness in this world, it is nothing in comparison to what the martyr would gain after martyrdom. Secondly, al-Rāzī goes in depth to counter the argument that the issue of martyrs being alive mentioned in 3:169 is about their resurrection in heaven after the day of judgment. He argues that this understanding is against the explicit meaning of the verse. He cites Qur'anic examples to demonstrate that true believers and even unbelievers will be alive right after they die, the former in eternal happiness and the latter being tormented.[67] He also draws on some traditions to demonstrate that every person who dies will experience the *al-barzakh*'s version of either hell or heaven. In addition, al-Rāzī argues that, in 3:170, the fact that martyrs are depicted as happy for the would-be martyrs proves they enjoy an enviable life after their death. al-Rāzī refutes the view of some other exegetes that the martyrs' happiness mentioned in 3:170 describes their feelings, after the resurrection on the day of judgment, for their fellow Muslims who are in lower ranks in heaven. In al-Rāzī's understanding, this is not true since such happiness is not specific to martyrs alone; rather, every believer in heaven will be happy for other blessed believers, and it is not something specific for the martyrs to be highlighted in the Qur'an.

Another verse that exegetes tend to link to the concept of martyrdom is 33:23.[68] According to some early *tafsīrs*, such as Muqātil's, the verse was explicitly revealed for Ḥamzah and the other martyrs of Badr and Uḥud.[69] However, this verse is especially exploited in sectarian literature. In Sunni *tafsīr*, the "some of them have fulfilled it by death" and "some are still waiting" are meant to refer to 'Uthman (the third Sunni Caliph) and Ṭalḥah, respectively (there are a number of sectarian traditions that try to identify the "martyrs" mentioned there in this way).[70] Moreover, in reference to this verse and in order to prove a martyr's life after death, some *tafsīrs* report that the Prophet saluted and prayed for the martyrs of Uḥud as if they were alive and could hear his voice.[71]

Muslim exegetes also tend to link some other verses containing the words *shahīd* and *shuhadā* to the concept of martyrdom. The first case is 3:140--1.[72] Translating *shuhadā* as "martyrs" here is not something out of context, although it is not explicit in the text. Understanding the words *shahīd* and *shuhadā* as "martyr(s)" in other verses, such as 2:143, 4:41, 4:69, and 57:19,[73] are less contextually obvious, yet many exegetes treat them as if the verses have to do with the concept of martyrdom.

Al-Ṭabarī says that verses 3:140–1 were revealed after the Muslims' defeat at the battle of Uḥud in which seventy of them died, so God wanted to honor them by calling them martyrs (*shuhadā*).[74] The verses are also used to prove the atoning consequence of martyrdom. Many exegetes link "for him to cleanse those who believe" to "for him to choose martyrs" and interpret it as proof that indeed God forgives the sins of martyrs to honor them.[75] However, al-Ṭabarī understands "for him to cleanse those who believe" as God's plan to test people with difficulties to distinguish true believers from unbelievers and hypocrites.[76]

Under 3:140, al-Rāzī argues that, according to the Qur'an, the position of martyrs is something so special that everyone would yearn to achieve it so that they join the special ranks. Based on this and some other verses (e.g., 3:169 and 4:69), he claims that those Muslims who were not martyred in the battle of Badr were desperately looking for a similar opportunity. al-Rāzī further says that, based on 4:69, martyrs stand in the third position behind that of the prophets and the truthful. So, this elevated position is well worth the effort to achieve martyrdom. In another argument, al-Rāzī raises the issue of the morality of seeking martyrdom. He argues that voluntary martyrdom is not moral where it involves putting Muslims in an inferior position to unbelievers. But if it is evident that the act of martyrdom has God's consent, it should be pursued without reservation. Here, al-Rāzī points to 3:140, in which we read, "for him to choose martyrs," and argues that real martyrdom is a kind of voluntary death that God approves. At the end of his discussion, al-Rāzī summarizes the reasons for calling the martyr *shahīd*. He enumerates four reasons for that: first, based on 3:169, we know that martyrs are alive, so unlike others they witness "the home of peace" (*dār al-salām*), hence they are called martyrs; secondly, God and his angels bore witness to heaven that is reserved for martyrs; thirdly, martyrs together with prophets and the truthful will bear witness to the truth on the day of judgment (as 2:143 shows us); and finally, martyrs are called *shuhadā* because, upon death, they go directly to heaven, just as unbelievers go to hell (though it is not convincing reasoning).[77] So, al-Rāzī sees martyrdom as an essential Qur'anic concept associated with the jihad verses. For him, God actually selected martyrs among the believer,s and this is part of the reason why martyrs in Islam are held in high respect.

Concerning verses like 2:143, most early exegetes read *shuhadā* in its literal understanding simply as the community of believers who will be witness to the truth on the day of judgment, and not "martyrs."[78] However, a much later nineteenth-century exegete, Maḥmūd al-Alūsī, maintains that *shuhadā* in 2:143 are in fact "martyrs." Here, he points to the tradition (as previously mentioned) which says that, if martyrs were only those killed in the path of God, they would have been few in number. Essentially, al-Alūsī uses the tradition and this verse to include the entire community of believers among the ranks of martyrs.[79]

As for 57:19, some exegetes tend to equate *shuhadā* with martyrs, or at least to include martyrs among the meanings of *shuhadā* in the verse. Muqātil defines *shuhadā* here as those who are killed (in the path of God).[80] Similarly, al-Ṭabarī understands *shuhadā* in this verse primarily in terms of martyrdom (e.g., those killed in the path of God, or even believers who die in bed).[81] al-Rāzī quotes Muqātil and al-Ṭabarī's views without any objection.[82] Abū al-Qasim Maḥmūd ibn 'Umar al-Zamakhsharī, an eleventh-century scholar, also reads *shuhadā* here as both those who witness the truth (of the prophecy of Muhammad) and martyrs in the path of God.[83] Abū al-Qāsim Sulaymān ibn Ahmad ibn Al-Tabarani (ninth and early tenth centuries) discusses two possibilities for *shuhadā*: first, the term means the prophets who will bear witness on the day of judgment; secondly, martyrs of the path of God.[84] Abū Ishāq Ahmad Ibn Muhammed Ibn Ibrāhīm al-Tha'labī (eleventh century) likewise mentions both the prophets and martyrs in his interpretation of *shuhadā* in this verse.[85] However, some other exegetes consider *shuhadā* only as those who bear witness, either the prophets (or a particular group of the Prophet's disciples)[86] or all believers.[87] Under 4:69, we find quite a similar discussion, and many exegetes understand the term *shuhadā* primarily to mean witnesses which include martyrs as well.[88]

There are also a few other verses in the Qur'an where there is no discussion of dying in the path of God or the words *shahīd* and *shuhadā*, yet still some exegetes take the opportunity to elaborate on the concept of martyrdom and connect it to the verses. The first group of verses speak about intercession, so the point here is that martyrs can be counted among those who can intercede.

One of the verses on intercession reads: "No one will have the power to intercede except for those who have permission from the lord of mercy" (19:87). The early *tafsīr* of Muqātil understands "those who have permission" to be a group of angels.[89] This is perhaps derived from another verse (21:28) that mentions that angels can intercede.[90] al-Ṭabarī sees 19:87 as a reference to the power of intercession of martyrs. He states that some groups of believers will intercede for other groups of believers on the day of judgment. al-Ṭabarī then narrates a tradition from the Prophet saying: "There is a man among my people that because of his intercession God enters so many believers (more than the population of the tribe of Bani Tamim) into paradise." al-Ṭabarī then quickly jumps to the tradition that "the martyr intercedes for seventy of his relatives," stating that martyrs can intercede.[91] He has the same discussion under 20:109.[92] Under 74:48, al-Ṭabarī counts martyrs as intercessors after angels and prophets.[93] With some variations, al-Tabarani, also under 74:48, says that on the day of judgment, at first, the prophets, then the truthful, and finally martyrs will intercede for sinners; and those not qualified to be interceded for will remain in hell.[94] Under 74:48, another early *tafsīr* by ibn Abī Zamānayn (tenth century) also narrates a tradition stating that on the day of judgment the prophet intercedes for his people, the martyr for his family, and the faithful for his family, too, before God himself intercedes for even more groups of people.[95]

There are other miscellaneous verses in different contexts where we see references to martyrdom in various *tafsīr*. These verses generally speak about otherworldly rewards for true believers. In *tafsīr* literature, such verses are usually followed by martyrdom traditions, implying that martyrs are the default and most notable recipients of such favors. al-Suyūtī, in his take on 14:27,[96] interprets the hereafter as referring to the state of being in the grave. After listing a number of traditions on the trial of the grave and the situation of believers there, he comes up with a tradition on martyrs quoting from the Prophet that only martyrs will be exempt from the terror and trial of the grave, and that is because they have already suffered enough due to their violent death in the path of God.[97] In 47:4–6, we also read that those who are killed in the path of God enter into heaven and they recognize it outright.[98] al-Rāzī explains this situation by adding: "Before martyrdom, the martyr would be shown his position in heaven in advance, and he would desire to reach that position"; hence, the phrase "he has already made known to them" in 47:4–6 can be understood.[99]

Verses on *ṣabr* ("patience" for the sake of God) are another occasion for the Qur'anic exegetes to highlight the merit of martyrdom. An example of this is 13:22–4.[100] al-Ṭabarī considers martyrs among those who show the virtue of *ṣabr* par excellence. Referring to the verse, he retells a *ḥadīth* saying that in heaven there is a castle called *'adn* that has 5,000 doors, and no one enters this castle other than the prophets, the truthful, martyrs, and the just imams (judges).[101] al-Suyūtī also narrates this tradition and in one of its variations adds that upon each door of *'adn* there are 25,000 "beautiful companions" (*ḥūr al-'ayn*).[102] Similar traditions are mentioned under 9:72,[103] where martyrs are counted as one of the main subjects of the verse as residences of the garden of *'adn*.[104]

Notes

Introduction

1 Jan Willem Van Henten, *The Maccabean Martyrs as Saviours of the Jewish People: A Study of 2 and 4 Maccabees*, vol. 57 (Leiden: Brill, 1997), 147; Friedrich Avemarie and Jan Willem Van Henten, *Martyrdom and Noble Death: Selected Texts from Graeco-Roman, Jewish and Christian Antiquity* (London: Routledge, 2002), 19.

2 Candida R. Moss, *Ancient Christian Martyrdom: Diverse Practices, Theologies, and Traditions* (New Haven: Yale University Press, 2012), 3.

3 Paul Middleton, "Early Christian voluntary martyrdom: A statement for the defence," *The Journal of Theological Studies* 64, no. 2 (2013).

4 Avemarie and Van Henten, *Martyrdom and Noble Death*, 3.

5 Arthur J. Droge and James D. Tabor, *A Noble Death: Suicide and Martyrdom among Christians and Jews in Antiquity* (San Francisco: Harpercollins, 1992), 75.

6 Brad Stephan Gregory, *Salvation at Stake: Christian Martyrdom in Early Modern Europe* (Cambridge, MA: Harvard University Press, 1999), 26.

7 David Cook, *Martyrdom in Islam* (Cambridge: Cambridge University Press, 2007), 1.

8 Mark Brettler, "Is there martyrdom in the Hebrew bible?," in *Sacrificing the Self: Perspectives on Martyrdom and Religion* (Atlanta: American Academy of Religion, 2002), 3.

9 William W. H. C. Frend, *Martyrdom and Persecution in the Early Church: A Study of Conflict from the Maccabees to Donatus* (Eugene, OR: Wipf and Stock, 2014), 65.

10 Glen Warren Bowersock, *Martyrdom and Rome* (Cambridge: Cambridge University Press, 2002), 10.

11 Daniel Boyarin, *Dying for God: Martyrdom and the Making of Christianity and Judaism* (Stanford: Stanford University Press, 1999), 93.

12 Boyarin, *Dying for God*, 94.

13 Paul Middleton, *Radical Martyrdom and Cosmic Conflict in Early Christianity* (London: A&C Black, 2006), 116.

14 See, for example, Droge and Tabor, *A Noble Death*; David Seeley, *The Noble Death: Graeco-Roman Martyrology and Paul's Concept of Salvation*, vol. 28, Journal for the Study of the New Testament (Sheffield: A&C Black, 1990); Shmuel Shepkaru, *Jewish Martyrs in the Pagan and Christian Worlds* (Cambridge: Cambridge University Press, 2006), 35.

15 Judith Perkins, "The Apocryphal Acts of the Apostles and Early Christian Martyrdom," *Arethusa* 18, no. 2 (1985).

16 Middleton, *Radical Martyrdom and Cosmic Conflict in Early Christianity*, 123.

17 2 Maccabees 6:26–9 (All biblical quotations are taken from the NRSV).

18 A. Cohen, *The Babylonian Talmud: Tractate Berakot* (London: Cambridge: University Press, 1921), 407. http://books.scholarsportal.info/viewdoc.html?id=/ebooks/oca1/11/babyloniantalmud00coheuoft

19 *The Martyrdom of Polycarp* 9:3. See the text in *Early Christian writings: The Apostolic Fathers*, ed. Maxwell Staniforth, Penguin Classics, L197 (Harmondsworth: Penguin, 1968), 158–9.

20 Abul-Qāsim ibn 'Asākir, *Tarjamat al-Imām al-Ḥusayn* (Qum: Majma' al-Thaqāfat al-Islāmīyyah, 1993), 314.

21 W. Wilson, *The Writings of Clement of Alexandria* (London: T&T Clark, 1869), 146. https://books.google.ca/books?id=5zM2AQAAMAAJ.

22 See also the discussion of fighting martyrs in Islam in Cook, *Martyrdom in Islam*, 23.

23 Some jihad verses in the Qur'an include, but are not limited to, 22:78; 29:69; 25:52; 22:39–40; 2:190; 4:95; 16:110; 3:144.

24 Asma Afsaruddin, *Striving in the Path of God: Jihad and Martyrdom in Islamic Thought* (Oxford: Oxford University Press, 2013), 119; Cook, *Martyrdom in Islam*, 36.

25 Arthur Jeffery, *The Foreign Vocabulary of the Qur'an* (Leiden: Brill, 2007), 187.

26 Another variation of the term is *shāhid* (شاهد) which means "witness" and knowledgeable; and its plural is *shāhidīn* (شاهدين).

27 "As for the believers, those who follow the Jewish faith, the Sabians, the Christians, the Magians, and the idolaters, God will judge between them on the day of resurrection; God witnesses all things" (22:17).

28 "Whoever obeys God and the Messenger will be among those he has blessed: the Prophets, the truthful, those who bear witness to the truth, and the righteous—what excellent companions these are! That is God's favour. No one knows better than him" (4:69–70).

29 "Those who believe in God and his messengers are the truthful ones who will bear witness before their Lord: they will have their reward and their light" (57:19).

30 "We have made you [believers] into a just community, so that you may bear witness [to the truth] before others and so that the Messenger may bear witness [to it] before you" (2:143); "God has called you Muslims—both in the past and in this [message]—so that the Messenger can bear witness about you and so that you can bear witness about other people" (22:78).

31 "Lord, we believe in what you have revealed, and we follow the messenger: record us among those who bear witness [to the truth]" (3:53); "These people are not given to arrogance, and when they listen to what has been sent down to the Messenger, you

will see their eyes overflowing with tears because they recognize the truth [in it]. They say, 'Our Lord, we believe, so count us amongst the witnesses'" (5:82–3).

32 "[A]nd in the end, you will be returned to the one who knows the seen and the unseen" (9:94); "Say [Prophet], 'Take action! God will see your actions—as will his Messenger and the believers—and then you will be returned to him who knows what is seen and unseen" (9:105); "He is God: there is no god other than him. It is he who knows what is hidden as well as what is in the open, he is the Lord of Mercy, the giver of mercy" (59:22); "[S]o say, 'the death you run away from will come to meet you and you will be returned to the one who knows the unseen as well as the seen: He will tell you everything you have done'" (62:8); "He knows the unseen, as well as the seen; He is the Almighty, the Wise" (64:18).

33 "Indeed, God has purchased from the believers their lives and their properties [in exchange] for that they will have paradise. They fight in the cause of God, so they kill and are killed. [It is] a true promise [binding] upon him in the Torah and the Gospel and the Qur'an. And who is truer to his covenant than God?" (9:111); "Do not think of those who have been killed in God's way as dead. They are alive with their Lord, well provided for, happy with what God has given them of his favour" (3:169–70).

34 "As for those who stayed behind, and said of their brothers, 'If only they had listened to us, they would not have been killed,' tell them [Prophet], 'ward off death from yourselves, if what you say is true'" (3:168).

35 See verses 2:25; 2:82; 4:57; 4:152; 4:69–70; 10:9; 14:23; 22:14; 57:12.

36 According to the following verse even those who have committed wrongdoing in the past may expect the otherworldly rewards in heaven provided they repent: "Those who give in prosperity and adversity, and those who restrain anger, and those who forgive people. God loves the doers of good. And those who, when they commit an indecency or wrong themselves, remember God and ask forgiveness for their sins—and who forgives sins except God? And they do not persist in their wrongdoing while they know. Those—their reward is forgiveness from their Lord, and gardens beneath which rivers flow, abiding therein forever. How excellent is the reward of the workers" (3:134–6).

37 Abū 'Alī Faḍl ibn Ḥasan Ṭabarsī, *Majma' al-Bayān fi-Tafsīr al-Qur'an*, ed. Hāshim Rasūlī, 10 vols. (Tehran: Nāṣir Khusru, 1993), 3: 111; Muhammad Ṣādiqī Tihrānī, *Al-Furqān fī Tafsīr al-Qur'an bil-Qur'an wa al-Sunnah*, 30 vols. (Qum: Farhang Islāmī, 2011), 7: 163; Hāshim al-Baḥrānī, *al-Burhān fī Tafsīr al-Qur'an*, 8 vols. (Beirut: Al-A'lamī, 2006), 2: 274–7; Muhammad ibn Jarīr al-Ṭabarī, *Jāmi' al-Bayān fī Tafsīr al-Qur'an*, 30 vols. (Beirut: Dār al-Ma'rifah, 1992), 5: 103; Ḥusayn ibn 'Alī Abul Futūh Rāzī, *Rawḍ al-Jinān wa Rūh al-Jinān fī Tafsīr al-Qur'an*, 20 vols., ed. Muhammad Mahdi Nasih (Mashhad: Āstān Quds Raḍavī, 1988), 6: 12–13;Muhammad ibn Shāh Murtaḍā Fayḍ Kāshānī, *Tafsīr al-Ṣāfī*, 5 vols., ed. Husayn A'lami (Tehran: Maktabah al-Ṣadr, 1995), 1: 468; Ahmad ibn Muhammad al-Tha'labi, *al-Kashf wa al-Bayan 'an*

Tafsir al-Qur'an, 10 vols. (Beirut: Ihya' al-Turath al-'Arabi, 2001), 3: 342; Mahmud ibn 'Abdullāh al-Ālūsī, *Rūḥ al-Ma'ānī fī Tafsīr al-Qur'an al-'Aẓīm wa al-Sab' al-Mathānī*, 16 vols., ed. Shams al-Din Sana' Bazi' (Beirut: Dār al-Kutub 'Ilmīyyah, 1995), 3: 75.

38 Muhammad Ḥusayn Ṭabāṭabāī, *al-Mīzān fī Tafsīr al-Qur'an*, 20 vols. (Qum: Ismā'īlīyān, 1992), 4: 408;Muhammad ibn 'Alī ibn 'Arabī, *Tafsīr ibn 'Arabī*, 2 vols., ed. Samir Mustafa Rubab (Beirut: Iḥyā' al-Turāth al-'Arabī, 2001), 1: 149.

39 See these verses: "Prophet, urge the believers to fight: if there are twenty of you who are steadfast, they will overcome two hundred, and a hundred of you, if steadfast, will overcome a thousand of the disbelievers, for they are people who do not understand" (8:65); "[F]ighting is ordained for you, though you dislike it. You may dislike something although it is good for you, or like something although it is bad for you: God knows and you do not" (2:216); and "[I]f we had ordered, 'lay down your lives' or 'leave your homes,' they would not have done so, except for a few—it would have been far better for them and stronger confirmation of their faith, if they had done as they were told" (4:66); and "[L]et those of you who are willing to trade the life of this world for the life to come, fight in God's way. To anyone who fights in God's way, whether killed or victorious, we shall give a great reward. Why should you not fight in God's cause and for those oppressed men, women, and children who cry out, 'Lord, rescue us from this town whose people are oppressors! By your grace, give us a protector and give us a helper!'? The believers fight for God's cause, while those who reject faith fight for an unjust cause. Fight the allies of Satan: Satan's strategies are truly weak" (4:74–6).

40 Afsaruddin, *Striving in the Path of God*, 165.

41 See verses 3:38–9: "There and then Zachariah prayed to his Lord, saying, 'Lord, from your grace grant me virtuous offspring: You hear every prayer.' The angels called out to him, while he stood praying in the sanctuary, 'God gives you news of John, confirming a word from God. He will be noble and chaste, a prophet, one of the righteous.'" Or see verses 19:12–15: "[We said], 'John, hold on to the Scripture firmly.' While he was still a boy, we granted him wisdom, tenderness from us, and purity. He was devout, kind to his parents, not domineering or rebellious. Peace was on him the day he was born, the day he died, and it will be on him the day he is raised to life again."

42 The Qur'an narrates the fate of Jesus this way: "[A]nd said, 'We have killed the Messiah, Jesus, son of Mary, the Messenger of God.' (They did not kill him, nor did they crucify him, though it was made to appear like that to them; those that disagreed about him are full of doubt, with no knowledge to follow, only supposition: they certainly did not kill him—God raised him up to himself. God is almighty and wise. There is not one of the people of the book who will not believe in [Jesus] before his death, and on the day of resurrection he will be a witness against them)" (4:157–9).

43 See verses 7:120–6: "The sorcerers fell to their knees and said, 'We believe in the Lord of the worlds, the Lord of Moses and Aaron!' but Pharaoh said, 'How dare you believe in him before I have given you permission? This is a plot you have hatched to drive the people out of this city! Soon you will see: I will cut off your alternate hands and feet and then crucify you all!' They said, 'And so we shall return to our Lord—Your only grievance against us is that we believed in the signs of our Lord when they came to us. Our Lord, pour steadfastness upon us and let us die in devotion to You.'" Or see verses 20:71–3: "Pharaoh said, 'How dare you believe in him before I have given you permission? This must be your master, the man who taught you witchcraft. I shall certainly cut off your alternate hands and feet, then crucify you on the trunks of palm trees. You will know for certain which of us has the fiercer and more lasting punishment.' They said, 'We shall never prefer you to the clear sign that has come to us, nor to him who created us. So, decide whatever you will: you can only decide matters of this present life—we believe in our Lord, [hoping] he may forgive us our sins and the sorcery that you forced us to practise—God is better and more lasting.'".

44 "A secret believer from Pharaoh's family said, 'How can you kill a man just for saying, "My Lord is God"? He has brought you clear signs from your Lord—if he is a liar, on his own head be it—and if he is truthful, then at least some of what he has threatened will happen to you. God does not guide any rebellious, outrageous liar. My people, as masters in the land you have the power today, but who will help us against God's might if it comes upon us?' But Pharaoh said, 'I have told you what I think; I am guiding you along the right path.' The believer said, 'My people, I fear your fate will be the fate of those others who opposed [their prophets]: the fate of the people of Noah, Ad, Thamud, and those who came after them—God never wills injustice on his creatures. My people, I fear for you on the day you will cry out to one another, the day you will turn tail and flee with no one to defend you from God! Whoever God leaves to stray will have no one to guide him'" (40:28–33).

45 "Damned were the makers of the trench, the makers of the fuel-stoked fire! They sat down to watch what they were doing to the believers. Their only grievance against them was their faith in God, the mighty, the praiseworthy, to whom all control over the heavens and earth belongs: God is witness over all things" (85:4–9).

46 Cook, *Martyrdom in Islam*, 20.

47 Many exegetes, however, interpret *shuhadā* in the Qur'an primarily as referring to Ḥamzah.

48 Abū al-Ḥasan ibn al-Athīr, *Al-Kāmil fī al-Tārīkh*, 2 vols. (Beirut: Dār al-Beirut, 1965), 2: 83.

49 David Cook on choosing the title of *sayyid al-shuhadā* for Ḥamzah points to the importance of his martyrdom for the early Muslims as an example of true martyrdom: "This title was accorded to him not because he was the first martyr—a title that arguably should go to Bilāl or one of those killed at earlier battles because

his life and death exemplified what a martyr should be. He demonstrated the qualities of a hero, fought bravely for the sake of Islam and died in a noble manner." Cook, *Martyrdom in Islam*, 25.

50 In a famous fourth-century *ḥadīth* book, there is a tradition from the Prophet regarding the future martyrdom of his grandson, Ḥusayn, saying that "he is master of the martyrs from the beginning to the end in this world and the world to come, and he is master of youth of all human beings in paradise." Ja'far b. Muhammad ibn Qūlawayh, *Kāmil al-Ziyārāt* (Qum: Nashr al-Faqāhah, 1996), 268.

51 Mahmoud Ayoub, *Redemptive Suffering in Islam: A Study of the Devotional Aspects of Ashura in Twelver Shi'ism* (The Hague: Walter de Gruyter, 1978); Wilferd; Jean Calmard; Peter Chelkowski Madelung, "Hosayn B. 'Ali," in *Encyclopaedia Iranica*, ed. Ehsan Yarshater (London: Routledge, 2004); Edith Szanto, "Beyond the Karbala Paradigm: Rethinking Revolution and Redemption in Twelver Shi'a Mourning Rituals," *Journal of Shi'a Islamic Studies* 6, no. 1 (2013).

52 Kamran Scot Aghaie, *The Martyrs Of Karbala: Shi'i Symbols and Rituals in Modern Iran* (Seattle University of Washington Press, 2004); James A. Bill and John Alden Williams, *Roman Catholics and Shi'i Muslims: Prayer, Passion, and Politics* (Chapel Hill: University of North Carolina Press, 2002).

53 Cook, *Martyrdom in Islam*; Meir Hatina, *Martyrdom in Modern Islam: Piety, Power, and Politics* (Cambridge: Cambridge University Press, 2014).

54 Afsaruddin, *Striving in the Path of God*;Bernard K. Freamon, "Martyrdom, Suicide, and the Islamic Law of War: A Short Legal History," *Fordham International Law Journal* 27, no. 1 (2003); Manochehr Dorraj, "Symbolic and Utilitarian Political Value of a Tradition: Martyrdom in the Iranian Political Culture," *The Review of Politics* 59, no. 3 (1997); Juan Ricardo Cole, *Sacred Space and Holy War: The Politics, Culture and History of Shi'ite Islam* (London: I.B. Tauris, 2002); Mia Bloom, *Dying to Kill: The Allure of Suicide Terror* (New York: Columbia University Press, 2005); Robert Pape, *Dying to Win: The Strategic Logic of Suicide Terrorism* (New York: Random House, 2005); Ami Pedahzur, *Suicide Terrorism* (Cambridge: Polity Press, 2004); Mohammed M. Hafez, *Manufacturing Human Bombs: The Making of Palestinian Suicide Bombers* (Washington, D.C.: United States Institute of Peace Press, 2006); Mohammed M. Hafez, *Suicide Bombers in Iraq: The Strategy and Ideology of Martyrdom* (Washington, D.C.: United States Institute of Peace Press, 2007); Massimo Campanini, "The party of god (Hizbullāh): Islamic opposition and martyrdom in contemporary imamite shiism," *Cristianesimo nella storia* 27, no. 1 (2006); Assaf Moghadam, *The Globalization of Martyrdom: Al Qaeda, Salafi Jihad, and the Diffusion of Suicide Attacks* (Baltimore: Johns Hopkins University Press, 2008); Meir Hatina and Meir Litvak, *Martyrdom and Sacrifice in Islam: Theological, Political and Social Contexts* (London: I.B. Tauris, 2017).

55 Wim Raven, "Martyrs," in *Encyclopedia of the Qur'an*, ed. Jane Dammen McAuliffe (Leiden: Brill, 2003); Etan Kohlberg, "Shahīd," in *Encyclopedia of Islam*, eds.

T. Bianquis P. Bearman, C. E. Bosworth, E. van Donzel, and W. P. Heinrichs (Leiden: Brill, 1997).

56 Hatina, *Martyrdom in Modern Islam*, 7.

57 Hatina, *Martyrdom in Modern Islam*, 99.

1 The Emergence of the Shīʿī form of Martyrdom

1 Cook, *Martyrdom in Islam*, 30.

2 ʿAbdul-Malik ibn-Hishām, *al-Sīrat al-Nabawīyya*, eds. ʿAbdul-Hāfiz Shiblī Muṣṭafā al-Saqqā and Ibrāhīm al-'Abyarī, 2 vols. (Beirut: Dār al-Maʾrifa), 1: 318; ʿIzz al-Dīn ʿAbu Ḥamid ibn abī al-Ḥadīd, *Sharḥ Nahj al-Balāghah*, 20 vols. (Qum: Maktabah Ayatollah al-Mar'ashī, 2004), 13: 273; Abū al-Ḥasan ibn al-Athīr, *Asad al-Ghābah fī Maʾrifat al-Ṣahābah*, 6 vols. (Beirut: Dār al-Fikr, 1989), 1: 243.

3 ibn al-Athīr, *Al-Kāmil fī al-Tārīkh*, 2: 67.

4 Hāshim Ḥasanī, *Sīrat al-Muṣṭafā*, trans. Hamid Taraqi Khah (Tehran: Ḥikmat, 1991), 165.

5 "With the exception of those who are forced to say they do not believe, although their hearts remain firm in faith, those who reject God after believing in him and open their hearts to disbelief will have the wrath of God upon them and a grievous punishment awaiting them" (16:106).

6 Ahmad Ibn Yahya al-Baladhuri, *Ansab al-Ashraf*, 13 vols. (Beirut: Dar al_fikr, 1996), 1: 159–60; Abū ʿAbdullāh ibn Saʾd, *al-Ṭabaqāt al-Kubrā* (Beirut: Dār al-Kutub al-'Ilmīyyah, 1990), 3: 190.

7 ibn al-Athīr, *Al-Kāmil fī al-Tārīkh*, 3: 309.

8 Aḥmad Ibn Yaḥyā al-Balādhūrī, *Ansāb al-ashrāf*, 13 vols. (Beirut: Dār al-fikr, 1996), 1: 168; Abu Hanifa Dinawari, *al-Akhbar al-Tiwal*, ed. ʿAbdul Mun'im ʿAmir (Qum: Manshurat al-Razi, 1989), 147; Aḥmad ibn Abū Yaʾqūb al-Yaʾqūbī, *Tārīkh al-Yaqūbī*, 2 vols. (Beirut: al-Aʾlamī, 2010), 2: 88.

9 al-Balādhūrī, *Ansāb al-ashrāf*, 1: 174.

10 al-Balādhūrī, *Ansāb al-ashrāf*, 1: 169; Muhammad ibn Jarīr al-Ṭabarī, *Tārīkh al-Ṭabarī*, 11 vols. (Beirut: Dār al-Turāth, 1967), 5: 41; Aḥmad ibn ʿAlī Ṭabarsī, *al-Iḥtijāj*, 2 vols. (Mashhad: al-Murtaḍā, 1982), 1: 182.
There are some speculations that the prophecy of ʿAmmār's martyrdom was fabricated by the anti-Umayyad front. See H. Reckendorf, "'Ammar b. Yasir," in *The Encyclopaedia of Islam* (Leiden: Brill, 1986).

11 ʿAlī Kūrānī ʿĀmilī, *Āyāt al-Ghadīr* (Qum: Markaz al-Muṣṭafā, 1998), 81; ʿAlī ibn ʿĪsā Bahāʾ al-Dīn al-Irbilī, *Kashf al-Ghummah fī Maʾrifat al-Aʾimma*, 3 vols. (Beirut: Dār al-Aḍwāʾ, 1985), 1: 360.

12 ibn al-Athīr, *Al-Kāmil fī al-Tārīkh*, 2: 76.

13 See appendix.

14 al-Ṭabarī, *Tārīkh al-Ṭabarī*, 2: 447.
15 al-Ṭabarī, *Tārīkh al-Ṭabarī*, 448.
16 al-Ṭabarī, *Tārīkh al-Ṭabarī*.
17 al-Ṭabarī, *Tārīkh al-Ṭabarī*, 3: 190.
18 Muhammad ibn Jarīr al-Ṭabarī, *Tārīkh al-Ṭabarī*, trans. Abulqasem Payandeh (Tehran: Asāṭīr, 1996), 5: 1859.
19 See appendix.
20 Muhammad Husayn Tihrānī, *Imām Shināsī*, 18 vols. (Tehran: 'Allāmih Ṭabāṭabāī, 2006), 3: 70.
21 Abū Ḥātam al-Rāzī, *Kitāb al-Zīnah fī al-Kalimāt al-Islāmīyyah al-'Arabīyyah*, 3 vols., ed. Husein al-Hamdani (Sana'a: Markaz al-Dirāsāt wal-Buḥūth al-'Arabī, 1994), 2: 83–4; Muhammad Kurd 'Alī, *Khitat al-Shām*, 6 vols. (Damascus: Maktabat al-Nūrī, 1983), 6: 245; Lothrop Stoddard, *Hadhir al-'Alim al-Islami*, trans. Shakib Arsalan, 2 vols. (Damascus: Dar al-Fikr, 1971), 1: 188.
22 Mālik al-Ashtar was 'Alī's right-hand man who was later killed by poison on his way to Egypt as designated governor. After Mu'āwīyah received the news of al-Ashtar's death, Ṭabarī narrates that he stood up and said to his court: "'Alī had two hands, one of them was cut at Ṣiffīn, that is 'Ammār, and the other [al-Ashtar] was cut today." al-Ṭabarī, *Tārīkh al-Ṭabarī*, 5: 96.
23 For more information refer to the appendix.
24 Lūt b. Yaḥyā Abū Mikhnaf, *Maqtal al-Ḥusayn*, ed. Ḥasan Qaffāri (Qum: 'Ilmīyyah, 1985), 119. For the translation I relied on Maria Massi Dakake, *The Charismatic Community: Shi'ite Identity in Early Islam* (Albany: SUNY Press, 2008), 83.
25 For a brief understanding of the Karbalā paradigm, see Aghaie, *The Martyrs Of Karbala: Shi'i symbols and Rituals in Modern Iran*, 3–14.
26 ibn Qūlawayh, *Kāmil al-Ziyārāt* 328–9. For the translation I relied on https://www.al-islam.org/gu/node/19489.
27 ibn Qūlawayh, *Kāmil al-Ziyārāt*, 329–30.
28 Ṭabarsī, *al-Iḥtijāj*, 367.
29 These titles can be found among the Shī'a as early as the fourth Islamic century: Ḥusayn b. Ḥamdān al-Khaṣībī, *al-Hidāyat al-Kubrā* (Beirut: al-Balāgh, 1998), 176.
30 al-Khaṣībī, *al-Hidāyat al-Kubrā*, 39.
31 Sulaym ibn Qays, *Kitāb Sulaym ibn Qays*, ed. Muhammad Ansari (Qum: al-Ḥādī, 1984), 584–8; Muhammad Bāqir b. Muhammad Taqī al-Majlisī, *Biḥār al-Anwār al-Jāmi'ah li-durar Akhbār al-A'immah al-Athār*, 110 vols. (Beirut: Dār 'Iḥyā' al-Turāth al-'Arabī, 1983), 43: 197.
32 Ayoub, *Redemptive Suffering in Islam*, 48.
33 Mir Riḍā Ḥusaynī Arḍī, *72 dāstān az shafā'at imam ḥusayn* (Mashhad: Hātif, 1998), 84–5; 15–120.

There are many websites and published treatises that tell tales of the appearance of Fāṭimah in dreams. For example, see https://goo.gl/ohTVy8.

34 Abū Ja'far Muhammad ibn 'Alī ibn Bābawayh al-Ṣadūq, *al-Amālī* (Tehran: Kitābchī, 1997), 18. Muhammad Bāqir b. Muhammad Taqī al-Majlisī, *Jalā' al-'Uyūn*, ed. Ali Emamian (Qum: Surūr, 2008), 280–1.
35 Kharijites were former followers of 'Alī who broke up with him when he agreed to arbitration with the then governor of Syria, Mu'āwīyah, during the battle of Ṣiffīn.
36 ibn Qūlawayh, *Kāmil al-Ziyārāt*, 95.
37 Dakake, *The Charismatic Community*, 71.
38 Dakake, *The Charismatic Community*, 71.
39 al-Ya'qūbī, *Tārīkh al-Yaqūbī*, 122.
40 Muhammad ibn Jarīr al-Ṭabarī al-Ṣaghīr, *Dalā'il al-Imāmah* (Qum: Bi'that, 1992), 166. In other sources we see different names who uttered this phrase regarding Ḥasan. It is not clear who was responsible for the phrase.
41 ibn abī al-Ḥadīd, *Sharḥ Nahj al-Balāghah*, 4: 56.
42 al-Ṭabarī, *Tārīkh al-Ṭabarī*, 5: 277.
43 Abū al-Ḥasan 'Alī ibn al-Ḥusayn ibn Alī Al-Mas'ūdi, *Murūj al-dhahab wa ma'ādin al-jawāhir*, 4 vols. (Qum: Dār al-Hijrah, 1988), 3: 3.
44 "Prophet's companion grave exhumation condemned." *Alalam*. May 3, 2013.
45 Al-Mas'ūdi, *Murūj al-dhahab wa ma'ādin al-jawāhir*, 2: 427.
46 Dakake, *The Charismatic Community*, 71.
47 al-Ṭabarī, *Tārīkh al-Ṭabarī*, 6: 187.
48 Abū Muhammad Aḥmad B. A'tham al Kūfī, *Kitāb al-Futūḥ*, 8 vols., ed. Ali Shiri (Beirut: Dār al-Aḍwā', 1991), 5: 28.
49 al Kūfī, *Kitāb al-Futūḥ*, 5: 32.
50 al Kūfī, *Kitāb al-Futūḥ*, 5: 64.
51 al Kūfī, *Kitāb al-Futūḥ*, 5: 69.
52 Ayoub, *Redemptive Suffering in Islam*, 91.
53 Ayoub, *Redemptive Suffering in Islam*, 105.
54 al Kūfī, *Kitāb al-Futūḥ*, 5: 87; al-Ṭabarī, *Tārīkh al-Ṭabarī*, 5: 411.
55 al-Ṭabarī, *Tārīkh al-Ṭabarī*, 5: 468.
56 al-Ṭabarī, *Tārīkh al-Ṭabarī*, 5: 464.
57 al-Ṭabarī, *Tārīkh al-Ṭabarī*, 5: 462.
58 al-Ṣadūq, *al-Amālī*, 168. However, considering reliable historical resources, it is not clear whether the captives returned to Karbalā directly from Syria or they went there on another occasion.
59 al-Ṭabarī, *Tārīkh al-Ṭabarī*, 5: 462.
60 al-Ṭabarī, *Tārīkh al-Ṭabarī*, 5: 462.
61 Muhammad Bāqir Majlisī, *Biḥār al-Anwār*, 110 vols. (Beirut: al-Wafā', 1983), 79: 102.
62 ibn Qūlawayh, *Kāmil al-Ziyārāt*, 326.
63 Majlisī, *Biḥār al-Anwār*, 46: 220.
64 Mīrzā Ḥusayn Nūrī Ṭabrasī, *Mustadrak al-Wasā'il wa Mustanbaṭ al-Masā'il*, 30 vols. (Beirut: Mu'ssisat Āl al-Bayt li 'Iḥyā' al-Turāth, 1987), 10: 318.

65 Āqā ibn ʿĀbid Fāḍil Darbandī, *Iksīr al-ʾIbādāt fī Asrār al-Shahādah*, 3 vols. (Manama: Shirkat al-Muṣṭafā, 1994), 1: 652.

66 "Death has been written on the son of Adam in such a suitable way like the elegance of a necklace around the neck of a young girl. I am so eager to meet my ancestors like the enthusiasm of Jacob to see Joseph. The divine fate has destined for me a place of killing to which I have to go. As if my body parts and members are torn between Nawāwīs and Karbalā to quench their thirst and hunger by killing me. There is no escape from such a divine fate. We, the household of the Prophet, are subservient to whatever God has destined us. We will be patient on this calamity which he has planned for us. Of course his Almighty will give us the reward of the patient. We are the body parts of the Prophet and his body parts will not separate from him. We will be surrounding the Prophet in paradise. By our departure from this world the Prophet will be delighted. The promises that have been given to us will be fulfilled. Now, whoever among us is ready for martyrdom and has prepared himself for death and is fond of meeting God will move with us. We will set out tomorrow; God willing." al-Sayyid Raḍī al-Dīn ibn Ṭāwūs, *Al-Luhūf ʿalā Qatla al-Ṭufūf* trans. Ahmad Fahri Zanjani (Tehran: Jahān, 1970), 61. (For the translation I relied on https://www.imamreza.net/old/eng/imamreza.php?id=7080; "Be patient O' the son of the nobles. Death is only a bridge which takes you from misery and loss to the vast Paradise and the eternal graces. Then, is there anyone among you who dislikes to be transferred from a prison to a palace? For your enemies death is the opposite, it is like being transferred from a palace to a prison to be tortured. Majlisī, *Biḥār al-Anwār*, 44: 297. (For the translation I relied on https://goo.gl/yYFXtR; "To me, death is nothing but happiness, and living under tyrants nothing but living in a hell." Abū Muhammad al-Ḥasan ibn ʿAli ibn al-Ḥusayn ibn Shu'ba al-Ḥarrānī, *Tuḥaf al-Uqūl*, ed. Ali Akbar Qaffari (Qum: Jāmi'at Mudarrisīn, 1984), 245.

67 "O' my mother, [Umm Salama, a Muhammad's widow], I also know that I will be wrongfully killed and God wants my family to be captive and my children be killed," Majlisī, *Biḥār al-Anwār*, 44: 231; "[Muhammad to Ḥusayn in a dream:] Certainly, God wants to see you be killed," Majlisī, *Biḥār al-Anwār*, 44: 364.

68 "My father received the prophecy of his murder and my murder from the Messenger of Allāh. He also revealed to me that my tomb will be near his," ibn Ṭāwūs, *Al-Luhūf ʿalā Qatla al-Ṭufūf*, 27.

69 This combination of love (*ḥub:* حُب) and hatred (*bughḍ* بُغض) in Shi'i teachings comes from some traditions that delineate the essence of faith as being summarized in the love of God, the Prophet, and the Imams (acknowledging their *wilāyah*), and hatred toward their enemies. One such tradition from the sixth Imām, Jaʿfar al-Sadiq, says: "Is faith anything but love and hatred?" Abū Ja'far Muhammad b. Ya'qūb al-Kulaynī, *al-Kāfī*, 8 vols. (Tehran: Dār al-Kutub al-Islāmīyyah, 1986),

2: 125. Other traditions specifically speak about the love of the Imams and hatred toward their enemies as the essence of Islam: "Everything has a foundation and the foundation of Islam is the love for us, the [*Ahlul-Bayt*]" M. Muhammadi Rayshahri, *The Scale of Wisdom: A Compendium of Shi'a Hadith*, trans. A. Kadhim N. Virjee, M. Dasht Bozorgi, Z. Alsalami, A. Virjee (London: ICAS Press, 2008), 538.

70 Majlisī, *Biḥār al-Anwār*, 45: 40.

71 Majlisī, *Biḥār al-Anwār*, 41.

72 al Kūfī, *Kitāb al-Futūḥ*, 5: 95.

73 'Abdul-Razzāq Mūsawī Muqarram, *Maqtal al-Ḥusayn* (Beirut: Mu'assisat al-Kharsan lil-Maṭbū'āt, 2007), 297.

74 Al-Sayyid Muhsin al-Amīn, *A'yān al-Shī'a*, 11 vols. (Beirut: Dār al-Ta'āruf, 1983), 1: 614; Majlisī, *Biḥār al-Anwār*, 45: 116.

75 al-Ṭabarī, *Tārīkh al-Ṭabarī*, 5: 552.

76 al-Ṭabarī, *Tārīkh al-Ṭabarī*, 5: 583.

77 al-Baladhuri, *Ansab al-Ashraf*, 6: 370.

78 Torsten Hylén, "New Meanings to Old Rituals: The Emergence of Mourning Rituals in Shi'ite Islam" (paper presented at the Middle East Studies Association Annual Meeting, Washington D.C., November 22–5, 2014).

79 al-Baladhuri, *Ansab al-Ashraf*.

80 al-Ṭabarī, *Tārīkh al-Ṭabarī*, 5: 590; Hylén, "New Meanings to Old Rituals."

81 See the appendix for more details.

82 al-Ṭabarī, *Tārīkh al-Ṭabarī*, 5: 589–90. (For the translation I relied on Hylén, "New Meanings to Old Rituals.")

83 Hylén, "New Meanings to Old Rituals."

84 al-Baladhuri, *Ansab al-Ashraf*, 6: 374.

85 al-Ṭabarī, *Tārīkh al-Ṭabarī*, 5: 561.

86 al-Ṭabarī, *Tārīkh al-Ṭabarī*, 6: 38–66.

87 al-Ṭabarī, *Tārīkh al-Ṭabarī*, 6: 93.

88 Majlisī, *Biḥār al-Anwār*, 45: 343, 86.

89 al-Baladhuri, *Ansab al-Ashraf*, 3: 140;al-Baladhuri, *Ansab al-Ashraf*, 4: 82; al-Baladhuri, *Ansab al-Ashraf*, 4: 138; al-Ṭabarī, *Tārīkh al-Ṭabarī*, 7: 390; al-Ṭabarī, *Tārīkh al-Ṭabarī*, 9: 7; Abul-Faraj Iṣfahāni, *Maqātil al-Ṭālibīyīn wa-Akhbāruhum*, ed. Bihzād Ja'farī (Beirut: Dār al-Ma'rifah), 428.

90 Abū 'Abdullāh Muhammad ibn al-Nu'mān al-Mufīd, *al-Irshād fī Ma'rifat Ḥujaj Allāh 'alā al-'Ibād*, 2 vols. (Qum: Kungirih Shaykh Mufīd, 1992), 2: 171.

91 al-Ṭabarī, *Tārīkh al-Ṭabarī*, 7: 182.

92 al-Mufīd, *al-Irshād fī Ma'rifat Ḥujaj Allāh 'alā al-'Ibād*, 2: 171–2; Majlisī, *Biḥār al-Anwār*, 46: 171; Majlisī, *Biḥār al-Anwār*, 46: 194–9.

93 Ṭabarsī, *al-Iḥtijāj*, 2: 373; Majlisī, *Biḥār al-Anwār*, 46: 252.

94 Abū Zayd ʿAbd al-Raḥmān ibn Muhammad ibn Khaldūn, *Tārīkh Ibn Khaldūn*, 8 vols. (Beirut: Dār al-Fikr, 1988), 1: 250.
95 Iṣfahāni, *Maqātil al-Ṭālibīyīn wa-Akhbāruhum*, 210–16.
96 al-Mufīd, *al-Irshād fī Maʾrifat Ḥujaj Allāh ʿalā al-ʾIbād*, 2: 192.
97 Iṣfahāni, *Maqātil al-Ṭālibīyīn wa-Akhbāruhum*, 366–7.
98 Majlisī, *Biḥār al-Anwār*, 48: 165.
99 We are talking about the premodern period, as we have seen a fresh drive for martyrdom in Sunni Islam by the rise of political Islam in modern times.
100 See the appendix.
101 ʿAbdul Ḥusayn Ṭayyib, *Aṭyab al-Bayān fī Tafsīr al-Qurʾan*, 14 vols. (Tehran: Islam, 1990), 2: 251.
102 Abulḥasan ʿAlī ibn ʿĪsa Irbilī, *Kashf al-Ghummah fī Maʾrifat al-ʾAʾimmah* (Tabriz: Banī Hāshimī, 2002), 1: 107.
103 al-Kulaynī, *al-Kāfī*, 5: 53.
104 al-Kulaynī, *al-Kāfī*, 2: 93; al-Kulaynī, *al-Kāfī*, 1: 354.
105 al-Kulaynī, *al-Kāfī*, 5: 52.
106 al-Kulaynī, *al-Kāfī*, 5: 54.
107 ʿAli ibn Mūsā al-Riḍā, *Ṣahifah Imām Riḍā*, ed. Muhammad Mahdi Najaf (Mashhad: Kungirih Jahāni Imām Riḍā, 1986), 92.
108 al-Riḍā, *Ṣahifah Imām Riḍā*, 93.
109 Ṭabāṭabāī, *al-Mīzān fī Tafsīr al-Qurʾan*, 4: 29; Fakhr al-Dīn al-Ṭurayḥī, *Majmaʾ al-Baḥrayn*, 6 vols., ed. Ahmad Ashkivari (Tehran: Murtaḍavī, 1997), 3: 78; Ṭabarsī, *Majmaʿ al-Bayān fī-Tafsīr al-Qurʾan*, 1: 416.
110 Ṭayyib, *Aṭyab al-Bayān fī Tafsīr al-Qurʾan*, 3: 368; Fayḍ Kāshānī, *Tafsīr al-Ṣāfī*, 1: 468; Muhammad Jawād Mughnīyyah, *Tafsīr al-Kāshif*, 7 vols. (Qum: Dār al-Kitāb al-Islāmī, 2003), 2: 164.
111 Aḥmad ibn Muhammad Barqī, *al-Maḥāsin*, 2 vols., ed. Jalal ad-Din Muhaddith (Qum: Dār al-Kutub al-Islāmīyyah, 1952), 1: 163–4; see also Muhammad ibn ʾAlī ibn Bābawayh al-Qummī, *Faḍāʾil al-Shīʿah* (Tehran: Aʿlamī), 38.
112 al-Kulaynī, *al-Kāfī*, 1: 354; Majlisī, *Biḥār al-Anwār*, 68: 94.
113 Barqī, *al-Maḥāsin*, 1: 172–4; al-Kulaynī, *al-Kāfī*, 8: 146; ibn Bābawayh al-Qummī, *Faḍāʾil al-Shīʿah*, 38.
114 Barqī, *al-Maḥāsin*, 1: 173.
115 Majlisī, *Biḥār al-Anwār*, 52: 125; Majlisī, *Biḥār al-Anwār*, 65: 142; Majlisī, *Biḥār al-Anwār*, 79: 173; Muhammad ibn Shāh Murtaḍā Fayḍ Kāshānī, *al-Wāfī*, 26 vols. (Isfahan: Kitābkhānih Imām ʿAmīr al-Muʾminīn, 1985), 2: 441–2; Muhammad ibn al-Ḥasan Al-Ḥurr al-ʾĀmilī, *Ithbāt al-hudāt bil-nuṣūṣ wal-muʿjizāt*, 5 vols. (Beirut: al-Aʿlamī, 2004), 5: 81.
116 In another *ḥadīth* from Imam Rida (the eight Imam), martyrs of the Shīʿa are said to be better than nine martyrs of other traditions. Majlisī, *Biḥār al-Anwār*, 26: 243.

117 Furāt ibn Ibrāhīm al-Kūfī, *Tafsīr Furāt al-Kūfī*, ed. Muhammad Hadhim (Tehran: Mu'assisat al-Ṭab' wal-Nashr, 1989), 284.
118 *Sibt* in Arabic means a descendant. In Shi'i terminology, *sibṭ al-nabi* particularly refers to either Ḥasan or Ḥusayn. *Sibt* then sometimes means "chosen" or "imam."
119 Muhammad ibn Jarīr ibn Rustam al-Ṭabarī Āmulī, *al-Mustarshad fī Imāmmat 'Alī ibn abī Ṭālib*, ed. Ahmad Mahmudi (Qum: Kūshanpūr, 1994), 613.
120 Al-Ḥurr al-'Āmilī, *Ithbāt al-hudāt bil-nuṣūṣ wal-mu'jizāt*, 4: 314; al-Ṣadūq, *al-Amālī*, 63.
121 'Alī ibn Muhammad Khazzāz Rāzī, *Kifāyat al-Athar*, ed. 'Abd al-Latif Husseini Kouhkamari (Qum: Bīdār, 1980), 183; al-Husaynī al-Shūshtarī Al-Sayyid Nūr Allāh, *Iḥqāq al-ḥaqq*, 23 vols. (Qum: Maktabah Ayatullah Mar'ashī, 1988), 3: 542.
122 Muhamad Riḍā Muẓaffar, *'Aqā'id al-Imāmīyyah* (Qum: Anṣārīān, 2008), 106.
123 al-Ṣadūq, *al-Amālī*, 129.
124 al-Kulaynī, *al-Kāfī*, 4: 581.
125 ibn Qūlawayh, *Kāmil al-Ziyārāt* 142.

2 Martyrdom Revival in Twelver Shī'īsm

1 James Piscatori and Amin Saikal, *Islam beyond Borders: The Umma in World Politics* (Cambridge: Cambridge University Press, 2019), 166.
2 Tony Bunting, "Siege of Vienna," in *Encyclopædia Britannica* (Encyclopædia Britannica, 2017). https://www.britannica.com/event/Siege-of-Vienna-1529
3 On the subject of Muslim countries falling behind Western Europe, Jared Rubin explains: "Middle Eastern rulers were strong, and the very thing that kept them strong—religious legitimation—discouraged them to negotiate with other potential propagating agents or to permit laws and policies capable of undermining the religious establishment. On the other hand, the relative weakness of Western European rulers encouraged them to engage in more costly negotiations with the economic elite. The unintended, path dependent consequences of these negotiations further weakened the capacity of the Church to legitimize rule, especially after the Reformation. This further encouraged Western European rulers to negotiate with the economic elite. Consequently, they enacted laws and policies more beneficial to the economy." Jared Rubin, *Rulers, Religion, and Riches: Why the West Got Rich and the Middle East Did Not* (New York: Cambridge University Press, 2017), 207.
4 Piscatori and Saikal, *Islam beyond Borders*, 25; Rudolph Peters, *Islam and Colonialism* (Berlin: De Gruyter Mouton, 1980), 39. https://www.degruyter.com/view/title/6260
5 One of the most important Muslim resistant movements in British-controlled India was led by Sayyid Ahmad Barelwi (1786–1831), a charismatic religious figure, though his short-lived movement was primarily against the Sikhs in Peshawar valley.

Benjamin D. Hopkins, "Islam and Resistance in the British Empire," in *Islam and the European Empires* (2013).

6 The Algerian resistance was led by 'Abd al-Qādir (1808–83), a religious figure, after the French army invaded Algeria in 1930. Despite his initial success against the French army, using guerrilla warfare, 'Abd al-Qādir was forced to surrender in 1847. Marcel Emerit, "Abdelkader," in *Encyclopædia Britannica* (September 2, 2020). https://www.britannica.com/biography/Abdelkader

7 The Mahdist movement was a reformist religious movement in the Sudan (1881–98), around the idea of Mahdi, the awaited eschatological figure who would renew religion at the end of time. The movement succeeded in toppling the Turco-Egyptian regime in Sudan, but finally was defeated by British forces in 1898 as they occupied Sudan. The Editors of Encyclopaedia Britannica, "Al-Mahdiyyah," in *Encyclopædia Britannica* (October 21, 2009). https://www.britannica.com/topic/al-Mahdiyyah

8 The Egyptian revolt (1879–82) was against British and French influence and intervention in Egypt and it was led by colonel 'Urabi. The revolt, that turned into jihad, was finally defeated as the British army occupied Egypt and the 'Urabi's "badly trained and insufficiently equipped army" was unable to withstand the British army. Peters, *Islam and Colonialism*, 79.

9 The Libyan uprising against Italian colonialism (1911–22) started with a call for jihad by the leader of the Sanusi Sufi order of the time. The Sanusi uprising was a sort of pan-Islamic jihadi movement, but remained loyal to the Ottoman Empire. Saima Raza, "Italian Colonisation & Libyan Resistance the Al-Sanusi of Cyrenaica (1911–1922)," *Ogirisi* 9, no. 1 (2012).

10 Peters, *Islam and Colonialism*, 156–7.

11 Daniel Brown, "Martyrdom in Sunni revivalist thought," *Sacrificing the Self: Perspectives on Martyrdom and Religion* (2001): 109–10.

12 Piscatori and Saikal, *Islam beyond Borders*, 2.

13 Piscatori and Saikal, *Islam beyond Borders*, 27.

14 Hamid Enayat, *Modern Islamic Political Thought: The Response of the Shi'i and Sunni Muslims to the Twentieth Century* (London: Bloomsbury, 2005), 70.

15 John Willis, "Debating the Caliphate: Islam and Nation in the Work of Rashid Rida and Abul Kalam Azad," *The International History Review* 32, no. 4 (2010).

16 Enayat, *Modern Islamic Political Thought*, 76–7.

17 Afsaruddin, *Striving in the Path of God*, 207.

18 James Heyworth-Dunne, "Religious and Political Trends in Modern Egypt," (1950): 54.

19 Afsaruddin, *Striving in the Path of God*, 212.

20 Piscatori and Saikal, *Islam beyond Borders*, 34.

21 S. Abul A'la Mawdudi, *Jihad in Islam* (Beirut: The Holy Koran Publishing House, 1980), 10.

22 Mawdudi, *Jihad in Islam*, 25.

23 Mawdudi, *Jihad in Islam*, 26.

24 Thomas Hegghammer, *The Caravan: Abdallah Azzam and the Rise of Global Jihad* (Cambridge: Cambridge University Press, 2020), 266.

25 Nir Arielli, *From Byron to Bin Laden* (Cambridge, MA: Harvard University Press, 2018), 2.

26 Moghadam, *The Globalization of Martyrdom.*

27 Hegghammer, *The Caravan*, 24.

28 Hatina, *Martyrdom in Modern Islam*, 139.

29 Hegghammer, *The Caravan*, 408.

30 Hatina, *Martyrdom in Modern Islam*, 142.

31 Hegghammer, *The Caravan*, 116.

32 Meir Hatina, "Warrior Saints: 'Abadallah 'Azzam's Reflections on Jihad and Karamat," in *Martyrdom and Sacrifice in Islam: Theological, Political and Social Contexts*, eds. Meir Hatina and Meir Litvak (London: I.B. Tauris, 2017), 252.

33 Hegghammer, *The Caravan*, 295.

34 Hegghammer, *The Caravan*, 296.

35 Hegghammer, *The Caravan*, 296.

36 Hegghammer, *The Caravan*, 450.

37 Hegghammer, *The Caravan*, 302.

38 Hegghammer, *The Caravan*, 300.

39 Hegghammer, *The Caravan*, 306.

40 Rafael Reuveny and Aseem Prakash, "The Afghanistan war and the breakdown of the Soviet Union," *Review of International Studies* (1999).

41 Metin Heper and Raphael Israeli, "'Ulamā' and Politics in Saudi Arabia," in *Islam and Politics in the Modern Middle East (RLE Politics of Islam)* (Routledge, 2014), 29.

42 Fouad Ajami, *Crosswinds: The Way of Saudi Arabia* (Stanford: Hoover Press, 2020).

43 Cole Bunzel, *The Kingdom and the Caliphate: Duel of the Islamic States* (Washington, D.C., Carnegie, 2016): 3.

44 Abu Bakr al-Baghdadi, "Wa-law kariha l-kafirun [Though the unbelievers be averse]," (November 13, 2014, September 27, 2020). https://archive.org/details/wlwCareha21

45 Raihan Ismail, "Reclaiming Saudi Salafism: The Saudi Religious Circles and the Threat of ISIS," *Journal of Arabian Studies* 9, no. 2 (2019).

46 Mapping the Global Muslim Population (Washington, D.C., Pew Research Center, published October 7, 2009). https://www.pewforum.org/2009/10/07/mapping-the-global-muslim-population/

47 Emmanuel Sivan, "Sunni radicalism in the Middle East and the Iranian Revolution," *International Journal of Middle East Studies* 21, no. 1 (1989): 10.

48 Muhammad Ḥusayn Ṭabāṭabāī, *Shī'a*, trans. Sayyid Husayn Nasr (Albany: State University of New York Press, 1977), 189.

49 Edward Wastnidge, "Iran's Own 'War on Terror': Iranian Foreign Policy Towards Syria and Iraq During the Rouhani Era," in *Foreign Policy of Iran under President Hassan Rouhani's First Term (2013–2017)* (Berlin: Springer, 2020), 118.

50 See, for example, this report from the Lashkar-e Taiba, a large Pakistan-based jihadi organization, on the pressure on the family of martyrs to avoid crying and showing weakness: Mariam Abou Zahab, "'I shall be waiting for you at the door of Paradise': the Pakistani Martyrs of the Lashkar-e Taiba (Army of the Pure)," in *The Practice of War: The Production, Reproduction and Communication of Armed Violence* (2008).

51 Thomas Hegghammer, *Jihadi culture* (Cambridge: Cambridge University Press, 2017), 19.

52 Seyyed Hossein Nasr, "Shi'ism and Sufism: Their Relationship in Essence and in History," *Religious Studies* 6, no. 3 (1970). http://www.jstor.org.libaccess.lib.mcmaster.ca/stable/20004827

53 Mohammad Ali Amir-Moezzi, *The Divine Guide in Early Shi'ism: The Sources of Esotericism in Islam*, trans. David Streight (Albany: State University of New York Press, 1994), 125.

54 Amir-Moezzi, *The Divine Guide in Early Shi'ism*, 125.

55 Enayat, *Modern Islamic Political Thought*, 82–3.

56 Amir-Moezzi, *The Divine Guide in Early Shi'ism*, 26.

57 Denis McEoin, "Aspects of militancy and quietism in Imami Shi'ism," *British Journal of Middle Eastern Studies* 11, no. 1 (1984).

58 'Alī ibn al-Ḥusayn Imām Zayn al-'Ābidīn, *The Psalms of Islam (al-Ṣaḥīfah al-kāmilah al-sajjādīyyah)*, trans. William C. Chittick (London: The Muhammadi Trust of Great Britain and Northern Ireland, 2006).

59 Muhammad ibn al-Ḥasan Al-Ḥurr al-'Āmilī, *Wasā'il al-Shi'ah ilā Tahsil Masā'il al-Shari'ah*, 29 vols. (Qum: Mu'assisat-i Aalul-bayt, 1988), 15: 52. Other such *ḥadīths* against armed rebellions without gaining the approval of the Imams can be found in the *Kitab al-Kāfī* that is held in the highest esteem by the Shī'a: al-Kulaynī, *al-Kāfī*, v.1, 174; v.8, 297.

60 Al-Ghadīr (20 volumes) is a collection of first-hand *ḥadīths* (taken from Sunni sources) from the first and second generations of the Prophet's disciples and followers on the event of Ghadīr and the appointment of 'Alī by the Prophet as his successor.

61 'Abdul Ḥusayn Amīnī, *Shuhadā' al-faḍīlah* (Beirut: Mu'assisat al-Wafā', 1983), preface.

62 ibn Qūlawayh, *Kāmil al-Ziyārāt* 330.

63 See appendix.

64 See, for example, Majlisī, *Biḥār al-Anwār*, 1: 178–84.

65 McEoin, "Aspects of militancy and quietism in Imami Shi'ism," 22.

66 See, for example, Abul-Faraj ibn al-Jawzī, *al-Muntaẓam*, 19 vols. (Beirut: Dār al-Kutub al-'Ilmīyyah, 1992), 15: 325; Abū 'Alī Ḥasan ibn 'Alī Ṭusī Niẓām al-Mulk, *Siyr al-Mulūk* (Tehran: Bungāh Tarjumih wa Nashr Kitāb, 1968), 221–2.

67 ibn al-Athīr, *Al-Kāmil fī al-Tārīkh*, 8: 549.

68 Ismā'īl ibn 'Umar ibn Kathīr, *Al-Bidāyat wa al-Nihāyah* (Beirut: Dār al-Fikr, 1986), 12: 62.

69 ibn al-Jawzī, *al-Muntaẓam*, 16: 8.

70 See ibn al-Jawzī, *al-Muntaẓam*, 14: 75; ibn al-Jawzī, *al-Muntaẓam*, 84; ibn al-Jawzī, *al-Muntaẓam*, 126; ibn al-Athīr, *Al-Kāmil fī al-Tārīkh*, 8: 221.

71 Derin Terzioğlu, "Sufis in the age of state-building and confessionalization," in *The Ottoman World*, ed. Christine Woodhead (London: Routledge, 2011), 94.

72 Suraiya Faroqhi, *The Ottoman Empire and the World Around It* (New York: I.B. Tauris, 2005), 34–6.

73 al-Kulaynī, *al-Kāfī*, 1: 338; Majlisī, *Biḥār al-Anwār*, 51: 135. On the contrary, in Sunni Islam, the Caliphate system was not something divinely planned, and the Prophet's caliphs were not supposed to be infallible and divinely guided persons. According to a prominent Sunni jurist, Abū al-Ḥasan al-Māwardī (d. 1058), the Caliphate was a temporal system "to replace prophecy in the defence of religion and the administration of the world." Wael B. Hallaq, "Caliphs, Jurists and the Saljūqs in the Political Thought of Juwayn?," *The Muslim World* 74, no. 1 (1984). Hence, for Sunnis, the successor to the Prophet would not necessarily need "exceptional spiritual qualities, but would merely have to be an exemplary Muslim, who could ably and virtuously direct the religious and political affairs of the community." Seyyed Vali Reza Nasr, *The Shia Revival: How Conflicts within Islam Will Shape the Future* (New York: W.W. Norton & Co., 2006), 35.

74 Ṭabāṭabāī, *Shī'a*, 189.

75 Husain Mohammad Jafri, *The Origins and Early Development of Shi 'a Islam* (Oxford: Oxford University Press, 2000), 294.

76 Sarvenaz Bahar, "Khomeinism, The Islamic Republic of Iran, and International Law: The Relevance of Islamic Political Ideology," *Harvard international law journal* 33, no. 1 (1992).

77 Hillel Fradkin, "The Paradoxes of Shiism," *Current Trends in Islamist Ideology* 8 (2009).

78 Abbas Amanat, *Apocalyptic Islam and Iranian Shi'ism* (London: I.B. Tauris, 2009), 150.

79 *Wilāyat-i faqīh* had its roots in a few traditions that gave qualified "*ulamā*" some kind of authority by recommending the believers to consult with them. One of the most important such traditions is known as *Maqbula* of Umar ibn-Hanzala, in which Imam Ja'far Sadiq emphasizes that it is forbidden for the Shi"a to refer their

disputes over legal issues to temporal rulers. Instead, the Imam commands the Shi'a to seek out those "who base themselves on the *hadith* (saying) and the guidance of the Imams on permissible and prohibited matters." Enayat, *Modern Islamic Political Thought: The Response of the Shi'i and Sunni Muslims to the Twentieth Century*, 172. Another tradition is part of an alleged decree from the Hidden Imam that is known as *Toqī' al-sharīf*. In that decree the Imam advises the Shi'a that "for new occurrences, refer in their regard to the transmitters of our Tradition; they are my proofs upon you, and I am the Proof of God upon them." The English translation of this tradition is from Saīd Amīr Arjomand, "Imam Absconditus and the Beginnings of a Theology of Occultation: Imami Shi'ism Circa 280–90 A. H./900 A. D," *Journal of the American Oriental Society* 117, no. 1 (1997). For a complete list of traditions that proponents of the theory of *wilāyat-i faqīh* refer to them, see Ahmad Vaezi, *Shia Political Thought* (London: Islamic Centre of England, 2004).

80 Mīrzā Abul-Qāsim Qā'im Maqām Farahānī, *Risālih Jahādīyyah* (Qum: Mu'ssisat Dā'irat al-Ma'ārif Fiqh al-Islāmī, 2005), 552–3.

81 Qā'im Maqām Farahānī, *Risālih Jahādīyyah*, 554.

82 Roy Mottahedeh, *The Mantle of the Prophet* (London: Oneworld, 2014), 210.

83 Historically, the root of *Akhbārī/Uṣūlī* division among the "*ulamā*" goes back to the severe crisis at the beginning of the Occultation of Imam Mahdī. In the absence of the infallible Imam, many who later became known as Akhbārīs held the Qur'an as well as the traditions of the Prophet and the Imams as the exclusive guides. For that purpose, "they collected enormous volumes of putative sayings, which they sought to put off-limits for reasoned examination."Cole, *Sacred Space and Holy War*, 193. The Akhbārīs confined the function of the "*ulamā*" to transmit those Shī'a traditions which are explicit in meaning. On the other hand, the rationalists (later known as Uṣūlīs) insisted that independent reasoning (*ijtihad*) as well as the consensus of the jurisprudents could also serve as sources of legal judgment. Bahar, "Khomeinism, The Islamic Republic of Iran, and International Law." In this way, the Uṣūlīs "divided all Shī'ites into formally trained jurisprudents (*mujtahids*) and laymen, stipulating that the ordinary believers must emulate the mujtahids in matters of subsidiary religious laws." Cole, *Sacred Space and Holy War*, 66.

In terms of the authority of "*ulamā*", also, the Uṣūlīs considered mujtahids, as the general deputy of the Imam, with authority to perform some tasks such as "rendering legal judgments," issuing fatwas, collecting *zakāt* and *khums* taxes, leading Friday prayers, and even, in some cases, mandating defensive jihads. In contrast, although the Akhbārīs generally accepted performing the function of judges by the "*ulamā*", they often disallowed doing the other functions during the Occultation. Cole, *Sacred Space and Holy War*, 66.Therefore, according to the Akhbārīs' line of thought, "the '*ulamā*' hold far less power both in religion and in politics." Nasr, *The Shia Revival*, 69.

84 al-Amīn, *A'yān al-Shī'a* 9: 443; Hamid Algar, *Religion and State in Iran, 1785–1906: The Role of the Ulama in the Qajar Period* (Berkeley: University of California Press, 1980), 88.
85 al-Amīn, *A'yān al-Shī'a*, 91.
86 Jahāngīr Mīrzā, *Tārīkhi Nu*, ed. Abbas Ighbal (Tehran: Kitābkhānih 'ALīakbar A'lamī, 1948), 15.
87 Ḥasan Fasāyī, *Fārs nāmih nāṣirī* (Tehran: Amīrkabīr, 2003), 731; 'Alīqulī Mīrzā I'tiḍād al-Salṭanah, *Iksīr al-Tawārīkh* (Tehran: Wīsman, 1991).
88 Fasāyī, *Fārs nāmih nāṣirī*, 732.
89 Hatina and Litvak, *Martyrdom and Sacrifice in Islam*, 6. All notable and influential Sunni Islamists of the twentieth century were not trained in traditional seminaries; they were journalists, writers, engineers, physicists, etc.: Hasan al-Bannā, Sayyid Qutb, Abul A'lā Maudūdī, Muhammad 'Abd-al-Salām Faraj, Bin-Laden, Ayman al-Zawahiri, to name a few.
90 Mihdī Malikzādih, *Tārīkh Inqilāb Mashrūṭīyyat Iran*, vol. 4–5 (Tehran: A'lamī, 1994), 870–9.
91 Rūḥullāh Khomeini, *Sahifih Imam*, 22 vols. (Tehran: Mu'assisah Tanzim wa Nashr Āthār Imām Khomeini), 13: 357–68. (For the translation of quotes from *Sahifih-i Imām*, I relied on its official website at http://emam.com.)
92 Amīnī, *Shuhadā' al-faḍīlah*, 367.
93 Khomeini, *Sahifih Imam*, 19: 73.
94 Hamid Hosseini, "Theocracy Versus Constitutionalism: Is Velayat-e-Faghih Compatible with Democracy," *Journal of Iranian Research and Analysis* 15, no. 2 (1999).
95 Mottahedeh, *The Mantle of the Prophet*, 237.
96 Farhang Rajaee, *Islamism and Modernism: The Changing Discourse in Iran* (Austin: University of Texas Press, 2007), 69.
97 Rajaee, *Islamism and Modernism*, 70.
98 Shahrough Akhavi, *Religion and Politics in Contemporary Iran: Clergy–State Relations in the Pahlavī Period* (Albany: State University of New York Press, 1980), 63.
99 Akhavi (1980, 119–20) has summarized the authors' views in these points:

> "(1) the need for an independent financial organization for the clergy; (2) the necessity of a *shūrā-yi fatvā*—i.e., a permanent committee of mujtahids [jurists], the members of which were to be drawn from the country at large, to issue collective authoritative opinions in matters of law; (3) the idea that no Shi'i society is possible without the delegation of the Imam's authority; (4) an interpretation of Islam as a total way of life, therefore incorporating social, economic and political issues into the religious ones; (5) the need to replace the central importance of *fqih* [jurisprudence] in the madrasah curricula with *akhlaq* (ethics), *'aqa'id* (ideology) and *falsafah* (philosophy); (6) the need for a

new concept of leadership of youth based on a correct understanding of responsibility; (7) the development of *ijtihad* as a powerful instrument for the adaptation of Islam to changing circumstances; (8) a revival of the nearly defunct principle of *al-amr bi-ma'rūf wa al-nahy 'an al-munkar* [enjoin what is good and forbid what is wrong] as a means of expressing a collective and public will; (9) specialization among mujtahids and making *taqlīd* (emulation of a mujtahid) contingent upon it; (10) the need for mutuality and communal spirit to overcome the individuality and mistrust that pervades Iranian culture." Akhavi, *Religion and Politics in Contemporary Iran*, 119–20.

100 Akhavi, *Religion and Politics in Contemporary Iran*, 120.

101 While, particularly since the triumph of the Uṣūlī school of *fiqh* (jurisprudence) over traditionalists (Akhbārīs), the rulings and reasonings of *mujtahids* have been binding for their followers, they have been diverse (or even contradictory at times), from one *mujtahid* to another, and also "deemed to die with [the *mujtahid*]." Sami Zubaida, *Law and Power in the Islamic World* (London: I.B. Tauris, 2005), 14. On the contrary, the new effort for the unification of the religious establishment, especially as implemented in the Islamic Republic of Iran in 1979 in the form of the *wilāyat-i faqīh*, made the authority of the unified religious establishment (as a single body of lawmaking) complete, autonomous, and long-lasting similar in functions to that of the Prophet and the Imams. This can be seen as part of the process of embracing the Sunni realism, that is, the Sunni idea that the collective body of religious scholars ("*ulamā*") would never go wrong (*ijmā'*), which helped the religious establishment to claim righteousness and collectively exercise the same authority as that of the Imam.

102 Khomeini, *Sahifih Imam*, 1: 177.

103 Khomeini, *Sahifih Imam*, 15: 328.

104 In Islamic terminology, these issues are called *umur al-hisbiyyah*.

105 Other issues include overseeing religious endowments, inheritance and funerals, etc.

106 Abul-Qāsim al-Khoei, "Sharḥ al-'Urwat al-Wuthqā," *Al-Khoei Foundation*: 360. http://www.al-khoei.us/books/index.php?id=120

107 Babak Rahimi, "The Discourse of Democracy in Shi'i Islamic Jurisprudence: The Two Cases of Montazeri and Sistani," *The Mediterranean Programme Series* (2008).

108 Ḥādī Ṭabāṭabāī, "Taqyīri sīāsī dar raftār marāji' shī'a," *Mubāhithāt* (2015), http://mobahesat.ir/9967; *Ayatollah Mar'ashī Najafī bi rivāyati asnādi sawāk*, 3 vols. (Tehran: Markaz-i barrisī-i asnād-i tārīkhī wizārat-i 'iṭṭilā'āt, 2009), 1.

109 Ervand Abrahamian, "Ali Shariati: ideologue of the Iranian revolution," *Merip Reports* 102 (1982).

110 Haleh Afshar, *Iran: A Revolution in Turmoil* (Basingstoke: Macmillan, 1985), 223; Forough Jahanbakhsh, *Islam, Democracy and Religious Modernism in Iran (1953–2000): From Bazargan to Soroush* (Leiden: Brill, 2001), 122.

111 Hamid Dabashi, *Theology of Discontent: The Ideological Foundations of the Islamic Revolution in Iran* (New Brunswick: Transaction Publishers, 2006), 112.
112 Dabashi, *Theology of Discontent*, 116.
113 'Alī Shariati, "After Shahādat," in *Jihād and Shahādat: Struggle and Martyrdom in Islam*, eds. Mehdi Abedi and Gary Legenhausen (Houston: Institute for Research and Islamic Studies, 1986), 247.
114 Shariati, "After Shahādat," 249.
115 Shariati, "After Shahādat," 251.
116 Shariati, "Thār."
117 https://web.archive.org/web/20160815113818/http://shariati.nimeharf.com/Shariati/article-442/
118 Evan Siegel, "The Politics of Shahid-e Javid," in *The Twelver Shia in Modern Times: Religious Culture and Political History* (Leiden: Brill, 2001), 150–1.
119 Siegel, "The Politics of Shahid-e Javid," 161.
120 Ni'matullāh Salehi Najafābādī, *Shahīd Jāwīd* (Tehran: Umīd Fardā, 1999), 159.
121 Ṣālihī Najafābādī, *Shahīd Jāwīd*, 400.
122 Mehdi Abedi and Gary Legenhausen, "Jihād and Shahādat: Struggle and Martyrdom in Islam," *The Institute for Research and Islamic Studies* (1986): 128.
123 Murtiḍā Muṭahharī, *Ḥimāsih Ḥusayni*, 3 vols. (Tehran: Ṣadrā, 2016), 2: 149.

3 Revolution, War, and Martyrdom

1 Ervand Abrahamian, *A History of Modern Iran* (New York: Cambridge University Press, 2008), 176.
2 Abrahamian, *A History of Modern Iran*, 161.
3 Amir Taheri, *The Spirit of Allah: Khomeini and the Islamic Revolution* (Chevy Chase: Adler & Adler Publishers, 1986), 223.
4 Meir Litvak, "Martyrdom is Bliss: The Iranian Concept of Martyrdom during the War with Iraq, 1981–88," in *Martyrdom and Sacrifice in Islam: Theological, Political and Social Contexts*, eds. Meir Hatina and Meir Litvak (London: I.B. Tauris, 2016), 117.
5 Maḥmūd Ṭāliqānī, "Jihād and shahādat," in *Jihad and Shahadat*, 70.
6 Muhammad Ḥusayn Mīr Abulqāsimī, *Ṭāliqānī, Faryādī Dar Sukūt*, 2 vols. (Tehran: Shirkat Sahāmī Intishār, 2003), 1: 263.
7 Ba'athism is an Arab nationalist ideology. Iraq's adoption of Ba'athism started in 1968 and ended in 2003 with the U.S.-led invasion of Iraq and the collapse of Saddam's regime.
8 Haggay Ram, "Mythology of Rage: Representations of the 'Self' and the 'Other' in Revolutionary Iran," *History and Memory* 8, no. 1 (1996): 55.

9 Roxanne Varzi, *Warring Souls: Youth, Media, and Martyrdom in Post-revolution Iran* (Durham, NC: Duke University Press, 2006), 50.

10 Al-Ḥurr al-'Āmilī, *Wasā'il al-Shi'ah ilā Tahsil Masā'il al-Shari'ah*, 15: 16.

11 Khomeini, *Sahifih Imam*, 13: 513.

12 The Qur'an, 3:169.

13 The Qur'an, 89:29–30.

14 Khomeini, *Sahifih Imam*, 21: 147.

15 Meir Litvak argues that "as military victory became increasingly unattainable, Khomeini portrayed martyrdom as an end in itself, whose occurrence meant the realization of a major goal of Iran's war against Iraq, namely the fight for Islam" (Litvak, "Martyrdom is Bliss," 118). However, Khomeini's speeches early in the war and during the revolution were replete with reference to martyrdom as a goal for the faithful.

16 Khomeini, *Sahifih Imam*, 21: 71–94.

17 It is a challenging task to find a neutral and true report of the whole issue of recruiting children for the war. Because of the ideological nature of the Islamic Republic of Iran, any such reports from within the state or those who defected from the regime should be considered with caution. For example, in an unverified account of a former Basīj member responsible for recruiting children, there are allegations of immoral methods of attracting and training school children to become killing machines and ready for martyrdom:

> If any children refused, we vilified them. We asked them if their parents perhaps weren't good Muslims, and wondered out loud whether we would have to send them to prison. Every evening, new children were standing in the barrack-yard: distraught, intimidated, and with no real idea of what lay ahead. There were panicking children; children who imagined they'd soon be with Muhammad, the Prophet, in Paradise and children who wanted to feed their families by serving in the war. For every child at the front, the parents receive 6,000 tuman[s], the monthly wage of an Iranian worker. If the child dies, the family is given a "certificate of martyrdom." This means privileges when buying groceries, clothes, and fridges and, above all, high prestige and social advancement in class-conscious Iranian society, with its finely wrought systems of rank and status.
>
> For ten hours every day, the children learnt to handle hand grenades and machine guns. Some children didn't survive even the first few days. They threw the hand grenades in the wrong direction or too late—and blew themselves up. After a couple of days, we had to test the youngsters for the first time. We drove dogs across the parade ground and shot them. The children had to catch the animals and slit their throats. Anyone who refused was given a rucksack full of stones and had to run with it on his back until he collapsed. After a week, all the children were ready to kill the dogs. Before the children went to the front, their parents were allowed to visit them twice. Any

boy who cried when they said good-bye had to cart the rucksack full of stones around again. Slogans of Khomeini decorated the huge dormitories, and the Qur'an lay on the narrow bedside table. There were no family photos, no toys, no teddy bears, no mementos—nothing of their own. After their two-week training, the children had to function like machines: without fear, hope, feelings. We were forbidden to play with little ones. If we'd played with them, they'd have become children again, children who laughed and cried. And such children don't go to war, say our superiors.

Christoph Reuter, *My life is a Weapon: A Modern History of Suicide Bombing* (Princeton: Princeton University Press, 2004), 45.

18 Khomeini, *Sahifih Imam*, 15: 386.
19 Varzi, *Warring Souls*, 58.
20 Baqer Moin, *Khomeini: Life of the Ayatollah* (London: I.B. Tauris, 1999), 249–50.
21 Khomeini, *Sahifih Imam*, 21: 189.
22 Muhammad Bāqir Ḥiydarī Kāshānī, *Nasl ṭūfān* (Qum: Zulāl-i Kuthar, 2007), 89.
23 Shariati, "A Discussion of Shahīd," 233.
24 Shariati, "A Discussion of Shahīd," 240.
25 Khomeini, *Sahifih Imam*, 14: 257.
26 Mahmoud Ayoub, "Martyrdom in Christianity and Islam," *Religious Resurgence: Contemporary Cases in Islam, Christianity, and Judaism* (1987); Hatina, *Martyrdom in Modern Islam*, 86.
27 On September 26, 1980, during the first Friday prayer after the start of the Iran–Iraq war, Ali Khamenei officially used the combination of "Saddam Yazīd." See http://farsi.khamenei.ir/speech-content?id=24582; Dhiaa Kareem, "Discourse of Wars and Conflicts: The Construction of Saddam Hussein in the Iraq–Iran War in the US Press," *Annual Review of Education, Communication & Language Sciences* 15 (2018).
28 Varzi, *Warring Souls*, 55.
29 Khomeini, *Sahifih Imam*, 15: 417.
30 Varzi, *Warring Souls*, 54–5.
31 *Thār Allāh* is a title used for Imam Ḥusayn.
32 Āshūrā occurred on the tenth day of the month of Muḥarram.
33 Muslim ibn ʿAqil was Ḥusayn's first cousin and his ambassador to Kūfa to confirm the loyalty of the Kūfan Shīʿa. He is widely revered by the Shīʿa as the first martyr of the tragedy of Karbalā, who was betrayed by the Kūfan Shīʿa and eventually was executed by the governor of Kūfa a few weeks before Āshūrā.
34 Even though "*Hal min nasirin yansuruni?*" is quoted frequently, in historical sources we see a different version: "*Ama min mughithen yughithuna bi wajh-i allāh?*" which means "Is there anyone to help us for the sake of God?" ibn Ṭāwūs, *Al-Luhūf ʿalā Qatla al-Ṭufūf*, 102.
35 Hatina, *Martyrdom in Modern Islam*, 87.

36 "Sukhanrani Shahid Hasan Baqeri," updated June 1, 2017, http://www.aparat.com/v/HQyf5.
37 Muhammad Salam, a Lebanese journalist described the aftermath of an Iranian offensive this way: "A Yugoslavian colleague and I set off from Basra at sunrise. At around nine o'clock, we reached the area where the Iranians had tried to break through. There were bodies lying there. Just bodies—that was all you could see as far as the horizon. We started to count them. We counted them all day. We gave up when we'd got to 23,000 because we were supposed to leave the area before dark. We hadn't finished. And yet all we'd done from 9 a.m. until evening was walk up and down counting the bodies. The offensive was called Karbalā IV or Karbalā V, I don't exactly recall which it was now." Reuter, *My Life is a Weapon*, 35.
38 https://goo.gl/aOqjS6.
39 Hatina, *Martyrdom in Modern Islam*, 89.
40 Khomeini, *Sahifih Imam*, 21: 284–5.
41 http://english.khamenei.ir/news/1820/Leader-s-Speech-to-Students.
42 https://goo.gl/jQPcRR.
43 George R. Pitman, *Why War?: An Inquiry into the Genetic and Social Foundations of Human Warfare* (Indianapolis: Dog Ear Publishing, 2016), 144.
44 https://goo.gl/VELPYZ.
45 Pitman, *Why War?*, 143.
46 Hatina, *Martyrdom in Modern Islam*, 86.
47 Khomeini, *Sahifih Imam*, 14: 71.
48 Abrahamian, *A History of Modern Iran*, 175.
49 Reuter, *My Life is a Weapon*, 11.
50 Varzi, *Warring Souls*, 59.
51 Muhammad Ḥusayn Shā'irī, *Jāmi'ih Shināsī Shahādat wa Angīzih hāyi Shahīdān* (Tehran: Shahīd, 2002), 170.
The statistical population of this study was composed of martyrs coming from the education sector.
52 حسین حسین، شعار ماست، شهادت افتخار ماست.
53 al-Kulaynī, *al-Kāfī*, 1: 337.
54 رهسپاریم با خمینی تا شهادت.
55 ما همه سرباز توییم خمینی، گوش به فرمان توییم خمینی.
56 با ولایت تا شهادت .
57 Litvak, "Martyrdom is Bliss," 118.
58 Abedi and Legenhausen, "Jihād and Shahādat," 19.
59 Shahrīyār Khunsārī, "Naqsh 'Aks dar Bāznamāī Ustūrih Shahādat dar Naqqāshī Dīvārī Shahr Tehran," *Manẓar* 36, no. 8 (2016). http://www.noormags.ir/view/fa/articlepage/1185497
60 تجدید پیمان با آرمانهای امام و شهدا.

61 از سر و جان بهر فتح نینوا باید گذشت

62 بانگ صلایت را شنیدم. راهت برادر برگزیدم. ای راهی کرب و بلا من هم رسیدم.

63 هرکه دارد هوس کرب و بـــلا بـســـم الله. هرکه دارد به سرش شور و نوا بسم الله. گرکه درسینه خود شوق شـــهـــادت داری. رود این قافله تا کرب و بـــــلا بسم الله. کاروانی شده آماده عشاق حسین. گر کنون پای طلب هست تو را بسم الله

64 ای لشکر صاحب زمان آماده باش آماده باش. بهر نبردی بی امان آماده باش آماده باش

65 Khomeini, *Sahifih Imam*, 15: 193.

66 “Spirit of God” is the literal meaning of Ayatollah Khomeini’s first name, Ruhollah.

67 هر که لبیک به فرمان خمینی گوید، به خداوند قسم راه حسینی پوید. هر که فرمان برد از روح خدا بسم الله. هرکه دارد هوس کرب وبلا بسم الله

68 رزمندگان جان به کف، روز شجاعت آمده. ای لشکر روح خدا، گاه شهادت آمده. ای لشگر روح خدا، گاه شهامت آمده. ای نیروی اسلامیان، تا بی نهایت آمده. از بهر دفع دشمنان، آماده باش، آماده باش

4 Civic Martyrdom

1 Ayatollah Khamenei’s speech to the IRGC Ground Forces servicemen, http://english.khamenei.ir/news/97/Leader-s-Speech-to-the-IRGC-Ground-Forces-Servicemen.

2 Leader’s address to the officials of the Kohgiluyeh Boyer-Ahmad and North Khorasan Martyrs Commemoration Congress, <http://english.khamenei.ir/news/4206/The-Enemy-Wants-to-Make-the-People-Indifferent-Towards-Ideals>.

3 Leader’s Address to War-Disabled Veterans, < http://english.khamenei.ir/news/74/Leader-s-Address-to-War-Disabled-Veteran>.

4 In Khamenei’s words, particularly the U.S., the U.K., and Israel, are the bullies and the global arrogance. See, for example, “Our problems with America are not solved by negotiations,”, <http://english.khamenei.ir/news/4052/Our-problems-with-America-are-not-solved-by-negotiations-Ayatollah>.

5 “Cultural Attacks By the Enemy Are More Dangerous than Military Attacks,” <http://english.khamenei.ir/news/4695/Cultural-Attacks-By-the-Enemy-Are-More-Dangerous-than-Military>.

6 Leader’s speech in meeting with families of the martyrs of 7th of Tir, <http://english.khamenei.ir/news/2089/Leader-s-speech-in-meeting-with-families-of-the-martyrs-of-7th>.

7 Leader’s speech in meeting with a group of martyr’s children, <http://farsi.khamenei.ir/speech-content?id=2166>.

8 “Leader Visits Families of Assassinated Scientists,” <http://english.khamenei.ir/news/1576/Leader-Visits-Families-of-Assassinated-Scientists>.

9 "Bullet-riddled cars and lush gardens: Iran's memorial to its 'nuclear martyrs,'" <https://www.theguardian.com/world/2015/jul/02/iran-memorial-museum-nuclear-martyrs>.

10 "Ayatollah Khamenei's Message in Praise of the Firefighters Martyred in the Plasco Incident," <http://english.khamenei.ir/news/4600/Ayatollah-Khamenei-s-Message-in-Praise-of-the-Firefighters-Martyred>.

11 "Leader's Speech to Members of Commemoration Congresses for Artist, Students and Education Martyrs," <http://english.khamenei.ir/news/2018/Leader-s-Speech-to-Members-of-Commemoration-Congresses-for-Artist>.

12 "Martyrs of the Green Movement," <http://www.pbs.org/wgbh/pages/frontline/tehranbureau/2010/06/martyrs-of-the-green-movement.html>.

13 Caspian Makan, "I cannot believe it yet. I still think I will see Neda again," <https://www.theguardian.com/world/2009/nov/15/iran-neda-caspian-makan-interview>.

14 Abū Muhammad 'Abdullāh ibn Muslim ibn Qutaybah, *al-Imāmat wa al-Siyāsah*, 2 vols. (Beirut: Dār al-Aḍwā', 1990), 1: 99.

15 <http://alef.ir/vdciqvazqt1auu2.cbct.html?108066>; <https://goo.gl/Ysx2Hv>.

16 *Ḥizbullāhi* in today's Iran is now a general term referring to the strict followers and advocates of *wilāyat-i faqīh* and the values of the Islamic Revolution. It is synonymous with the term *Basījī*.

17 جانم فدای رهبر.

18 ما اهل کوفه نیستیم علی تنها بماند.

19 خونی که در رگ ماست، هدیه به رهبر ماست.

20 Leader's speech in meeting with youth in the great mosque of Tehran, <http://farsi.khamenei.ir/speech-content?id=3003>.

21 William Beeman, "Martyrdom, Shi'a Islam, Ta'ziya: Political Symbolism in Shi'a Islam," in *Martyrdom and Sacrifice in Islam: Theological, Political and Social Contexts*, eds. Meir Hatina and Meir Litvak (London: I.B. Tauris, 2016), 242.

22 <https://crcms.ir/ghanoon/2393>.

23 Khomeini, *Sahifih Imam*, 19: 146–61.

24 <https://goo.gl/6ZfU6s>.

25 Hamid Dabashi, *Iran, the Green Movement and the USA: The Fox and the Paradox* (New York: Zed Books, 2013), 202.

26 "Leader Meets with Officials of Ministry of Intelligence," <http://english.khamenei.ir/news/861/Leader-Meets-with-Officials-of-Ministry-of-Intelligence>.

5 Martyrdom Reimagined

1 <https://goo.gl/f3thw4>. Extract translated by the author.

2 Khomeini, *Sahifih Imam*, 13: 483–90.

3 Marius Deeb, "Shia movements in Lebanon: Their formation, ideology, social basis, and links with Iran and Syria," *Third World Quarterly* 10, no. 2 (1988).
4 Deeb, "Shia movements in Lebanon."
5 The Syrian government also was not happy with the military presence of Iran in southern Lebanon as it would undermine Syrian influence in Lebanon. It is reported that Iran's withdrawal of most of its troops from Lebanon in part was to satisfy Syria because Iran needed Syrian support in the war with Iraq. Shireen T. Hunter, "Iran and the spread of revolutionary Islam," *Third World Quarterly* 10, no. 2 (1988).
6 راه قدس از کربلا می گذرد.
7 Khomeini, *Sahifih Imam*, 16: 343–57.
8 Pape, *Dying to Win*, 129.
9 Simon Haddad, "A comparative study of Lebanese and Palestinian perceptions of suicide bombings: The role of militant Islam and socio-economic status," *International Journal of Comparative Sociology* 45, no. 5 (2004).
10 Pape, *Dying to Win*, 132.
11 Haddad, "A comparative study of Lebanese and Palestinian perceptions of suicide bombings."
12 See, for example, Ḥasan ibn Yūsuf Al-Ḥillī, *Tabsirat al-Muta'allimīn fī Aḥkām al-Dīn*, ed. Muhammad Ḥādī Yūsufi Gharawī (Tehran: Chāpp wa Nashr, 1990), 88; Muhammad Ḥasan al-Najafī, *Jawāhir al-Kalām*, ed. 'Abbās Quchānī, 43 vols. (Beirut: Dār 'ihyā' al-Turāth al-'Arabī, 1983), 21: 70; Muhammad Muṣṭafā Al-Zaḥilī and Aḥmad Mu'az Al-Khātīb, *Al-'Amaliyyāt al-"istishhādīyah fī al-Mīzān al-Fiqhī* (Damascus: Dār al-Fikr, 1997), 89.
13 Mashru'iyyat-i 'Amaliyat Esteshhadi az Didgah-i Fuqahaye Mu'aser Shī'ah va Sunni, in *hawzah.net*, https://goo.gl/5Akky9.
14 Mashru'iyyat-i 'Amaliyat Esteshhadi az Didgah-i Fuqahaye Mu'aser Shī'ah va Sunni, in *hawzah.net*, https://goo.gl/5Akky9.
15 The definition of "civilian," though, turned out to be very subjective as the Shī'a coalition involved in Syria has never conceded killing civilians in their attack against ISIS and other Salafī militias while the Syrian opposition front believe the otherwise. See the Middle East Institute report of December 15, 2016, "Civilians Massacred in Aleppo by Iranian Backed Militia," http://www.mei.edu/content/is/civilians-massacred-aleppo-iranian-backed-militia.
16 *Al-Monitor*, http://www.al-monitor.com/pulse/originals/2013/12/suicide-bombing-increase-shiite.html.
17 Zaynab, along with other women among the followers of Ḥusayn in Karbala, survived the massacre and was sent to Yazīd's court as a prisoner.
18 In Shī'a terminology, *Ahlul-Bayt* ("People of the House") refers to the immediate family of the Prophet and it is extended to mean all twelve Imams.

19 See Fatima Ayub, *The Gulf and Sectarianism* (European Council on Foreign Relations [ECFR], 2013), 11; Nasr, *The Shia Revival*, 236; Susanne Olsson, "Shia as Internal Others: A Salafi Rejection of the 'Rejecters,'" *Islam and Christian–Muslim Relations* 28, no. 4 (2017); Elaine Sciolino, "Where the Prophet Trod, He Begs, Tread Lightly," *The New York Times* (2002).

20 This duality of pro- and anti-government countries and groups is not entirely accurate since their stance on the issue of the Syrian civil war depends on their interests. This means we cannot depict a black-and-white picture of the two opposing sides. For example, Turkey started with strong anti-Russian and anti-Assad rhetoric. Still, later its position against them became softer because the real factor behind Turkey's involvement in Syria is the issue of Kurdish groups. Moreover, the Trump administration had an ambivalent stance regarding Syria's Assad and Russian involvement in the Syrian conflict.

21 "Syrian Observatory says war has killed more than half a million," Reuters, 12 March 2018, https://www.reuters.com/article/us-mideast-crisis-syria/syrian-observatory-says-war-has-killed-more-than-half-a-million-idUSKCN1GO13M.

22 Edward Wastnidge, "Iran and Syria: An Enduring Axis," *Middle East Policy* 24, no. 2 (2017), https://doi.org/10.1111/mepo.12275, http://dx.doi.org/10.1111/mepo.12275.

23 Saleem A. Salih Al-Dulaimi, Mohammad Kamal, and Dalal Mahmoud Elsayed, "The Impact of Sectarian Conflict in Syria on Iran-Gulf Relations," *Asian Social Science* 13, no. 7 (2017).

24 Ewan Stein, "Ideological Codependency and Regional Order: Iran, Syria, and the Axis of Refusal," *PS: Political Science & Politics* 50, no. 3 (2017).

25 Wastnidge, "Iran and Syria"; Emile El-Hokayem, "Hizballah and Syria: Outgrowing the Proxy Relationship," *Washington Quarterly* 30, no. 2 (2007).

26 Wastnidge, "Iran and Syria."

27 Al-Dulaimi, Kamal, and Elsayed, "The Impact of Sectarian Conflict in Syria on Iran-Gulf Relations."

28 Geneive Abdo, *The New Sectarianism: The Arab Uprisings and the Rebirth of the Shi'a–Sunni Divide* (New York: Oxford University Press, 2016), 60.

29 Khamenei in his message on the day of the attack to the Samarra shrine wrote: "I express my condolence over this tragic incident to the holy Prophet of Islam (peace be upon him and his infallible household) and to his holiness Imam of the age—may our souls be sacrificed for his sake—and also to all the Shīʿas throughout the world and to all devoted and vigilant Muslims and the adherents of the holy Prophet's immaculate household (greetings be upon them), and I declare a week of public mourning in the country. I deem it necessary to emphatically ask the mournful people in Iran and Iraq and other parts of the world to strictly avoid any action that is likely to foment conflict and hostility among Muslim brethren. Surely certain

hands are at work trying to incite Shī'a Muslims to attack the mosques and other sites revered by Sunni Muslims. Any action in this direction will help to further the goals of the enemies of Islam and the enemies of Muslim nations and is religiously prohibited." "Leader's Message on Desecration of holy 'Askarīya Shrine in Samarra," https://goo.gl/ZaZqVR.

30 The U.S. president, his ambassador in Iraq, and the British foreign secretary along with Iraqi officials, were quick to condemn the attack and tried to calm down both sides for fear of a new wave of sectarian conflict and possibly a civil war. In response to the attack, "U.S. Ambassador Zalmay Khalilzad and the top American commander in Iraq, Gen. George Casey, called the bombing a deliberate attempt to foment sectarian strife, and warned it was a critical moment for Iraq." Robert F. Worth, "Blast destroys shrine in Iraq, setting off sectarian fury," *The New York Times*, February 23, 2006, https://www.nytimes.com/2006/02/23/world/middleeast/blast-at-shiite-shrine-sets-off-sectarian-fury-in-iraq.html.

31 Dahr Jamail and Arkan Hamed, "In Iraq, Mosque Outrage Also Brings Solidarity," *The Washington Report on Middle East Affairs* 25, no. 3 (2006). Muqtada al-Sadr, a leading cleric and (now former) militia in Iraq echoed this unity strategy and blamed the Americans for the attack: "It was not the Sunnis who attacked the shrine of Imam al-Hadi, God's peace be upon him, but rather the occupation [forces] and Ba'athists . . . God damn them. We should not attack Sunni mosques. I have ordered the al-Mahdī Army to protect both Shi'i and Sunni shrines." Jamail and Hamed, "In Iraq, Mosque Outrage Also Brings Solidarity."

32 Lucian Harris, "Conservation: Iran takes the lead in restoration of Samarra mosque," *The art newspaper* 15, no. 168 (2006).

33 Alummah.ir, 7 October, 2018, https://bit.ly/3kE511w

34 Hamid Algar, *Wahhabism: A Critical Essay* (BookBaby, 2015), 43.

35 See, for example, this news story on the anniversary of the demolition of al-Baqī' at yjc.ir, published on August 5, 2014: https://www.yjc.ir/00KhaD.

36 Robert F. Worth, "Blast destroys shrine in Iraq, setting off sectarian fury.".

37 See this news story published by isna.ir on February 24, 2006: https://www.isna.ir/news/8412-02463/.

38 Mariam Karouny, "Shiite Fighters Rally to Defend Damascus Shrine," *Reuters*, March 3, 2013, https://goo.gl/efCrNe.

39 Thomas Erdbrink, "Iran Warns Syrian Rebels After Report of Shrine Desecration," *The New York Times*, May 6, 2013, https://www.nytimes.com/2013/05/07/world/middleeast/iran-warns-syrian-rebels-after-report-of-shrine-desecration.html.

40 Zafer Kızılkaya, "Hizbullah's Moral Justification of Its Military Intervention in the Syrian Civil War," *The Middle East Journal* 71, no. 2 (2017). Watch full Naṣrallāh's speech with live English translation on YouTube here: https://www.youtube.com/watch?v=dFXbliX3h5w.

41 “Iranian Casualties in Syria and the Strategic Logic of Intervention”, *The Washington Institute*, https://goo.gl/Kn8NX6.
42 “Iran Aims to Boost Prestige of Beleaguered Afghan Proxy Force in Syria”, *Radio Free Europe*, https://goo.gl/GLYYyp.
43 Phillip Smyth, *The Shiite Jihad in Syria and Its Regional Effects* (Washington, D.C.: Washington Institute for Near East Policy, 2015), 8.
44 Jubin M, Goodarzi, “Iran and the Syrian civil war,” in *The War for Syria* (Routledge, 2019), 144.
45 Goodarzi, “Iran and the Syrian civil war,” 146; Thomas Juneau, “Iran’s costly intervention in Syria: A pyrrhic victory,” *Mediterranean Politics* 25, no. 1 (2020).
46 See these speeches made by Ayatollah Khamenei in defense of fighting against *takfīrīs* in Iraq and Syria: New Year speech to state officials on April 10, 2017, http://farsi.khamenei.ir/news-content?id=36176; speech to families of martyred shrine defenders published on March 13, 2019, http://farsi.khamenei.ir/speech-content?id=41853; http://farsi.khamenei.ir/speech-content?id=30791.
47 However, Ayatollah Khamenei sees *takfīrī* movements as being secretly formed and backed by Zionists and the U.S., i.e., conspiracies to make Islam and Islamic countries disreputable. See, for example, Khamenei’s speech in meeting with participants of International Congress on Takfirism, November 25, 2014, http://english.khamenei.ir/news/1985/Leader-s-Speech-in-Meeting-with-Participants-of-International; Khamenei’s speech in a meeting with the Iraqi Prime Minister, Mr. Haider Al-Abadi on June 20, 2017, http://english.khamenei.ir/news/4930/Iran-opposes-the-partitioning-of-Iraq-Ayatollah-Khamenei; Khamenei’s speech on October 18, 2017 in a meeting with outstanding students, members of the Elite Foundation and the winners of scientific competitions and entrance exams in Iran, http://english.khamenei.ir/news/5222/US-Europe-gave-Saddam-WMD-have-no-right-meddle-in-our-missile; Khamenei’s speech in a meeting with senior commanders of the armed forces on April 9, 2017, http://english.khamenei.ir/news/4753/The-US-made-a-strategic-mistake-by-attacking-Syria-Ayatollah.
48 “Leader’s speech in the meeting with the families of martyrs of the borders and shrine defenders,” Khmenei.ir: http://farsi.khamenei.ir/speech-content?id=36894.
49 This quote is from a recent book (*zulfaqār*), first published in 2019 (in Farsi), that collected oral memories of Suleimani. I got the excerpt from mehrnews.com/xSvTx.
50 Smyth, *The Shiite Jihad in Syria and Its Regional Effects*, 1.
51 *Defapress.ir*, published on January 26, 2016, http://dnws.ir/67744; *Parsine.com*, May 7, 2013, parsine.com/000QtX.
52 Wastnidge, “Iran and Syria.”
53 <http://dnws.ir/67744>; <https://goo.gl/MbfzzV>.
54 However, it should be noted here that, in Khamenei’s understanding, Salafism/Wahhabism is not the main enemy facing the Shī’as; rather, for him the main enemy

are the U.S., Zionism, and Western intelligent services that have tried to create and invoke groups with a Salafi/Wahhabi mindset to divide the Islamic world. See. for example. his speech at the twenty-fifth anniversary of the death of Ayatollah Khomeini on June 4, 2014: http://farsi.khamenei.ir/news-content?id=26612. See also his speech for families of martyred shrine defenders on March 13, 2019: http://farsi.khamenei.ir/speech-content?id=41853.

55 Leader's speech in the meeting with the families of martyred shrine defenders, http://farsi.khamenei.ir/speech-content?id=35136.

56 Habib ibn Mazahir was one of the most famous companions of Imam Ḥusayn. He was martyred in Karbalā in old age.

57 See the video here: www.islamicideology.net/view_video.php?viewkey=158969548&page=&viewtype=&category=.

58 See, for example, this manifesto issued by Iran's Freedom Movement on December 22, 1985, criticizing the Islamic Republic's policy of the continuation of the war with Iraq until the collapse of Saddam: http://www.mizankhabar.net/asnad/bayanieh/64/html/64_52.htm.

59 Muhammad Reza Akhgarī, *Wilāyatī-hāyi bī wilāyat* (Tehran: Akhgarī, 1988), 79; Zia'uddin Ulyanasab and Salman Alavi Nik, *Jaryanshenasi anjoman hujjatiyyih* (Tehran: Zulal kuthar, 2008), 175.

60 See Ayatollah Wahīd Khurāsanī's lecture on May 15, 2013, published on his official website: https://bit.ly/3wIAILV.

61 "Grand Ayatollah Sistani Calls on 'Everyone' in Iraq to Expel Takfīrīs," *ABNA24*, https://goo.gl/TMtd7Y.

62 "Grand Ayatollah Sistani's son joins volunteers to defend holy shrines against ISIL militants in Iraq," *ABNA24*, https://goo.gl/LYzZzr.

63 Wastnidge, "Iran's Own 'War on Terror,'" 119.

64 Smyth, *The Shiite Jihad in Syria and Its Regional Effects*, 15–16.

65 Smyth, *The Shiite Jihad in Syria and Its Regional Effects*, 9.

66 See, for example, these YouTube videos: <https://www.youtube.com/watch?v=FUPkvUJ7g50; https://www.youtube.com/watch?v=NuS-bf_FK6g>.

67 al-Khaṣībī, *al-Hidāyat al-Kubrā*, 39.

68 Ayoub, *Redemptive Suffering in Islam*, 16.

69 The "People of the Cloak" (*ahlul-kisa'*), in accordance with a long and famous tradition, refers to Muhammad, 'Alī, Fāṭimah, Ḥasan, and Ḥusayn.

70 Syed Akbar Hyder, *Reliving Karbala: Martyrdom in South Asian Memory* (Oxford: Oxford University Press, 2006), 95.

71 Imam Ḥusayn's harem is mostly understood as female relatives of Ḥusayn who were present in Karbalā with him.

72 *Ziyārat Mufji'a of Bībī Zaynab.*

73 Muwaffaq b. Aḥmad al-Khwārazmī, *Maqtal al-Ḥusayn (by al-Khwārazmī)*, 2 vols. (Qum: Anwār al-Ḥudā, 2002), 2: 34.

74 "Ziyārat Mufji'a of Bībī Zaynab," *Ziarat.org*, https://www.ziaraat.org/syria/zainab.php.

75 Smyth, *The Shiite Jihad in Syria and Its Regional Effects*, 6 and 27; also see these videos: https://www.youtube.com/watch?v=FUPkvUJ7g50; https://youtu.be/pYCjRAaG_Ns; https://goo.gl/tBLAzu.

76 "Iran's Foreign Legion: The Role of Iraqi Shiite Militias in Syria," *The Washington Institute*, <https://goo.gl/d2xq97>.

77 Hyder, *Reliving Karbala*, 95.

78 In the popular storytelling of the event of Karbalā, Zaynab is depicted as the spiritual heir of Fāṭimah. A particularly moving scene in Āshūrā lamentations is when Ḥusayn bade farewell to Zaynab before going to the battle for the last time. At the end of the dialogue, Zaynab stopped him to perform Fāṭimah's will by kissing his neck.

6 Shrine Defenders: A New Beginning

1 *Mashregh News*, March 6, 2017, mshrgh.ir/698569

2 Ali Fathollah-Nejad, *Aljazeera*. May 2, 2018. https://www.aljazeera.com/opinions/2018/5/2/iranians-respond-to-the-regime-leave-syria-alone.

3 Julia Masterson, "Iranian Public Opinion Under 'Maximum Pressure,'" *Arms Control Today* 49, no. 10 (2019).

4 Afshin Shahi and Ehsan Abdoh-Tabrizi, "Iran's 2019–2020 Demonstrations: The Changing Dynamics Of Political Protests In Iran," *Asian Affairs* 51, no. 1 (01/02/2020); Saeed Ghasseminejad, Behnam Ben Taleblu, and Eliora Katz, "Evolution Toward Revolution: The Development Of Street Protests In The Islamic Republic Of Iran," *Journal of International Affairs* 73, no. 2 (2020).

5 Juneau, "Iran's costly intervention in Syria."

6 Juneau, "Iran's costly intervention in Syria."

7 The irony was that prior to the Syrian conflicts, Iran had called the popular uprisings that became known as the "Arab Spring" the "Islamic awakening." So, when the Syrian uprising started, Iran's leaders were caught off guard and found themselves in an awkward position on how to respond to the conflict that was rapidly escalating. Wastnidge, "Iran and Syria."

8 Goodarzi, "Iran and the Syrian civil war," 140.

9 Goodarzi, "Iran and the Syrian civil war," 143.

10 Wastnidge, "Iran's Own 'War on Terror,'" 120.

11 Goodarzi, "Iran and the Syrian civil war," 143.

12 Juneau, "Iran's costly intervention in Syria."

13 "Iran's Revolutionary Guards: We Have Armed 200,000 Fighters in the Region," *Middle East Monitor*, January 15, 2016, https://www.middleeastmonitor.com/20160115-irans-revolutionary-guards-we-havearmed-200000-fighters-in-the-region.

14 David Cook, "Messianism in the Shiite crescent," *Current trends in Islamist ideology* 11 (2011).

15 Ali Ansari, "Iran under Ahmadinejad: populism and its malcontents," *International Affairs* 84, no. 4 (2008), https://dx.doi.org/10.1111/j.1468-2346.2008.00732.x.

16 Shirin Saeidi, "Hojaji's Gaze: Civilizational Aspirations and the Reclamation of Space in Contemporary Iran," *International Journal of Middle East Studies* 52, no. 2 (2020).

17 Saeidi, "Hojaji's Gaze."

18 https://web.archive.org/web/20171020095928/https://www.al-monitor.com/pulse/originals/2017/08/iran-mohsen-hojjajji-irgc-beheading-isis-syria-iraq.html.

19 https://english.khamenei.ir/news/5203/Martyr-Mohsen-Hojaji-Is-the-Spokesperson-for-All-Innocent-Martyrs

20 Florin Diaconu, "Iranian Grand Strategy In The Greater Middle East, The IRGC and General Qassem Soleimani" (paper presented at the International Scientific Conference Strategies XXI, 2017).

21 Maysam Behravesh, "Qassem Soleimani: Guardian of Iran's regional interests," *Middle East Eye (MEE)* (2020).

22 Fanar Haddad, "Understanding Iraq's Hashd al-Sha 'bi: State and Power in Post-2014 Iraq," *The Century Foundation* (2018).

23 Bozorgmehr Sharafedin, "General Qasem Soleimani: Iran's Rising Star," *BBC Persian Service* (2015).

24 See the video of Qasem Suleimani's speech on how he came up with the name of "shrine defenders" here: https://snn.ir/0036Dp.

25 Khamenei.ir, "A severe revenge awaits the criminal killers of General Soleimani," January 3, 2020, https://english.khamenei.ir/news/7270/A-severe-revenge-awaits-the-criminal-killers-of-General-Soleimani.

26 ISNA, February 10, 2020. https://www.isna.ir/news.

27 Michael Safi, "Iran: dozens dead in stampede at Suleimani burial procession." *The Guardian*, January 7, 2020, https://www.theguardian.com/world/2020/jan/07/qassem-suleimani-burial-iran-general-home-town.

28 Nakissa Jahanbani, "Beyond Soleimani: Implications for Iran's Proxy Network in Iraq and Syria," *CTC Perspectives* (2020).

29 https://english.khamenei.ir/news/8203/Martyr-Soleimani-is-a-champion-of-the-Iranian-nation-and-of-the.

30 IRNA.ir, "Major General Salami: we take hard and remorseful revenge," January 7, 2020. www.irna.ir/news/83624000/.

31 The animation video is available at: Mehrnews.com, "VIDEO: 'Hard Revenge' animation." January 2, 2021, https://en.mehrnews.com/news/167952/VIDEO-Hard-Revenge-animation.
32 Irna.ir, "The message of Iran's health minister," September 20, 2020, www.irna.ir/news/84046431/.
33 Traditionally the *Haft-Sīn* table has the following seven items that start with the Persian letter 'س': *sabzeh*, *samanu* (wheat germ sweet pudding), *senjed* (Persian olive), *serkeh* (vinegar), *sīb* (apple), *sīr* (garlic), and *somāq* (sumac, a common Persian condiment).
34 Speech by Mahdi Faqih Imami, https://web.archive.org/web/20210810062331if_/https://graphics.reuters.com/world-coronavirus-tracker-and-maps/countries-and-territories/iran/.
35 https://www.youtube.com/watch?v=DNTzYD8i55A.

7 From Karbalā to Damascus

1 *Saqīfah Banī Sā'idah* was a roofed building in Medina that became famous because, after the Prophet's death, a number of influential disciples of the Prophet gathered there and finally selected Abu Bakr as the first Caliph and successor to the Prophet. Abd al-Malik Ibn Hishām, "The life of Muhammad: a translation of Isḥāq's Sīrat rasūl Allāh / with introduction and notes by A. Guillaume," (New York: Oxford University Press, 1997), 683. That is why, for the Shī'a, *saqīfah* became the single most important symbol of the betrayal of the family of the Prophet and the beginning of the deviation of Islam from its right path and harbinger of calamities that followed, most importantly the martyrdom of Fāṭimat al-Zahrā and the events of Āshūrā. For a good grasp of the Shī'ī interpretation of the *saqīfah*, see a work of Sayyid Murtadā Sharīf 'Askarī (1914–2007), an erudite Shī'ī scholar, who presented a detailed history of *saqīfah* and its consequences. In that book (written in Farsi), with a strong sectarian tone and numerous references to both Sunni and Shī'a sources, 'Askarī intended to demonstrate how *saqīfah* had to be blamed for the calamities that faced the Imams and the community of the Shī'a: Sayyid Murtadā Sharīf 'Askarī, *Saqīfah*, ed. Mahdī Dashtī (Qum: Daneshkadeh Uṣūl al-dīn, 2008).
2 Ayoub, *Redemptive Suffering in islam*, 27–37.
3 Āshūrā occurred on the tenth day of the lunar month of Muharram. So, traditionally, Shī'ites mourn for Imam Ḥusayn during the whole two months of Muharram and Safar.
4 Khomeini, *Sahifih Imam*, 15: 326–37.
5 Among prominent ultra-traditionalists, Ayatollahs Mohammad Hussaini-Shirazi (d. 2001), Hassan Tabataba'i-Qomi (d. 2006), Muhammad Ruhani (d. 1997), and

Sadeq Ruhani, each have had some sort of confrontation with the Islamic Republic's brand of Shīʿism and faced condemnation from the ruling religious leaders.

6 Mahmoud Sadri, "Ḥojjatiya," *Encyclopaedia Iranica* (2004). http://www.iranicaonline.org/articles/hojjatiya

7 Rajaee, *Islamism and Modernism*, 86.

8 One of the best-written works of the the pro-Hujjatiyeh doctrine of *intiẓār* is Muhammad Bani-Hashemi, *Ma'refat-e Emam-e 'Asr [Cognition of the Imam of the Time]* (Tehran: Nik Ma'aref, 2007).

9 During its early years, the Hujjatiyeh developed rapidly among Iran's religious sectors such that many of its members joined the 1979 revolution and abandoned the group (Nasr 2006, 133). Even Halabi unsuccessfully became a candidate for the first Assembly of Experts, though never fully embraced the Revolution's cause (for details of his activities, see Jafarian 1385/2006, 368–78).

10 Nasr, *The Shia Revival*, 133.

11 Jolyon P. Mitchell, *Promoting Peace, Inciting Violence: The Role of Religion and Media* (Routledge, 2012), 59.

12 ibn Qūlawayh, *Kāmil al-Ziyārāt.*

13 The full video of the lamentation in Farsi with English subtitles is accessible at: https://goo.gl/VEZ3Yy.

14 Khomeini, *Sahifih Imam*, 19: 146; Khomeini, *Sahifih Imam*, 8: 374.

15 Khomeini, *Sahifih Imam*, 18: 269.

16 Khomeini, *Sahifih Imam*, 14: 472.

17 See, for example, Khamenei's speech during an assembly with commanders and personnel of the Islamic Republic of Iran's Army Air Force: A. Khamenei, "The new U.S. President reveals the true nature of the United States of America," Khamenei.ir, February 7, 2017, http://english.khamenei.ir/news/4625/The-new-U-S-President-reveals-the-true-nature-of-the-United.

18 As discussed in Chapter 3, the Iranian soldiers of the war with Iraq also in their mottos considered themselves as part of the army of al-Mahdī, aiming to avenge the blood of Ḥusayn. However, the circumstances of the war and its ending meant, in reality, they mostly set their eyes on the scene of Karbalā as inspiration for martyrdom in an "imposed" and "unjust war."

Appendix: Martyrdom in Classical Islam

1 Roberta Denaro, "Definitions and Narratives of Martyrdom in Sunni Hadith Literature," in *Twenty-first Century Jihad: Law, Society and Military Action*, eds. Elisabeth Kenall and Ewan Stein (London: I.B. Tauris, 2015).

2 'Abdullāh ibn Mubārak, *Kitāb al-Jihād*, ed. Nazih Hammaad (Jidah: Dār al-Matbū'āt al-Ḥadithah), 62.

3 ibn Mubārak, *Kitāb al-Jihād*, 129–30.
4 ibn Mubārak, *Kitāb al-Jihād*, 64, no. 9.
5 Abul-Ḥusayn Muslim ibn al-Ḥajjāj, *Ṣaḥīḥ Muslim* (Beirut: Dār al-Ḥadīth, 1991), 1513–14, no. 905. I relied on the translation by Jibril Mohammed, *Above the Law 360°* (Bloomington: AuthorHouse, 2013).
6 ibn Mubārak, *Kitāb al-Jihād*, 128–9.
7 ibn Mubārak, *Kitāb al-Jihād*, 85–6.
8 ibn Mubārak, *Kitāb al-Jihād*, 172; ibn Mubārak, *Kitāb al-Jihād*, 86.
9 See David Nicolle, *The Great Islamic Conquests AD 632–750* (Oxford: Osprey Publishing, 2009), 56–8.
10 Abū 'Abdullah Muhammad ibn Mājah al-Rab'ī al-Qazwīnī, *Sunan ibn Mājah*, ed. Muhammad Fu'ad 'Abdul Baghi (Cairo: Dār al-Iḥyā' al-Kutub al-'Arabīyyah, 1954), 928, no. 2778.
11 ibn Mubārak, *Kitāb al-Jihād*, 110.
12 ibn Mubārak, *Kitāb al-Jihād*, 83, no. 45.
13 ibn Mubārak, *Kitāb al-Jihād*, 87, no. 52.
14 ibn Mubārak, *Kitāb al-Jihād*, 74, no. 26; ibn Mubārak, *Kitāb al-Jihād*, 75, no. 28; Abū Zakarīā Muḥyi al-Dīn Yaḥyā Ibn Sharaf al-Nawawī, *Rīyāḍ al-Sāliḥīn* (Cairo: Dār al-Ma'ārif), 335, no. 1311; Muslim ibn al-Ḥajjāj, *Ṣaḥīḥ Muslim*, 1498, no. 877. For the translation I relied on *The Termination of the Afflictions and Fierce Battles—Ibn Kathir*, trans. Abd el Qader al-Azeez (Mansoura: Dar al-Ghad al-Gadeed, 2005), 562.
15 Muhammad al-Bukhārī, *Ṣahīh al-Bukhārī* (Riyadh: Maktabah al-Rushd, 2006), 994, no. 7226–7; al-Bukhārī, *Ṣahīh al-Bukhārī*, 12, no. 36. I relied on the translation by Andrew G. Bostom, *The Legacy of Jihad: Islamic Holy War and the Fate of Non-Muslims* (Amherst, NY: Prometheus Books, 2010), 137.
16 In Islamic eschatological literature, *al-ṣirāṭ is* the hair-narrow bridge which every person must pass on the day of judgement to enter paradise. Those with impurities and misdeeds will have difficulties passing that bridge and will fall into hell.
17 ibn Mubārak, *Kitāb al-Jihād*, 165, no. 81.
18 ibn Mubārak, *Kitāb al-Jihād*, 165, no. 82.
19 ibn Mubārak, *Kitāb al-Jihād*, 74, no. 25.
20 *Al-Ṣiḥāḥ al-Ṣittah* are the collection these books: al-Bukhari, Muslim, al-Tirmidhi, Abū Dawud, al-Nasa'i, and ibn Maja.
21 Aḥmad ibn Shu'ayb al-Nasā'ī, *Sunan al-Nasā'ī*, ed. Muhammad ibn Salih al-Rajihi (Riyadh: Bayt al-Afkār al-Dawlīyyah), 430, no. 4094–6; Abū Bakr Muhammad ibn Isḥāq ibn Khuzaymah, *Ṣaḥiḥ Ibn Khuzaymah*, ed. Muhammad Mustafa al-A'zimi (Riyadh: al-Maktab al-Islāmi, 2003), 1121, no. 2336; Jalāl al-Dīn al-Suyūtī, *Abwāb al-Sa'ādah fī Asbāb al-Shahādah*, ed. Najm 'Abd al-Rahman Khalaf (Cairo: al-Maktabah al-Qayyimah, 1987), 47–9, no. 21–3.
22 ibn Mubārak, *Kitāb al-Jihād*, 94, no. 68. See similar *ḥadīths* naming different types of martyrs: ibn Mubārak, *Kitāb al-Jihād*, 173, no. 98; al-Nasā'ī, *Sunan al-Nasā'ī*, 338, no.

3194; al-Bukhārī, *Ṣaḥīh al-Bukhārī*, 383, no. 2829; Muhammad ibn Īsā al-Tirmidhī, *Jāmi' al-Tirmidhī*, ed. Ahmad Muhammad Shakir (Cairo: Maktabah Muṣṭfā al-Bābi al-Ḥalbī, 1975), 368, no. 1063; Sulaymān ibn al-Ash'ath Abū Dāwūd, *Sunan Abī Dāwūd* (Riyadh: Bayt al-Afkār al-Dawlīyyah), 352, no. 3111; al-Nasā'ī, *Sunan al-Nasā'ī*, 211, no. 1846; ibn Mājah al-Rab'ī al-Qazwīnī, *Sunan ibn Mājah*, 937, no. 2803; al-Suyūtī, *Abwāb al-Sa'ādah fī Asbāb al-Shahādah*, 36–7, no. 1–2; al-Suyūtī, *Abwāb al-Sa'ādah fī Asbāb al-Shahādah*, 42–3, no. 9–12; al-Suyūtī, *Abwāb al-Sa'ādah fī Asbāb al-Shahādah*, 47, no. 20; al-Suyūtī, *Abwāb al-Sa'ādah fī Asbāb al-Shahādah*, 66, no. 58. For the translation, I relied on https://sunnah.com/nasai/21.

23 al-Suyūtī, *Abwāb al-Sa'ādah fī Asbāb al-Shahādah*, 44, no. 13; al-Suyūtī, *Abwāb al-Sa'ādah fī Asbāb al-Shahādah*, 55–6, no. 34–5.

24 al-Suyūtī, *Abwāb al-Sa'ādah fī Asbāb al-Shahādah*, 44, no. 14.

25 al-Suyūtī, *Abwāb al-Sa'ādah fī Asbāb al-Shahādah*, 45, no. 15.

26 al-Suyūtī, *Abwāb al-Sa'ādah fī Asbāb al-Shahādah*, 65, no. 56.

27 al-Suyūtī, *Abwāb al-Sa'ādah fī Asbāb al-Shahādah*, 61–2, no. 50.

28 al-Suyūtī, *Abwāb al-Sa'ādah fī Asbāb al-Shahādah*, 52–3, no. 28.

29 al-Suyūtī, *Abwāb al-Sa'ādah fī Asbāb al-Shahādah*, 52–3, no. 30–1.

30 ibn Mubārak, *Kitāb al-Jihād*, 101, no. 83.

31 Abū Dāwūd, *Sunan Abī Dāwūd*, 284, no. 2499. See also al-Suyūtī, *Abwāb al-Sa'ādah fī Asbāb al-Shahādah*, 46, no. 16; al-Suyūtī, *Abwāb al-Sa'ādah fī Asbāb al-Shahādah*, 46–7, no. 18–19; al-Suyūtī, *Abwāb al-Sa'ādah fī Asbāb al-Shahādah*, 50–1, no. 25.

32 Abū Dāwūd, *Sunan Abī Dāwūd*, 181, no. 1520. See also al-Suyūtī, *Abwāb al-Sa'ādah fī Asbāb al-Shahādah*, 67, no. 60–1; al-Suyūtī, *Abwāb al-Sa'ādah fī Asbāb al-Shahādah*, 68, no. 63; al-Tirmidhī, *Jāmi' al-Tirmidhī*, 183, no. 1653; Muslim ibn al-Ḥajjāj, *Ṣaḥīḥ Muslim*, 1517, no. 908–9; ibn Mājah al-Rab'ī al-Qazwīnī, *Sunan ibn Mājah*, 935, no. 2797.

33 al-Suyūtī, *Abwāb al-Sa'ādah fī Asbāb al-Shahādah*, 58, no. 39.
Salat al-duha is a special morning prayer practiced by Sunni Muslims. *Salat al-witr* is a special night prayer practiced by both Sunni and Shī'a Muslims, considered as one of the highest signs of piety.

34 al-Suyūtī, *Abwāb al-Sa'ādah fī Asbāb al-Shahādah*, 57, no. 37 (though, the chain of narration consists of unknown and untruthful narrators; see 'Alī ibn Abū Bakr al-Haythamī, *Majma' al-Zawā'id*, 12 vols., ed. Muhammad 'Abd al-Ghadir Ahmad 'Ata (Beirut: Dār al-Kutub al-'Ilmīyyah, 2001), 5: 390.

35 al-Suyūtī, *Abwāb al-Sa'ādah fī Asbāb al-Shahādah*, 59, no. 42; al-Suyūtī, *Abwāb al-Sa'ādah fī Asbāb al-Shahādah*, 62–5, no. 52–5.

36 al-Tirmidhī, *Jāmi' al-Tirmidhī*, 5: 644, no. 3739.
Ṭalḥah bin 'Ubaydullāh was a close companion of the Prophet who later fought 'Alī ibn Abītālib, the fourth Caliph and first Shī'a Imām, over the problem of leadership.

37 ibn Mājah al-Rab'ī al-Qazwīnī, *Sunan ibn Mājah*, 724, no. 2139; also see: al-Suyūtī, *Abwāb al-Sa'ādah fī Asbāb al-Shahādah*, 59, no. 43.

38 al-Suyūtī, *Abwāb al-Sa'ādah fī Asbāb al-Shahādah*, 58, no. 40.

39 al-Suyūtī, *Abwāb al-Sa'ādah fī Asbāb al-Shahādah*, 60, no. 46.

40 al-Suyūtī, *Abwāb al-Sa'ādah fī Asbāb al-Shahādah*, 58, no. 41.

41 Jalāl al-Dīn al-Suyūtī, *al-Muḥāḍirāt wa al-Muḥāwirāt*, ed. Yahya al-Jabouri (Beirut: Dār al-Gharb al-Islāmī, 2003), 374.

42 ibn Mubārak, *Kitāb al-Jihād*, 95, no. 69; al-Nasā'ī, *Sunan al-Nasā'ī*, 338, no. 3194; ibn Mājah al-Rab'ī al-Qazwīnī, *Sunan ibn Mājah*, 937, no. 2803; al-Suyūtī, *Abwāb al-Sa'ādah fī Asbāb al-Shahādah*, 39, no. 4; al-Suyūtī, *Abwāb al-Sa'ādah fī Asbāb al-Shahādah*, 47, no. 20; al-Suyūtī, *Abwāb al-Sa'ādah fī Asbāb al-Shahādah*, 57, no. 37; al-Suyūtī, *Abwāb al-Sa'ādah fī Asbāb al-Shahādah*, 66, no. 57; al-Suyūtī, *Abwāb al-Sa'ādah fī Asbāb al-Shahādah*, 67, no. 59.

43 This could be a case of *ḥadīth* fabrication, which is a big issue in the study of the authenticity of *ḥadīth*.

44 ibn Mubārak, *Kitāb al-Jihād*, 132, no. 29.

45 al-Bukhārī, *Ṣahīh al-Bukhārī*, 551, no. 4046. See also al-Bukhārī, *Ṣahīh al-Bukhārī*, 1026, no. 7463; al-Bukhārī, *Ṣahīh al-Bukhārī*, 1036, no. 7530.

46 Abū Dāwūd, *Sunan Abī Dāwūd*, 354, no. 3135.

47 See Cook, *Martyrdom in Islam*, 38.

48 al-Nasā'ī, *Sunan al-Nasā'ī*, 335, no. 3161. For the translation I relied on https://sunnah.com/nasai/25/77.

49 ibn Mājah al-Rab'ī al-Qazwīnī, *Sunan ibn Mājah*, 935, no. 2798. See also ibn Mubārak, *Kitāb al-Jihād*, 70, no. 20. For the translation I relied on https://sunnah.com/urn/1276470.

Hullah means a very special and decent piece of cloth.

50 "The martyr has six things (in store) with Allāh: He is forgiven from the first drop of his blood that is shed; he is shown his place in Paradise; he is spared the torment of the grave; he is kept safe from the great fright; he is adorned with a garment of faith; he is married to (wives) from among the wide-eyed *hūrīs*; and he is permitted to intercede for seventy of his relatives" (ibn Mājah al-Rab'ī al-Qazwīnī, *Sunan ibn Mājah*, 935–6, no. 2799.).

51 Muhammad ibn 'Abdullāh ibn-abī-Zamanayn, *Qudwat al-Ghāzī*, ed. 'A'ishah al-Sulaymani (Beirut: Dār al-Gharb al-Islāmī, 1989), 241, no. 111.

52 Muslim ibn al-Ḥajjāj, *Ṣaḥīḥ Muslim*, 1502, no. 886.

53 al-Nawawī, *Rīyāḍ al-Sāliḥīn*, 81–2, no. 216; Muslim ibn al-Ḥajjāj, *Ṣaḥīḥ Muslim*, 107, no. 14. For the translation I relied on https://sunnah.com/riyadussaliheen/1/216.

54 al-Suyūtī, *Abwāb al-Sa'ādah fī Asbāb al-Shahādah*, 49, no. 23.

55 Abū Dāwūd, *Sunan Abī Dāwūd*, 286, no. 2522.

56 *Tafasir* is the plural of *tafsir* (Qur'anic exegesis).

57 Most exegetes believe these verses were revealed after the battle of Uhud (seventy Muslims are said to have died in the battle). See al-Tha'labi, *al-Kashf wa al-Bayan 'an*

Tafsir al-Qur'an 3: 200; Muhammad ibn 'Umar Fakhr al-Dīn al-Rāzī, *Tafsīr al-Kabīr*, 32 vols. (Beirut: Iḥyā' al-Turāth al-'Arabī, 1999), 9: 425; al-Ālūsī, *Rūḥ al-Ma'ānī fī Tafsīr al-Qur'an al-'Aẓīm wa al-Sab' al-Mathānī*, 2: 333; Jalāl al-Dīn al-Suyūtī, *al-Dur al-Manthūr fī Tafsīr Bil-Ma'thūr*, 6 vols. (Qum: Kitābkhānih Ayatollah Mar'ashī Najafī, 1984), 2: 94; abū 'Abdullāh al-Qurṭubī, *Al-Jami' li Ahkām al-Qur'an*, 20 vols. (Tehran: Nasir Khusru, 1985), 4: 268.

58 Muqātil ibn Sulaymān al-Balkhī, *Tafsīr Muqātil*, 5 vols., ed. 'Abdullah Mahmuoud al-Shahatah (Beirut: Dār Ihya' al-Turāth al-'Arabiī, 2003), 1: 150–1.

59 The tradition of the dialogue between God and martyrs is found in other *tafasir* such as al-Tha'labi, *al-Kashf wa al-Bayan 'an Tafsir al-Qur'an*, 3: 201.

60 al-Ṭabarī, *Jāmi' al-Bayān fī Tafsīr al-Qur'an*, 4: 114.

61 *Al-barzakh* in Islamic eschatology means the stage between death and the day of judgment in which the souls supposedly will be awaiting the final resurrection.

62 al-Ṭabarī, *Jāmi' al-Bayān fī Tafsīr al-Qur'an*, 2: 24.
Abū Hayyān al-Andulusī, a fourteenth-century exegete, also understands under 3:169–70 that the difference between martyrs and other believers is that the former will be provided even before the day of judgment. See Abū Ḥayyān al-Andulusī, *al-Baḥr al-Muḥīt fī al-Tafsīr*, 11 vols., ed. Sidghi Muhammad Jamil (Damascus: Dar al-Fikr, 1999), 2: 53–4.

63 al-Tha'labi, *al-Kashf wa al-Bayan 'an Tafsir al-Qur'an* 3: 201.

64 al-Tha'labi, *al-Kashf wa al-Bayan 'an Tafsir al-Qur'an* 2: 22. See also Abū al-Qāsim Sulaymān ibn Aḥmad al-Ṭabarānī, *Tafsīr al-Ṭabarānī*, 6 vols. (Irbid: Dār al-Kitāb al-Thighafī, 2008), 1: 271.

65 al-Qurṭubī, *Al-Jami' li Ahkām al-Qur'an*, 4: 276.

66 Fakhr al-Dīn al-Rāzī, *Tafsīr al-Kabīr*, 9: 425–30.

67 "They were drowned and sent to hell for their evildoings: they found no one to help them against God" (Qur'an, 71:25); "'[But] you, soul at peace: return to your Lord well pleased and well pleasing; go in among my servants; and into my garden'" (89:27–30).

68 "There are men among the believers who honored their pledge to God: some of them have fulfilled it by death, and some are still waiting. They have not changed in the least" (33:23).

69 ibn Sulaymān al-Balkhī, *Tafsīr Muqātil*, 3: 484.

70 al-Ālūsī, *Rūḥ al-Ma'ānī fī Tafsīr al-Qur'an al-'Aẓīm wa al-Sab' al-Mathānī*, 11: 169; al-Ṭabarī, *Jāmi' al-Bayān fī Tafsīr al-Qur'an*, 21: 94; 'Abdullāh ibn Muhammad ibn abī Ḥātam, *Tafsīr al-Qur'an al-'Aẓīm (ibn abī Ḥātam)*, 13 vols., ed. As'ad Muhammad Tabib (Riyadh: Maktabah Nazār Mustafā al-Bāz, 1998), 9: 3124; al-Ṭabarānī, *Tafsīr al-Ṭabarānī*, 5: 181; al-Tha'labi, *al-Kashf wa al-Bayan 'an Tafsir al-Qur'an*, 8: 24; 'Abdul-Haqq ibn Ghalib ibn 'Atīyyah Andulūsī, *al-Muḥarrar al-Wajīz fī Tafsīr al-Kitāb al-'Azīz*, 6 vols., ed. 'Abdussalam 'Abdusshafi Muhammad (Beirut: Dār

al-Kutub al-'Ilmīyyah, 2001), 4: 378; Abul-Faraj ibn al-Jawzī, *Zād al-Masīr fī 'Ilm al-Tafsīr*, 4 vols., ed. Mahdi 'Abdul Razzagh (Beirut: Dār al-Kutub al-'Arabī, 2001), 3: 456; Abū al-Qāsim Maḥmūd ibn 'Umar al-Zamakhsharī, *Al-Kashshāf 'an Ḥaqā'iq al-Tanzīl*, 4 vols., ed. Mustafa Hussein Ahmad (Beirut: Dār al-Kutub al-'Arabī, 1987), 3: 532; Ismā'īl ibn 'Umar ibn Kathīr, *Tafsīr al-Qur'an al-'Aẓīm (ibn Kathīr)*, 9 vols., ed. Shams al-Din Muhammad Hussein (Beirut: Dār al-Kutub al-'Ilmīyyah, 1998), 6: 353; Ismā'īl Ḥaqqī al-Brūsawī, *Tafsīr Rūh al-Bayān*, 10 vols. (Beirut: Dār al-Fikr), 7: 159.

71 Qāḍī Thanā'ullāh al-Maẓharī, *Tafsīr al-Maẓharī*, 10 vols. (Quetta: Maktabah Rāshidīyyah, 1992), 2: 170.

72 "If you have suffered a blow, they too have suffered one like it. We deal out such days among people in turn, for God to find out who truly believes, for him to choose martyrs [*shuhadā*] from among you—God does not love evildoers; for him to cleanse those who believe and for him to destroy the disbelievers" (3:140–1).

73 "We have made you [believers] into a just community, so that you may bear witness [to the truth] before others and so that the Messenger may bear witness [to it] before you" (2:143); "What will they do when we bring a witness from each community, with you [Muhammad] as a witness against these people?" (4:41); "Whoever obeys God and the Messenger will be among those he has blessed: the messengers, the truthful, those who bear witness to the truth, and the righteous—what excellent companions these are!" (4:69); "Those who believe in God and his messengers are the truthful ones who will bear witness before their Lord: they will have their reward and their light. But those who disbelieve and deny our revelations are the inhabitants of hell" (57:19).

74 al-Ṭabarī, *Jāmi' al-Bayān fī Tafsīr al-Qur'an*, 4: 69. See also ibn abī Ḥātam, *Tafsīr al-Qur'an al-'Aẓīm (ibn abī Ḥātam)*, 3: 773–4; al-Ṭabarānī, *Tafsīr al-Ṭabarānī*, 2: 134; al-Tha'labi, *al-Kashf wa al-Bayan 'an Tafsir al-Qur'an* 3: 134; ibn 'Atīyyah Andulūsī, *al-Muḥarrar al-Wajīz fī Tafsīr al-Kitāb al-'Azīz*, 1: 234, 69; al-Zamakhsharī, *Al-Kashshāf 'an Ḥaqā'iq al-Tanzīl*, 1: 420; al-Qurṭubī, *Al-Jami' li Ahkām al-Qur'an*, 4: 218.

75 Fakhr al-Dīn al-Rāzī, *Tafsīr al-Kabīr*, 9: 374; ibn 'Atīyyah Andulūsī, *al-Muḥarrar al-Wajīz fī Tafsīr al-Kitāb al-'Azīz*, 1: 234, 69; al-Zamakhsharī, *Al-Kashshāf 'an Ḥaqā'iq al-Tanzīl*, 420; 'Abdullāh ibn 'Umar al-Bayḍāwī, *Anwār al-Tanzīl wa Asrār al-Ta'wīl*, 5 vols. (Beirut: Dār al-'Ihyā' al-Turāth al-'Arabī, 1997), 2: 40; al-Tha'labi, *al-Kashf wa al-Bayan 'an Tafsir al-Qur'an*, 3: 174; ibn Kathīr, *Tafsīr al-Qur'an al-'Aẓīm (ibn Kathīr)*, 2:110.

76 al-Ṭabarī, *Jāmi' al-Bayān fī Tafsīr al-Qur'an*, 4: 70. See also ibn abī Ḥātam, *Tafsīr al-Qur'an al-'Aẓīm (ibn abī Ḥātam)*, 3: 775.

77 Fakhr al-Dīn al-Rāzī, *Tafsīr al-Kabīr*, 9: 374. al-Qurtubī also has a similar argument here: al-Qurṭubī, *Al-Jami' li Ahkām al-Qur'an*, 4: 218.

78 al-Ṭabarī, *Jāmi' al-Bayān fī Tafsīr al-Qur'an*, 2: 6–7; ibn abī Ḥātam, *Tafsīr al-Qur'an al-'Aẓīm (ibn abī Ḥātam)*, 1: 249–50; al-Tha'labi, *al-Kashf wa al-Bayan '*

an Tafsir al-Qur'an, 2: 8; al-Zamakhsharī, *Al-Kashshāf 'an Ḥaqā'iq al-Tanzīl*, 1: 199, 512; al-Ṭabarī, *Jāmi' al-Bayān fī Tafsīr al-Qur'an*, 5: 59; ibn Sulaymān al-Balkhī, *Tafsīr Muqātil*, 1:145, 373.

79 al-Ālūsī, *Rūḥ al-Ma'ānī fī Tafsīr al-Qur 'an al-'Aẓīm wa al-Sab' al-Mathānī*, 3: 75.

80 ibn Sulaymān al-Balkhī, *Tafsīr Muqātil*, 4:243.

81 al-Ṭabarī, *Jāmi' al-Bayān fī Tafsīr al-Qur'an*, 27: 133–4.

82 Fakhr al-Dīn al-Rāzī, *Tafsīr al-Kabīr*, 29: 463. Others also translate *shuhadā* as "martyrs" in this verse. SeeAbū Mansūr al-Māturīdī, *Ta'wīlāt Ahl al-Sunnah*, 10 vols. (Beirut: Dār al-Kutub al-'Ilmīyyah, 2005), 3: 248.

83 al-Zamakhsharī, *Al-Kashshāf 'an Ḥaqā'iq al-Tanzīl*, 4: 478.

84 al-Ṭabarānī, *Tafsīr al-Ṭabarānī*, 6: 210–11.

85 al-Tha'labi, *al-Kashf wa al-Bayan 'an Tafsir al-Qur'an* 9: 243. See also ibn 'Atīyyah Andulūsī, *al-Muḥarrar al-Wajīz fī Tafsīr al-Kitāb al-'Azīz*, 2: 1069.

86 These early disciples are Abū Bakr, 'Umar, 'Uthman, 'Alī, Ḥamzah, Ṭalḥah, Zubayr, Sa'd, and Zayd (see ibn al-Jawzī, *Zād al-Masīr fī 'Ilm al-Tafsīr*, 4: 236).

87 ibn al-Jawzī, *Zād al-Masīr fī 'Ilm al-Tafsīr*, 4: 236. See also abū-Muslim al-Iṣfahānī, *Mawsū'at Tafāsīr al-Mu'tazilah*, 5 vols. (Beirut: Dār al-Kutub al-'Ilmīyyah, 2009), 1: 96.

88 See, for example, Fakhr al-Dīn al-Rāzī, *Tafsīr al-Kabīr*, 10: 135; al-Ālūsī, *Rūḥ al-Ma'ānī fī Tafsīr al-Qur 'an al-'Aẓīm wa al-Sab' al-Mathānī*, 3: 75.

89 ibn Sulaymān al-Balkhī, *Tafsīr Muqātil*, 2:639.

90 "He knows what is before them and what is behind them, and they cannot intercede without his permission" (21:28).

91 al-Tha'labi, *al-Kashf wa al-Bayan 'an Tafsir al-Qur'an*, 10: 77. A similar discussion can be found in al-Ṭabarī, *Jāmi' al-Bayān fī Tafsīr al-Qur'an*, 16: 97.

92 "On that day, intercession will be useless except from those to whom the Lord of mercy has granted permission and whose words he approves" (20:109).

93 "No intercessor's plea will benefit them now" (74:48). See al-Ṭabarī, *Jāmi' al-Bayān fī Tafsīr al-Qur'an*, 29: 105.

94 al-Ṭabarānī, *Tafsīr al-Ṭabarānī*, 6: 389.

95 Muhammad ibn 'Abdullāh ibn-abī-Zamanayn, *Tafsīr ibn-abī-Zamanayn*, 2 vols. (Beirut: Dār al-Kutub al-'Ilmīyyah, 2003), 1: 465. See also Aḥmad ibn Muhammad Rashīduddīn Miybudī, *Kashf al-Asrār wa 'Uddat al-Abrār*, 10 vols., ed. Ali Asghar Hikmat (Tehran: Amīrkabīr, 1992), 1: 693.

96 "God will give firmness to those who believe in the firmly rooted word, both in this world and the hereafter, but the evildoers he leaves to stray: God does whatever he will" (14:27).

97 al-Suyūtī, *al-Dur al-Manthūr fī Tafsīr Bil-Ma'thūr*, 4: 84.

98 "He will not let the deeds of those who are killed for his cause come to nothing; he will guide them and put them into a good state; he will admit them into the garden he has already made known to them" (47:4–6).

99 Fakhr al-Dīn al-Rāzī, *Tafsīr al-Kabīr*, 28: 42.

100 "Who remain steadfast through their desire for the face of their Lord; who keep up the prayer; who give secretly and openly from what we have provided for them; who repel evil with good. These will have the reward of the [true] home: they will enter perpetual gardens [*'adn*], along with their righteous ancestors, spouses, and descendants; the angels will go in to them from every gate, peace be with you, because you have remained steadfast" (13:22–4).

101 al-Ṭabarī, *Jāmi' al-Bayān fī Tafsīr al-Qur'an*, 13: 95. See also ibn Kathīr, *Tafsīr al-Qur'an al-'Aẓīm (ibn Kathīr)*, 4: 387.

102 al-Suyūtī, *al-Dur al-Manthūr fī Tafsīr Bil-Ma'thūr*, 4: 57.

103 "God has promised the believers, both men and women, gardens graced with flowing streams where they will remain; good, peaceful homes in gardens of lasting bliss [*'adn*]; and—greatest of all—God's good pleasure" (9:72).

104 See ibn 'Atīyyah Andulūsī, *al-Muḥarrar al-Wajīz fī Tafsīr al-Kitāb al-'Azīz*, 3: 58; al-Tha'labi, *al-Kashf wa al-Bayan 'an Tafsir al-Qur'an*, 5: 68; al-Zamakhsharī, *Al-Kashshāf 'an Ḥaqā'iq al-Tanzīl*, 2: 289; Fakhr al-Dīn al-Rāzī, *Tafsīr al-Kabīr*, 16: 102; al-Qurṭubī, *Al-Jami' li Ahkām al-Qur'an*, 8: 204.

Bibliography

Abdo, Geneive. *The New Sectarianism: The Arab Uprisings and the Rebirth of the Shi'a–Sunni Divide*. New York: Oxford University Press, 2017.

Abedi, Mehdi, and Gary Legenhausen. "Jihād and Shahādat: Struggle and Martyrdom in Islam." *The Institute for Research and Islamic Studies* (1986).

Abou Zahab, Mariam. "'I Shall Be Waiting for You at the Door of Paradise': The Pakistani Martyrs of the Lashkar-E Taiba (Army of the Pure)." *The Practice of War: The Production, Reproduction and Communication of Armed Violence* (2008): 133–58.

Abrahamian, Ervand. "Ali Shariati: Ideologue of the Iranian Revolution." *Merip Reports* 102 (1982): 24–8.

Abrahamian, Ervand. *A History of Modern Iran*. New York: Cambridge University Press, 2008.

Abū Dāwūd, Sulaymān ibn al-Ash'ath. *Sunan Abī Dāwūd*. Riyadh: Bayt al-Afkār al-Dawlīyyah, n.d.

Abū Mikhnaf, Lūt b. Yaḥyā. *Maqtal Al-Ḥusayn*. Edited by Ḥasan Qaffāri. Qum: 'Ilmīyyah, 1985.

Abul Futūh Rāzī, Ḥusayn ibn 'Alī. *Rawḍ Al-Jinān Wa Rūh Al-Jinān Fī Tafsīr Al-Qur'an*. Edited by Muhammad Mahdi Nasih. 20 vols. Mashhad: Āstān Quds Raḍavī, 1988.

Afsaruddin, Asma. *Striving in the Path of God: Jihad and Martyrdom in Islamic Thought*. Oxford: Oxford University Press, 2013.

Afshar, Haleh. *Iran: A Revolution in Turmoil*. Basingstoke: Macmillan, 1985.

Aghaie, Kamran Scot. *The Martyrs of Karbala: Shi'i Symbols and Rituals in Modern Iran*. Seattle: University of Washington Press, 2004.

Ajami, Fouad. *Crosswinds: The Way of Saudi Arabia*. Stanford: Hoover Press, 2020.

Akhavi, Shahrough. *Religion and Politics in Contemporary Iran: Clergy-State Relations in the Pahlavī Period*. Albany: State University of New York Press, 1980.

Akhgarī, Muhammad Reza. *Wilāyatī-Hāyi Bī Wilāyat*. Tehran: Akhgarī, 1988.

al-Ālūsī, Mahmud ibn 'Abdullāh. *Rūḥ Al-Ma'ānī Fī Tafsīr Al-Qur'an Al-'Aẓīm Wa Al-Sab' Al-Mathānī*. Edited by Shams al-Din Sana' Bazi'. 16 vols. Beirut: Dār al-Kutub 'Ilmīyyah, 1995.

al-Amīn, Al-Sayyid Muhsin *A'yān Al-Shī'a* 11 vols. Beirut: Dār al-Ta'āruf, 1983.

al-Andulusī, Abū Ḥayyān. *Al-Baḥr Al-Muḥīt Fī Al-Tafsīr*. Edited by Sidghi Muhammad Jamil. 11 vols. Damascus: Dar al-Fikr, 1999.

al-Baghdadi, Abu Bakr. "Wa-Law Kariha L-Kafirun [Though the Unbelievers Be Averse]." November 13, 2014, September 27, 2020, https://archive.org/details/wlwCareha21.

al-Baḥrānī, Hāshim. *Al-Burhān Fī Tafsīr Al-Qur'an*. 8 vols. Beirut: Al-A'lamī, 2006.

al-Balādhūrī, Aḥmad Ibn Yaḥyā. *Ansāb Al-Ashrāf*. 13 vols. Beirut: Dār al-fikr, 1996.

al-Bayḍāwī, 'Abdullāh ibn 'Umar. *Anwār Al-Tanzīl Wa Asrār Al-Ta'wīl*. 5 vols. Beirut: Dār al-'Ihyā' al-Turāth al-'Arabī, 1997.

al-Brūsawī, Ismā'īl Ḥaqqī. *Tafsīr Rūh Al-Bayān*. 10 vols. Beirut: Dār al-Fikr.

al-Bukhārī, Muhammad. *Ṣahīh Al-Bukhārī*. Riyadh: Maktabah al-Rushd, 2006.

al-Dulaimi, Saleem A. Salih, Mohammad Kamal, and Dalal Mahmoud Elsayed. "The Impact of Sectarian Conflict in Syria on Iran-Gulf Relations." *Asian Social Science* 13, no. 7 (2017): 92.

al-Ḥarrānī, Abū Muhammad al-Ḥasan ibn 'Ali ibn al-Ḥusayn ibn Shu'ba. *Tuḥaf Al-Uqūl* Edited by Ali Akbar Qaffari. Qum: Jāmi'at Mudarrisīn, 1984.

al-Haythamī, 'Alī ibn Abū Bakr. *Majma' Al-Zawā'id*. Edited by Muhammad 'Abd al-Ghadir Ahmad 'Ata. 12 vols. Beirut: Dār al-Kutub al-'Ilmīyyah, 2001.

al-Ḥillī, Ḥasan ibn Yūsuf. *Tabsirat Al-Muta'allimīn Fī Aḥkām Al-Dīn*. Edited by Muhammad Ḥādī Yūsufi Gharawī. Tehran: Chāpp wa Nashr, 1990.

al-Ḥurr al-'Āmilī, Muhammad ibn al-Ḥasan. *Ithbāt Al-Hudāt Bil-Nuṣūṣ Wal-Mu'jizāt*. 5 vols. Beirut: al-A'lamī, 2004.

al-Ḥurr al-'Āmilī, Muhammad ibn al-Ḥasan. *Wasā 'il Al-Shi'ah Ilā Tahsil Masā 'il Al-Shari'ah*. 29 vols. Qum: Mu'assisat-i Aalul-bayt, 1988.

al-Iṣfahānī, abū-Muslim. *Mawsū'at Tafāsīr Al-Mu'tazilah*. 5 vols. Beirut: Dār al-Kutub al-'Ilmīyyah, 2009.

al-Khaṣībī, Ḥusayn b. Ḥamdān. *Al-Hidāyat Al-Kubrā*. Beirut: al-Balāgh, 1998.

al-Khoei, Abul-Qāsim. "Sharḥ Al-'Urwat Al-Wuthqā." *Al-Khoei Foundation*. http://www.al-khoei.us/books/index.php?id=120.

al-Khwārazmī, Muwaffaq b. Aḥmad. *Maqtal Al-Ḥusayn (by Al-Khwārazmī)*. 2 vols. Qum: Anwār al-Ḥudā, 2002.

al-Kūfī, Furāt ibn Ibrāhīm. *Tafsīr Furāt Al-Kūfī*. Edited by Muhammad Hadhim. Tehran: Mu'assisat al-Ṭab' wal-Nashr, 1989.

al-Kulaynī, Abū Ja'far Muhammad b. Ya'qūb. *Al-Kāfī*. 8 vols. Tehran: Dār al-Kutub al-Islāmīyyah, 1986.

al-Majlisī, Muhammad Bāqir b. Muhammad Taqī. *Biḥār Al-Anwār Al-Jāmi'ah Li-Durar Akhbār Al-A'immah Al-Athār*. 110 vols. Beirut: Dār 'Iḥyā' al-Turāth al-'Arabī, 1983.

al-Majlisī, Muhammad Bāqir b. Muhammad Taqī. *Jalā' Al-'Uyūn*. Edited by Ali Emamian. Qum: Surūr, 2008.

al-Mas'ūdi, Abū al-Ḥasan 'Alī ibn al-Ḥusayn ibn Alī. *Murūj Al-Dhahab Wa Ma'ādin Al-Jawāhir*. 4 vols. Qum: Dār al-Hijrah, 1988.

al-Māturīdī, Abū Mansūr. *Ta'wīlāt Ahl Al-Sunnah*. 10 vols. Beirut: Dār al-Kutub al-'Ilmīyyah, 2005.

al-Maẓharī, Qāḍī Thanā'ullāh. *Tafsīr Al-Maẓharī*. 10 vols. Quetta: Maktabah Rāshidīyyah, 1992.

al-Mufīd, Abū 'Abdullāh Muhammad ibn al-Nu'mān. *Al-Irshād Fī Ma'rifat Ḥujaj Allāh 'Alā Al-'Ibād*. 2 vols. Qum: Kungirih Shaykh Mufīd, 1992.

al-Najafī, Muhammad Ḥasan. *Jawāhir Al-Kalām*. Edited by 'Abbās Quchānī. 43 vols. Vol. 21, Beirut: Dār 'ihyā' al-Turāth al-'Arabī, 1983.
al-Nasā'ī, Aḥmad ibn Shu'ayb. *Sunan Al-Nasā'ī*. Edited by Muhammad ibn Salih al-Rajihi. Riyadh: Bayt al-Afkār al-Dawlīyyah.
al-Nawawī, Abū Zakarīā Muḥyi al-Dīn Yaḥyā Ibn Sharaf. *Rīyāḍ Al-Sāliḥīn*. Beirut: Dār al-Minhāj, 2015.
al-Qurṭubī, abū 'Abdullāh. *Al-Jami' Li Ahkām Al-Qur'an*. 20 vols. Tehran: Nasir Khusru, 1985.
al-Rāzī, Abū Ḥātam. *Kitāb Al-Zīnah Fī Al-Kalimāt Al-Islāmīyyah Al-'Arabīyyah*. Edited by Husein al-Hamdani. 3 vols. Sana'a: Markaz al-Dirāsāt wal-Buḥūth al-'Arabī, 1994.
al-Riḍā, 'Ali ibn Mūsā. *Ṣahifah Imām Riḍā*. Edited by Muhammad Mahdi Najaf. Mashhad: Kungirih Jahāni Imām Riḍā, 1986.
al-Ṣadūq, Abū Ja'far Muhammad ibn 'Alī ibn Bābawayh. *Al-Amālī*. Tehran: Kitābchī, 1997.
al-Sayyid Nūr Allāh, al-Husaynī al-Shūshtarī. *Iḥqāq Al-Ḥaqq*. 23 vols. Qum: Maktabah Ayatullah Mar'ashī, 1988.
al-Suyūtī, Jalāl al-Dīn. *Abwāb Al-Sa'ādah Fī Asbāb Al-Shahādah*. Edited by Najm 'Abd al-Rahman Khalaf. Cairo: al-Maktabah al-Qayyimah, 1987.
al-Suyūtī, Jalāl al-Dīn. *Al-Dur Al-Manthūr Fī Tafsīr Bil-Ma'thūr*. 6 vols. Qum: Kitābkhānih Ayatollah Mar'ashī Najafī, 1984.
al-Suyūtī, Jalāl al-Dīn. *Al-Muḥāḍirāt Wa Al-Muḥāwirāt*. Edited by Yahya al-Jabouri. Beirut: Dār al-Gharb al-Islāmī, 2003.
al-Ṭabarānī, abū al-Qāsim Sulaymān ibn Aḥmad. *Tafsīr Al-Ṭabarānī*. 6 vols. Irbid: Dār al-Kitāb al-Thighafī, 2008.
al-Ṭabarī, Muhammad ibn Jarīr. *Tārīkh Al-Ṭabarī*. 11 vols. Beirut: Dār al-Turāth, 1967.
al-Ṭabarī, Muhammad ibn Jarīr. *Tārīkh Al-Ṭabarī*. Translated by Abulqasem Payandeh. Tehran: Asāṭīr, 1996.
al-Ṭabarī al-Ṣaghīr, Muhammad ibn Jarīr. *Dalā'il Al-Imāmah*. Qum: Bi'that, 1992.
al-Ṭabarī Āmulī, Muhammad ibn Jarīr ibn Rustam. *Al-Mustarshad Fī Imāmmat 'Alī Ibn Abī Ṭālib*. Edited by Ahmad Mahmudi. Qum: Kūshanpūr, 1994.
al-Ṭabarī, Muhammad ibn Jarīr. *Jāmi' Al-Bayān Fī Tafsīr Al-Qur'an*. 30 vols. Beirut: Dār al-Ma'rifah, 1992.
al-Tha'labi, Ahmad ibn Muhammad. *Al-Kashf Wa Al-Bayan 'an Tafsir Al-Qur'an*. 10 vols. Beirut: Ihya' al-Turath al-'Arabi, 2001.
al-Tirmidhī, Muhammad ibn Īsā. *Jāmi' Al-Tirmidhī*. Edited by Ahmad Muhammad Shakir. Cairo: Maktabah Muṣṭfā al-Bābi al-Ḥalbī, 1975.
al-Ṭurayḥī, Fakhr al-Dīn. *Majma' Al-Baḥrayn*. Edited by Ahmad Ashkivari. 6 vols. Tehran: Murtaḍavī, 1997.
al-Ya'qūbī, Aḥmad ibn Abū Ya'qūb. *Tārīkh Al-Yaqūbī*. 2 vols. Beirut: al-A'lamī, 2010.
al-Zaḥilī, Muhammad Muṣṭafā, and Aḥmad Mu'az Al-Khātīb. *Al-'Amaliyyāt Al-"Istishhādīyah Fī Al-Mīzān Al-Fiqhī*. Damascus: Dār al-Fikr, 1997.
al-Zamakhsharī, Abū al-Qāsim Maḥmūd ibn 'Umar. *Al-Kashshāf 'an Ḥaqā'iq Al-Tanzīl*. Edited by Mustafa Hussein Ahmad. 4 vols. Beirut: Dār al-Kutub al-'Arabī, 1987.

al-Kūfī, Abū Muhammad Aḥmad B. A'tham. *Kitāb Al-Futūḥ*. Edited by Ali Shiri. 8 vols. Beirut: Dār al-Aḍwā', 1991.

Algar, Hamid. *Religion and State in Iran, 1785–1906: The Role of the Ulama in the Qajar Period*. Berkeley: University of California Press, 1980.

Algar, Hamid. *Wahhabism: A Critical Essay*. BookBaby, 2015.

Amanat, Abbas. *Apocalyptic Islam and Iranian Shi'ism*. London: I.B. Tauris, 2009.

Amīnī, 'Abdul Ḥusayn. *Shuhadā' Al-Faḍīlah*. Beirut: Mu'assisat al-Wafā', 1983.

Amir-Moezzi, Mohammad Ali. *The Divine Guide in Early Shi'ism: The Sources of Esotericism in Islam*. Translated by David Streight. Albany: State University of New York Press, 1994.

Ansari, Ali. "Iran under Ahmadinejad: Populism and Its Malcontents." *International Affairs* 84, no. 4 (2008): 683–700. https://dx.doi.org/10.1111/j.1468-2346.2008.00732.x.

Arielli, Nir. *From Byron to Bin Laden*. Harvard University Press, 2018.

Arjomand, Saïd Amīr. "Imam Absconditus and the Beginnings of a Theology of Occultation: Imami Shiʿism Circa 280-90 A. H./900 A. D." *Journal of the American Oriental Society* 117, no. 1 (1997): 1–12.

Avemarie, Friedrich, and Jan Willem Van Henten. *Martyrdom and Noble Death: Selected Texts from Graeco-Roman, Jewish and Christian Antiquity*. London: Routledge, 2002.

Ayatollah Mar'ashī Najafī Bi Rivāyati Asnādi Sawāk. 3 vols. Vol. 1, Tehran: Markaz-i barrisī-i asnād-i tārīkhī wizārat-i 'iṭṭilā'āt, 2009.

Ayoub, Mahmoud. "Martyrdom in Christianity and Islam." *Religious Resurgence: Contemporary Cases in Islam, Christianity, and Judaism* (1987): 67–76.

Ayoub, Mahmoud. *Redemptive Suffering in Islam: A Study of the Devotional Aspects of Ashura in Twelver Shi'ism*. The Hague: Walter de Gruyter, 1978.

Ayub, Fatima. *The Gulf and Sectarianism*. European Council on Foreign Relations (ECFR), 2013.

Bahā' al-Dīn al-Irbilī, 'Alī ibn 'Īsā. *Kashf Al-Ghummah Fī Ma'rifat Al-A'imma*. 3 vols. Vol. 1, Beirut: Dār al-Aḍwā', 1985.

Bahar, Sarvenaz. "Khomeinism, the Islamic Republic of Iran, and International Law: The Relevance of Islamic Political Ideology." *Harvard international law journal* 33, no. 1 (1992): 145.

Bahar, Sarvenaz. "Khomeinism, the Islamic Republic of Iran, and International Law: The Relevance of Islamic Political Ideology." *Harvard international law journal* 33, no. 1 (1992).

Bani-Hashemi, Muhammad. *Ma'refat-E Emam-E 'Asr [Cognition of the Imam of the Time]*. Tehran: Nik Ma'aref, 2007.

Barqī, Aḥmad ibn Muhammad. *Al-Maḥāsin*. Edited by Jalal ad-Din Muhaddith. 2 vols. Qum: Dār al-Kutub al-Islāmīyyah, 1952.

Beeman, William. "Martyrdom, Shi'a Islam, Ta'ziya: Political Symbolism in Shi'a Islam." In *Martyrdom and Sacrifice in Islam: Theological, Political and Social Contexts*, edited by Meir Hatina and Meir Litvak. London: I.B. Tauris, 2016.

Behravesh, Maysam. "Qassem Soleimani: Guardian of Iran's Regional Interests." *Middle East Eye (MEE)* (2020).

Bill, James A., and John Alden Williams. *Roman Catholics and Shi'i Muslims: Prayer, Passion, and Politics*. Chapel Hill: University of North Carolina Press, 2002.

Bloom, Mia. *Dying to Kill: The Allure of Suicide Terror*. New York: Columbia University Press, 2005.

Bostom, Andrew G. *The Legacy of Jihad: Islamic Holy War and the Fate of Non-Muslims*. Amherst, NY: Prometheus Books, 2010.

Bowersock, Glen Warren. *Martyrdom and Rome*. Cambridge: Cambridge University Press, 2002.

Boyarin, Daniel. *Dying for God: Martyrdom and the Making of Christianity and Judaism*. Stanford: Stanford University Press, 1999.

Brettler, Mark. "Is There Martyrdom in the Hebrew Bible?". In *Sacrificing the Self: Perspectives on Martyrdom and Religion*. Washington, D.C.: American Academy of Religion, 2002.

Britannica, The Editors of Encyclopaedia. "Al-Mahdiyyah." In *Encyclopædia Britannica*, October 21, 2009. https://www.britannica.com/topic/al-Mahdiyyah.

Brown, Daniel. "Martyrdom in Sunni Revivalist Thought." *Sacrificing the Self: Perspectives on Martyrdom and Religion* (2001): 107–17.

Bunting, Tony. "Siege of Vienna." In *Encyclopædia Britannica*, Encyclopædia Britannica, 2017. https://www.britannica.com/event/Siege-of-Vienna-1529.

Bunzel, Cole. "The Kingdom and the Caliphate." *Duel of the Islamic States, Washington, Carnegie* (2016).

Campanini, Massimo. "The Party of God (Hizbullāh): Islamic Opposition and Martyrdom in Contemporary Imamite Shiism." *Cristianesimo nella storia* 27, no. 1 (2006): 319–34.

Cohen, A. *The Babylonian Talmud: Tractate Berakot*. London: Cambridge: University Press, 1921. http://books.scholarsportal.info/viewdoc.html?id=/ebooks/oca1/11/babyloniantalmud00coheuoft.

Cole, Juan Ricardo. *Sacred Space and Holy War: The Politics, Culture and History of Shi'ite Islam*. London: I.B. Tauris, 2002.

Cook, David. *Martyrdom in Islam*. Cambridge: Cambridge University Press, 2007.

Cook, David. "Messianism in the Shiite Crescent." *Current trends in Islamist ideology* 11 (2011): 91–103.

Dabashi, Hamid. *Iran, the Green Movement and the USA: The Fox and the Paradox*. New York: Zed Books, 2013.

Dabashi, Hamid. *Theology of Discontent: The Ideological Foundations of the Islamic Revolution in Iran*. New Brunswick: Transaction Publishers, 2006.

Dakake, Maria Massi. *The Charismatic Community: Shi'ite Identity in Early Islam*. Albany: State University of New York Press, 2008.

Deeb, Marius. "Shia Movements in Lebanon: Their Formation, Ideology, Social Basis, and Links with Iran and Syria." *Third World Quarterly* 10, no. 2 (1988): 683–98.

Denaro, Roberta. "Definitions and Narratives of Martyrdom in Sunni Hadith Literature." In *Twenty-First Century Jihad: Law, Society and Military Action*, edited by Elisabeth Kenall and Ewan Stein, 82–96. London: I.B.Tauris, 2015.

Diaconu, Florin. "Iranian Grand Strategy in the Greater Middle East, the IRGC and General Qassem Soleimani." Paper presented at the International Scientific Conference Strategies XXI, 2017.

Dinawari, Abu Hanifa. *Al-Akhbar Al-Tiwal*. Edited by 'Abdul Mun'im 'Amir. Qum: Manshurat al-Razi, 1989.

Dorraj, Manochehr. "Symbolic and Utilitarian Political Value of a Tradition: Martyrdom in the Iranian Political Culture." *The Review of Politics* 59, no. 3 (1997): 489–522.

Droge, Arthur J., and James D. Tabor. *A Noble Death: Suicide and Martyrdom among Christians and Jews in Antiquity*. San Francisco: HarperCollins, 1992.

Early Christian Writings: The Apostolic Fathers. Penguin Classics, L197. Edited by Maxwell Staniforth. Harmondsworth: Penguin, 1968.

El-Hokayem, Emile. "Hizballah and Syria: Outgrowing the Proxy Relationship." *Washington Quarterly* 30, no. 2 (2007): 35–52.

Emerit, Marcel. "Abdelkader." In *Encyclopædia Britannica*, September 2, 2020. https://www.britannica.com/biography/Abdelkader.

Enayat, Hamid. *Modern Islamic Political Thought: The Response of the Shi'i and Sunni Muslims to the Twentieth Century*. London: Bloomsbury, 2005.

Fāḍil Darbandī, Āqā ibn 'Ābid *Iksīr Al-'Ibādāt Fī Asrār Al-Shahādah*. 3 vols. Manama: Shirkat al-Muṣṭafā, 1994.

Fakhr al-Dīn al-Rāzī, Muhammad ibn 'Umar. *Tafsīr Al-Kabīr*. 32 vols. Beirut: Iḥyā' al-Turāth al-'Arabī, 1999.

Faroqhi, Suraiya. *The Ottoman Empire and the World around It*. New York: I.B. Tauris, 2005.

Fasāyī, Ḥasan. *Fārs Nāmih Nāṣirī*. Tehran: Amīrkabīr, 2003.

Fayḍ Kāshānī, Muhammad ibn Shāh Murtaḍā. *Al-Wāfī*. 26 vols. Isfahan: Kitābkhānih Imām 'Amīr al-Mu'minīn, 1985.

Fayḍ Kāshānī, Muhammad ibn Shāh Murtaḍā. *Tafsīr Al-Ṣāfī*. Edited by Husayn A'lami. 5 vols. Tehran: Maktabah al-Ṣadr, 1995.

Fradkin, Hillel. "The Paradoxes of Shiism." *Current Trends in Islamist Ideology* 8 (2009): 5–25.

Freamon, Bernard K. "Martyrdom, Suicide, and the Islamic Law of War: A Short Legal History." *Fordham International Law Journal* 27, no. 1 (2003): 299–369.

Frend, William W. H. C. *Martyrdom and Persecution in the Early Church: A Study of Conflict from the Maccabees to Donatus*. Eugene: Wipf and Stock, 2014.

Ghasseminejad, Saeed, Behnam Ben Taleblu, and Eliora Katz. "Evolution toward Revolution: The Development of Street Protests in the Islamic Republic of Iran." Article. *Journal of International Affairs* 73, no. 2 (2020): 147–61.

Goodarzi, Jubin M. "Iran and the Syrian Civil War." In *The War for Syria*, 138–55. London: Routledge, 2019.

Gregory, Brad Stephan. *Salvation at Stake: Christian Martyrdom in Early Modern Europe*. Cambridge, MA: Harvard University Press, 1999.

Haddad, Fanar. "Understanding Iraq's Hashd Al-Sha 'Bi: State and Power in Post-2014 Iraq." *The Century Foundation* (2018).

Haddad, Simon. "A Comparative Study of Lebanese and Palestinian Perceptions of Suicide Bombings: The Role of Militant Islam and Socio-Economic Status." *International Journal of Comparative Sociology* 45, no. 5 (2004): 337–63.

Hafez, Mohammed M. *Manufacturing Human Bombs: The Making of Palestinian Suicide Bombers*. Washington, D.C.: United States Institute of Peace Press, 2006.

Hafez, Mohammed M. *Suicide Bombers in Iraq: The Strategy and Ideology of Martyrdom*. Washington, D.C.: United States Institute of Peace Press, 2007.

Hallaq, Wael B. "Caliphs, Jurists and the Saljūqs in the Political Thought of Juwayn?". *The Muslim World* 74, no. 1 (1984): 26–41.

Harris, Lucian. "Conservation: Iran Takes the Lead in Restoration of Samarra Mosque." *The art newspaper* 15, no. 168 (2006): 32.

Ḥasanī, Hāshim. *Sīrat Al-Muṣṭafā*. Translated by Hamid Taraqi Khah. Tehran: Ḥikmat, 1991.

Hatina, Meir. *Martyrdom in Modern Islam: Piety, Power, and Politics*. Cambridge: Cambridge University Press, 2014.

Hatina, Meir. "Warrior Saints: 'Abadallah 'Azzam's Reflections on Jihad and Karamat." In *Martyrdom and Sacrifice in Islam: Theological, Political and Social Contexts*, edited by Meir Hatina and Meir Litvak, 244–58. London: I.B. Tauris, 2017.

Hatina, Meir, and Meir Litvak. *Martyrdom and Sacrifice in Islam: Theological, Political and Social Contexts*. London: I.B. Tauris, 2017.

Hegghammer, Thomas. *The Caravan: Abdallah Azzam and the Rise of Global Jihad*. Cambridge: Cambridge University Press, 2020.

Hegghammer, Thomas. *Jihadi Culture*. Cambridge: Cambridge University Press, 2017.

Heper, Metin, and Raphael Israeli. "'Ulamā' and Politics in Saudi Arabia." In *Islam and Politics in the Modern Middle East (RLE Politics of Islam)*, 41–75. London: Routledge, 2014.

Heyworth-Dunne, James. "Religious and Political Trends in Modern Egypt." Washington, D.C.: Published by the Author, 1950.

Ḥiydarī Kāshānī, Muhammad Bāqir. *Nasl Ṭūfān*. Qum: Zulāl-i Kuthar, 2007.

Hopkins, Benjamin D. "Islam and Resistance in the British Empire." *Islam and the European Empires* (2013): 150–69.

Hosseini, Hamid. "Theocracy Versus Constitutionalism: Is Velayat-E-Faghih Compatible with Democracy." *Journal of Iranian Research and Analysis* 15, no. 2 (1999): 84–96.

Hunter, Shireen T. "Iran and the Spread of Revolutionary Islam." *Third World Quarterly* 10, no. 2 (1988): 730–49.

Ḥusaynī Arḍī, Mir Riḍā. *72 Dāstān Az Shafā'at Imam Ḥusayn*. Mashhad: Hātif, 1998.

Hyder, Syed Akbar. *Reliving Karbala: Martyrdom in South Asian Memory*. Oxford: Oxford University Press, 2006.

Hylén, Torsten. "New Meanings to Old Rituals: The Emergence of Mourning Rituals in Shi'ite Islam." Paper presented at the Middle East Studies Association Annual Meeting, Washington D.C., November 22–25, 2014.

I'tiḍād al-Salṭanah, 'Alīqulī Mīrzā. *Iksīr Al-Tawārīkh*. Tehran: Wīsman, 1991.

ibn abī al-Ḥadīd, 'Izz al-Dīn 'Abu Ḥamid. *Sharḥ Nahj Al-Balāghah*. 20 vols. Qum: Maktabah Ayatollah al-Mar'ashī, 2004.

ibn abī Ḥātam, 'Abdullāh ibn Muhammad. *Tafsīr Al-Qur'an Al-'Aẓīm (Ibn Abī Ḥātam)*. Edited by As'ad Muhammad Tabib. 13 vols. Riyadh: Maktabah Nazār Mustafā al-Bāz, 1998.

ibn-abī-Zamanayn, Muhammad ibn 'Abdullāh. *Qudwat Al-Ghāzī*. Edited by 'A'ishah al-Sulaymani. Beirut: Dār al-Gharb al-Islāmī, 1989.

ibn-abī-Zamanayn, Muhammad ibn 'Abdullāh. *Tafsīr Ibn-Abī-Zamanayn*. 2 vols. Beirut: Dār al-Kutub al-'Ilmīyyah, 2003.

ibn al-Athīr, Abū al-Ḥasan. *Al-Kāmil Fī Al-Tārīkh*. 2 vols. Beirut: Dār al-Beirut, 1965.

ibn al-Athīr, Abū al-Ḥasan. *Asad Al-Ghābah Fī Ma'rifat Al-Ṣahābah*. 6 vols. Beirut: Dār al-Fikr, 1989.

ibn al-Jawzī, Abul-Faraj. *Al-Muntaẓam*. 19 vols. Beirut: Dār al-Kutub al-'Ilmīyyah, 1992.

ibn al-Jawzī, Abul-Faraj. *Zād Al-Masīr Fī 'Ilm Al-Tafsīr*. Edited by Mahdi 'Abdul Razzagh. 4 vols. Beirut: Dār al-Kutub al-'Arabī, 2001.

ibn 'Arabī, Muhammad ibn 'Alī. *Tafsīr Ibn 'Arabī*. Edited by Samir Mustafa Rubab. 2 vols. Beirut: Iḥyā' al-Turāth al-'Arabī, 2001.

ibn 'Asākir, Abul-Qāsim. *Tarjamat Al-Imām Al-Ḥusayn*. Qum: Majma' al-Thaqāfat al-Islāmīyyah, 1993. http://shiaweb.org/books/al-imam_al-hussain/pa1.html.

ibn 'Atīyyah Andulūsī, 'Abdul-Haqq ibn Ghalib. *Al-Muḥarrar Al-Wajīz Fī Tafsīr Al-Kitāb Al-'Azīz*. Edited by 'Abdussalam 'Abdusshafi Muhammad. 6 vols. Beirut: Dār al-Kutub al-'Ilmīyyah, 2001.

ibn Bābawayh al-Qummī, Muhammad ibn 'Alī. *Faḍā'il Al-Shī'ah*. Tehran: A'lamī.

ibn-Hishām, 'Abdul-Malik. *Al-Sīrat Al-Nabawīyya*. Edited by 'Abdul-Hāfiz Shiblī Muṣṭafā al-Saqqā and Ibrāhīm al-'Abyarī. 2 vols. Beirut: Dār al-Ma'rifa.

ibn Hishām, Abd al-Malik. "The Life of Muhammad: A Translation of Isḥāq's Sīrat Rasūl Allāh / with Introduction and Notes by A. Guillaume." New York: Oxford University Press, 1997.

ibn Kathīr, Ismā'īl ibn 'Umar. *Al-Bidāyat Wa Al-Nihāyah*. Beirut: Dār al-Fikr, 1986.

ibn Kathīr, Ismā'īl ibn 'Umar. *Tafsīr Al-Qur'an Al-'Aẓīm (Ibn Kathīr)*. Edited by Shams al-Din Muhammad Hussein. 9 vols. Beirut: Dār al-Kutub al-'Ilmīyyah, 1998.

ibn Khaldūn, Abū Zayd 'Abd al-Raḥmān ibn Muhammad. *Tārīkh Ibn Khaldūn*. 8 vols. Beirut: Dār al-Fikr, 1988.

ibn Khuzaymah, Abū Bakr Muhammad ibn Isḥāq. *Ṣaḥiḥ Ibn Khuzaymah*. Edited by Muhammad Mustafa al-A'zimi. Riyadh: al-Maktab al-Islāmi, 2003.

ibn Mājah al-Rab'ī al-Qazwīnī, Abū 'Abdullah Muhammad. *Sunan Ibn Mājah*. Edited by Muhammad Fu'ad 'Abdul Baghi. Cairo: Dār al-Iḥyā' al-Kutub al-'Arabīyyah, 1954.

ibn Mubārak, 'Abdullāh. *Kitāb Al-Jihād*. Edited by Nazih Hammaad. Jidah: Dār al-Matbū'āt al-Ḥadithah.

ibn Qays, Sulaym. *Kitāb Sulaym Ibn Qays*. Edited by Muhammad Ansari. Qum: al-Ḥādī, 1984.

ibn Qūlawayh, Ja'far b. Muhammad. *Kāmil Al-Ziyārāt* Qum: Nashr al-Faqāhah, 1996.

ibn Qutaybah, Abū Muhammad 'Abdullāh ibn Muslim. *Al-Imāmat Wa Al-Siyāsah*. 2 vols. Beirut: Dār al-Aḍwā', 1990.

ibn Sa'd, Abū 'Abdullāh. *Al-Ṭabaqāt Al-Kubrā*. Beirut: Dār al-Kutub al-'Ilmīyyah, 1990.

ibn Sulaymān al-Balkhī, Muqātil. *Tafsīr Muqātil*. Edited by 'Abdullah Mahmuoud al-Shahatah. 5 vols. Beirut: Dār Ihya' al-Turāth al-'Arabiī, 2003.

ibn Ṭāwūs, al-Sayyid Raḍī al-Dīn. *Al-Luhūf 'Alā Qatla Al-Ṭufūf* Translated by Ahmad Fahri Zanjani. Tehran: Jahān, 1970.

Imām Zayn al-'Ābidīn, 'Alī ibn al-Ḥusayn. *The Psalms of Islam (Al-Ṣaḥīfah Al-Kāmilah Al-Sajjādīyyah)*. Translated by William C. Chittick. London: The Muhammadi Trust of Great Britain and Northern Ireland, 2006.

Irbilī, Abulḥasan 'Alī ibn 'Īsa. *Kashf Al-Ghummah Fī Ma'rifat Al-'A'immah*. Tabriz: Banī Hāshimī, 2002.

Iṣfahāni, Abul-Faraj. *Maqātil Al-Ṭālibīyīn Wa-Akhbāruhum*. Edited by Bihzād Ja'farī. Beirut: Dār al-Ma'rifah.

Ismail, Raihan. "Reclaiming Saudi Salafism: The Saudi Religious Circles and the Threat of Isis." *Journal of Arabian Studies* 9, no. 2 (2019): 164–81.

Jafri, Husain Mohammad. *The Origins and Early Development of Shi 'a Islam*. Oxford: Oxford University Press, 2000.

Jahanbakhsh, Forough. *Islam, Democracy and Religious Modernism in Iran (1953–2000): From Bazargan to Soroush*. Leiden: Brill, 2001.

Jahanbani, Nakissa. "Beyond Soleimani: Implications for Iran's Proxy Network in Iraq and Syria." *CTC Perspectives* (2020).

Jamail, Dahr, and Arkan Hamed. "In Iraq, Mosque Outrage Also Brings Solidarity." *The Washington Report on Middle East Affairs* 25, no. 3 (2006): 11.

Jeffery, Arthur. *The Foreign Vocabulary of the Qur'an*. Leiden: Brill, 2007.

Juneau, Thomas. "Iran's Costly Intervention in Syria: A Pyrrhic Victory." *Mediterranean Politics* 25, no. 1 (2020): 26–44.

Kareem, Dhiaa. "Discourse of Wars and Conflicts: The Construction of Saddam Hussein in the Iraq–Iran War in the US Press." *Annual Review of Education, Communication & Language Sciences* 15 (2018).

Khazzāz Rāzī, 'Alī ibn Muhammad. *Kifāyat Al-Athar*. Edited by 'Abd al-Latif Husseini Kouhkamari. Qum: Bīdār, 1980.

Khomeini, Rūḥullāh. *Sahifih Imam*. 22 vols. Tehran: Mu'assisah Tanzim wa Nashr Āthār Imām Khomeini.

Khunsārī, Shahrīyār "Naqsh 'Aks Dar Bāznamāī Ustūrih Shahādat Dar Naqqāshī Dīvārī Shahr Tehran." [In Farsi]. *Manẓar* 36, no. 8 (2016): 12–19. http://www.noormags.ir/view/fa/articlepage/1185497.

Kızılkaya, Zafer. "Hizbullah's Moral Justification of Its Military Intervention in the Syrian Civil War." *The Middle East Journal* 71, no. 2 (2017): 211–28.

Kohlberg, Etan. "Shahīd." In *Encyclopedia of Islam*, edited by T. Bianquis P. Bearman, C. E. Bosworth, E. van Donzel, and W. P. Heinrichs, 203–7. Leiden: Brill, 1997.

Kūrānī 'Āmilī, 'Alī. *Āyāt Al-Ghadīr*. Qum: Markaz al-Muṣṭafā, 1998.

Kurd 'Alī, Muhammad. *Khitat Al-Shām*. 6 vols. Vol. 6, Damascus: Maktabat al-Nūrī, 1983.

Litvak, Meir. "Martyrdom Is Bliss: The Iranian Concept of Martyrdom During the War with Iraq, 1981–88." In *Martyrdom and Sacrifice in Islam: Theological, Political and Social Contexts*, edited by Meir Hatina and Meir Litvak. London: I.B. Tauris, 2016.

Madelung, Wilferd, Jean Calmard, and Peter Chelkowski. "Hosayn B. 'Ali." In *Encyclopaedia lranica*, edited by Ehsan Yarshater, 493–506. London: Routledge, 2004.

Majlisī, Muhammad Bāqir. *Biḥār Al-Anwār*. 110 vols. Beirut: al-Wafā', 1983.

Malikzādih, Mihdī. *Tārīkh Inqilāb Mashrūṭīyyat Iran*. Vols. 4–5, Tehran: A'lamī, 1994.

Masterson, Julia. "Iranian Public Opinion Under 'Maximum Pressure.'" *Arms Control Today* 49, no. 10 (2019): 34.

Mawdudi, S. Abul A'la. *Jihad in Islam*. Beirut: The Holy Koran Publishing House, 1980.

McEoin, Denis. "Aspects of Militancy and Quietism in Imami Shi'ism." *British Journal of Middle Eastern Studies* 11, no. 1 (1984): 18–27.

Middleton, Paul. "Early Christian Voluntary Martyrdom: A Statement for the Defence." *The Journal of Theological Studies* 64, no. 2 (2013): 556–73.

Middleton, Paul. *Radical Martyrdom and Cosmic Conflict in Early Christianity*. London: A&C Black, 2006.

Mīr Abulqāsimī, Muhammad Ḥusayn. *Ṭāliqānī, Faryādī Dar Sukūt*. 2 vols. Tehran: Shirkat Sahāmī Intishār, 2003.

Mīrzā, Jahāngīr. *Tārīkhi Nu*. Edited by Abbas Ighbal. Tehran: Kitābkhānih 'ALīakbar A'lamī, 1948.

Mitchell, Jolyon P. *Promoting Peace, Inciting Violence: The Role of Religion and Media*. London: Routledge, 2012.

Moghadam, Assaf. *The Globalization of Martyrdom: Al Qaeda, Salafi Jihad, and the Diffusion of Suicide Attacks*. Baltimore: Johns Hopkins University Press, 2008.

Mohammed, Jibril. *Above the Law 360°*. Bloomington: AuthorHouse, 2013.

Moin, Baqer. *Khomeini: Life of the Ayatollah*. London: I.B. Tauris, 1999.

Moss, Candida R. *Ancient Christian Martyrdom: Diverse Practices, Theologies, and Traditions*. New Haven: Yale University Press, 2012.

Mottahedeh, Roy. *The Mantle of the Prophet*. London: Oneworld, 2014.

Mughnīyyah, Muhammad Jawād. *Tafsīr Al-Kāshif*. 7 vols. Qum: Dār al-Kitāb al-Islāmī, 2003.

Mūsawī Muqarram, 'Abdul-Razzāq. *Maqtal Al-Ḥusayn*. Beirut: Mu'assisat al-Kharsan lil-Maṭbū'āt, 2007.

Muslim ibn al-Ḥajjāj, Abul-Ḥusayn. *Ṣaḥīḥ Muslim*. Beirut: Dār al-Ḥadīth, 1991.

Muṭahharī, Murtiḍā. *Ḥimāsih Ḥusayni*. 3 vols. Vol. 2, Tehran: Ṣadrā, 2016.

Muẓaffar, Muhamad Riḍā. *'Aqā'id Al-Imāmīyyah*. Qum: Anṣāriān, 2008.

Nasr, Seyyed Hossein. "Shi'ism and Sufism: Their Relationship in Essence and in History." *Religious Studies* 6, no. 3 (1970): 229–42. http://www.jstor.org.libaccess.lib.mcmaster.ca/stable/20004827.

Nasr, Seyyed Vali Reza. *The Shia Revival: How Conflicts within Islam Will Shape the Future*. New York: W.W. Norton & Co., 2006.

Nicolle, David. *The Great Islamic Conquests AD 632–750*. Oxford: Osprey Publishing, 2009.

Niẓām al-Mulk, Abū 'Alī Ḥasan ibn 'Alī Ṭusī *Siyr Al-Mulūk*. Tehran: Bungāh Tarjumih wa Nashr Kitāb, 1968.

Nūrī Ṭabrasī, Mīrzā Ḥusayn. *Mustadrak Al-Wasā'il Wa Mustanbaṭ Al-Masā'il*. 30 vols. Beirut: Mu'ssisat Āl al-Bayt li 'Iḥyā' al-Turāth, 1987.

Olsson, Susanne. "Shia as Internal Others: A Salafi Rejection of the 'Rejecters.'" *Islam and Christian–Muslim Relations* 28, no. 4 (2017): 409–30.

Pape, Robert. *Dying to Win: The Strategic Logic of Suicide Terrorism*. New York: Random House, 2005.

Pedahzur, Ami. *Suicide Terrorism*. Cambridge: Polity Press, 2004.

Perkins, Judith. "The Apocryphal Acts of the Apostles and Early Christian Martyrdom." *Arethusa* 18, no. 2 (1985): 211.

Peters, Rudolph. *Islam and Colonialism*. Berlin: De Gruyter Mouton, 1980. doi:https://doi.org/10.1515/9783110824858. https://www.degruyter.com/view/title/6260.

Piscatori, James, and Amin Saikal. *Islam Beyond Borders: The Umma in World Politics*. Cambridge: Cambridge University Press, 2019.

Pitman, George R. *Why War?: An Inquiry into the Genetic and Social Foundations of Human Warfare*. Indianapolis: Dog Ear Publishing, 2016.

Qā'im Maqām Farahānī, Mīrzā Abul-Qāsim. *Risālih Jahādīyyah*. Qum: Mu'ssisat Dā'irat al-Ma'ārif Fiqh al-Islāmī, 2005.

Rahimi, Babak. "The Discourse of Democracy in Shi'i Islamic Jurisprudence: The Two Cases of Montazeri and Sistani." *The Mediterranean Programme Series* (2008).

Rajaee, Farhang. *Islamism and Modernism: The Changing Discourse in Iran*. Austin: University of Texas Press, 2007.

Ram, Haggay. "Mythology of Rage: Representations of the 'Self' and the 'Other' in Revolutionary Iran." *History and Memory* 8, no. 1 (1996): 67–87.

Rashīduddīn Miybudī, Aḥmad ibn Muhammad. *Kashf Al-Asrār Wa 'Uddat Al-Abrār*. Edited by Ali Asghar Hikmat. 10 vols. Tehran: Amīrkabīr, 1992.

Raven, Wim. "Martyrs." In *Encyclopedia of the Qur'an*, edited by Jane Dammen McAuliffe, 281–7. Leiden: Brill, 2003.

Rayshahri, M. Muhammadi. *The Scale of Wisdom: A Compendium of Shi'a Hadith*. Translated by A. Kadhim N. Virjee, M. Dasht Bozorgi, Z. Alsalami, and A. Virjee. London: ICAS Press, 2008.

Raza, Saima. "Italian Colonisation & Libyan Resistance the Al-Sanusi of Cyrenaica (1911–1922)." *Ogirisi: a new journal of African studies* 9, no. 1 (2012): 1–43.

Reckendorf, H. "'Ammar B. Yasir." In *The Encyclopaedia of Islam*. Leiden: Brill, 1986. http://go.galegroup.com/ps/i.do?id=GALE%7CCX2686300725&v=2.1&u=ocul_mcmaster&it=r&p=GVRL&sw=w&asid=aa81b1fce866d6194aba4d72de7634a8.

Reuter, Christoph. *My Life Is a Weapon: A Modern History of Suicide Bombing*. Princeton: Princeton University Press, 2004.

Reuveny, Rafael, and Aseem Prakash. "The Afghanistan War and the Breakdown of the Soviet Union." *Review of International Studies* (1999): 693–708.

Rubin, Jared. *Rulers, Religion, and Riches: Why the West Got Rich and the Middle East Did Not*. Cambridge: Cambridge University Press, 2017.

Ṣādiqī Tihrānī, Muhammad. *Al-Furqān Fī Tafsīr Al-Qur'an Bil-Qur'an Wa Al-Sunnah*. 30 vols. Qum: Farhang Islāmī, 2011.

Sadri, Mahmoud. "Ḥojjatiya." *Encyclopaedia Iranica*. (2004). http://www.iranicaonline.org/articles/hojjatiya.

Saeidi, Shirin. "Hojaji's Gaze: Civilizational Aspirations and the Reclamation of Space in Contemporary Iran." *International Journal of Middle East Studies* 52, no. 2 (2020): 356–61.

Ṣāliḥī Najafābādī, Ni'matullāh. *Shahīd Jāwīd*. Tehran: Umīd Fardā, 1999.

Sciolino, Elaine. "Where the Prophet Trod, He Begs, Tread Lightly." *The New York Times* (2002): A4.

Seeley, David. *The Noble Death: Graeco-Roman Martyrology and Paul's Concept of Salvation*. Journal for the Study of the New Testament. Vol. 28, Sheffield: A&C Black, 1990.

Shā'irī, Muhammad Ḥusayn. *Jāmi'ih Shināsī Shahādat Wa Angīzih Hāyi Shahīdān*. Tehran: Shahīd, 2002.

Shahi, Afshin, and Ehsan Abdoh-Tabrizi. "Iran's 2019–2020 Demonstrations: The Changing Dynamics of Political Protests in Iran." *Asian Affairs* 51, no. 1 (01/02/2020): 1–41.

Sharafedin, Bozorgmehr. "General Qasem Soleimani: Iran's Rising Star." *BBC Persian Service* (2015).

Shariati, Ali. "After Shahādat." In *Jihād and Shahādat: Struggle and Martyrdom in Islam*, edited by Mehdi Abedi and Gary Legenhausen, 244–52. Houston: Institute for Research and Islamic Studies, 1986.

Shariati, Ali. "A Discussion of Shahīd." In *Jihād and Shahādat: Struggle and Martyrdom in Islam*, edited by Mehdi Abedi and Gary Legenhausen, 230–43. Houston: Institute for Research and Islamic Studies, 1986.

Shariati, Ali. "Thār." In *Jihād and Shahādat: Struggle and Martyrdom in Islam*, edited by Mehdi Abedi and Gary Legenhausen, 253–63. Houston: Institute for Research and Islamic Studies, 1986.

Sharīf 'Askarī, Sayyid Murtadā. *Saqīfah*. Edited by Mahdī Dashtī. Qum: Daneshkadeh Uṣūl al-dīn, 2008.

Shepkaru, Shmuel. *Jewish Martyrs in the Pagan and Christian Worlds*. Cambridge: Cambridge University Press, 2006.

Siegel, Evan. "The Politics of Shahid-E Javid." In *The Twelver Shia in Modern Times: Religious Culture & Political History*, 150–77. Leiden: Brill, 2001.

Sivan, Emmanuel. "Sunni Radicalism in the Middle East and the Iranian Revolution." *International Journal of Middle East Studies* 21, no. 1 (1989): 1–30.

Smyth, Phillip. *The Shiite Jihad in Syria and Its Regional Effects*. Washington, D.C.: Washington Institute for Near East Policy 2015.

Stein, Ewan. "Ideological Codependency and Regional Order: Iran, Syria, and the Axis of Refusal." *PS: Political Science & Politics* 50, no. 3 (2017): 676–80.

"Sukhanrani Shahid Hasan Baqeri." Updated June 1, 2017 http://www.aparat.com/v/HQyf5.

Stoddard, Lothrop. *Hadhir Al-'Alim Al-Islami*. Translated by Shakib Arsalan. 2 vols. Vol. 1, Damascus: Dar al-Fikr, 1971.

Szanto, Edith. "Beyond the Karbala Paradigm: Rethinking Revolution and Redemption in Twelver Shi'a Mourning Rituals." *Journal of Shi'a Islamic Studies* 6, no. 1 (2013): 75–91.

Ṭabarsī, Abū 'Alī Faḍl ibn Ḥasan. *Majma' Al-Bayān Fī-Tafsīr Al-Qur'an*. Edited by Hāshim Rasūlī. 10 vols. Tehran: Nāṣir Khusru, 1993.

Ṭabarsī, Aḥmad ibn 'Alī. *Al-Iḥtijāj*. Translated by Jafari. Vol. 1, Tehran: Islāmīyyah, 2002.

Ṭabarsī, Aḥmad ibn 'Alī. *Al-Iḥtijāj*. 2 vols. Mashhad: al-Murtaḍā, 1982.

Ṭabāṭabāī, Ḥādī. "Taqyīri Sīāsī Dar Raftār Marāji' Shī'a." [In Farsi]. *Mubāhithāt* (2015). http://mobahesat.ir/9967.

Ṭabāṭabāī, Muhammad Ḥusayn. *Al-Mīzān Fī Tafsīr Al-Qur'an*. 20 vols. Qum: Ismā'īlīyān, 1992.

Ṭabāṭabāī, Muhammad Ḥusayn. *Shī'a*. Translated by Sayyid Husayn Nasr. Albany: State University of New York Press, 1977.

Taheri, Amir. *The Spirit of Allah: Khomeini and the Islamic Revolution*. Chevy Chase: Adler & Adler Publishers, 1986.

Ṭāliqānī, Maḥmūd. "Jihād and Shahādat." In *Jihad and Shahadat: Struggle and Martyrdom in Islam*, edited by Mehdi Abedi and Gary Legenhausen, 47–80. Houston: Institute for Research and Islamic Studies, 1986.

Ṭayyib, 'Abdul Ḥusayn. *Aṭyab Al-Bayān Fī Tafsīr Al-Qur'an*. 14 vols. Tehran: Islam, 1990.

The Termination of the Afflictions and Fierce Battles–Ibn Kathir. Translated by Abd el Qader al-Azeez. Mansoura: Dar al-Ghad al-Gadeed, 2005.

Terzioğlu, Derin. "Sufis in the Age of State-Building and Confessionalization." In *The Ottoman World*, edited by Christine Woodhead. London: Routledge, 2011.

Tihrānī, Muhammad Husayn. *Imām Shināsī*. 18 vols. Tehran: 'Allāmih Ṭabāṭabāī, 2006.

Ulyanasab, Zia'uddin, and Salman Alavi Nik. *Jaryanshenasi Anjoman Hujjatiyyih*. Tehran: Zulal kuthar, 2008.

Vaezi, Ahmad. *Shia Political Thought*. London: Islamic Centre of England, 2004.

Van Henten, Jan Willem. *The Maccabean Martyrs as Saviours of the Jewish People: A Study of 2 and 4 Maccabees*. Vol. 57, Leiden: Brill, 1997.

Varzi, Roxanne. *Warring Souls: Youth, Media, and Martyrdom in Post-Revolution Iran*. Durham, NC: Duke University Press, 2006.

Wastnidge, Edward. "Iran and Syria: An Enduring Axis." *Middle East Policy* 24, no. 2 (2017): 148–59. https://doi.org/10.1111/mepo.12275. http://dx.doi.org/10.1111/mepo.12275.

Wastnidge, Edward. "Iran's Own 'War on Terror': Iranian Foreign Policy Towards Syria and Iraq During the Rouhani Era." In *Foreign Policy of Iran under President Hassan Rouhani's First Term (2013–2017)*, 107–29: Springer, 2020.

Willis, John. "Debating the Caliphate: Islam and Nation in the Work of Rashid Rida and Abul Kalam Azad." *The International History Review* 32, no. 4 (2010): 711–32.

Wilson, W. *The Writings of Clement of Alexandria*. London: T&T Clark, 1869. https://books.google.ca/books?id=5zM2AQAAMAAJ.

Worth, Robert F. "Blast Destroys Shrine in Iraq, Setting Off Sectarian Fury." *The New York Times* 22 (2006).

Zubaida, Sami. *Law and Power in the Islamic World*. London: I.B. Tauris, 2005.

Index

References to endnotes are given in the format 169 n73, referring to note 73 on page 169.

'Abbās ibn 'Alī 30–1, 110–11
Abū al-Faraj Isfahāni 35
Abul A'la Mawdudi *see* Mawdudi, Abul A'la
Afghanistan 45–6, 47–50
Afsaruddin, Asma 6, 11
Ahmadinejad, Mahmoud 116
Akiva, Rabbi 4
al-Alūsī, Mahmud 149–50
al-Assad, Bashar 100, 101, 104
al-Balādhurī, Aḥmad Ibn Yaḥyā 16
al-Bannā, Hassan 44
al-Ḥakīm, Mohammad Bāqir 102
al-Ḥurr al-'Amilī, Muhammad ibn al-Ḥasan 57
al-Khoei, Ayatollah Abul-Qāsim 69
al-Mas'ūdi, Abū al-Ḥasan 'Alī ibn al-Ḥusayn ibn Alī 23–4
Al-Qaida 47, 49
al-Qurṭubī, Abū 'Abdullāh 147
al-Rāzi, Abū Ḥātam 18
al-Sūyuti, Jalāl al-Dīn 142, 143, 151
al-Tabarani, Abū al-Qāsim Sulaymān ibn Ahmad 150
al-Ṭabarī, Muhammad ibn Jarīr 17, 26, 147, 149, 150–1
al-Tha'labi, Ahmad ibn Muhammad 147, 150
al-Zamakhsharī, Abū al-Qasim Maḥmūd ibn 'Umar 150
al-Zuhayr ibn al-Qayn 19
'Alī 18–19, 20–1, 22–3, 24, 93
'Alī ibn Mūsā al-Rida 39
Amīnī, 'Abdul Ḥusayn 57–8, 65
'Ammār 15–17
anti-colonial movements 42
Āqā-Sultān, Neda 92
  Iran-Iraq war (1980–8) and 79, 81
  love of God 31
  public mourning rituals 28, 59, 126–7, 131
  significance of 26–7, 29–30, 129, 130
  zīyārat 'āshūrā prayer 19–20
  see also Karbalā, massacre at
assassinations 48, 90, 102, 121
Avemarie, Friedrich 2
Azzam, Abdullah 46–9, 54

Ba'athism 75, 173 n7
balance of power 41–2
Bāqerī, Ḥasan 81
Basīj 77–8, 79, 81, 82, 105
Bilāl 15
Bin-Laden, Osama 47, 49
Black Friday massacre (1978) 73–5
Bowersock, Glen 3
Boyarin, Daniel 3
Brown, Daniel 42
Burūjirdī, Ayatollah Seyyed-Hossein 67
Buyid dynasty 59

Caliphate system 43–4, 60, 169 n73
chants and songs 85, 86, 93
civic martyrdom 89–95
civilian targets 99
Clement of Alexandria 5
clerical martyrs 64
Companions of the Pit 9, 157 n45
Cook, David 3, 6, 10
Covid-19 pandemic *123*, 124–7, *125–6*

Dakake, Maria Massi 23
decline of the Islamic world 41–2
Denaro, Roberta 137
Droge, Arthur 2

Eleazar 4
emotions, public display of 53–4
  see also mourning
Enayat, Hamid 55
enjoining what is right and forbidding of 94

Fadā'iyān-i Islam 55
Fahmideh, Muhammad Husayn 83
Fakhr al-Dīn al-Rāzī 147–8, 149, 150, 151
Faraj, 'Abd al-Salām 44–5
Fāṭimah 21–2
fatwas
against Israeli citizens 99
in defence of shrines 108
jihad in Afghanistan 47, 48
jihad with Russian Empire 61–2
first wronged person 22–3
forgiveness of sins 32, 39, 146
Frend, William 3
funerals 86, 105, *119*, *121*, 122

Green Movement martyrs 92
Gregory, Brad 2–3

ḥadīth literature 137–51
definitions of martyrdom 138–40
merits of martyrdom 140–1
rewards of martyrdom 145–6, 151
Sunni *tafsīrs* 146–51
Sunni traditions 137–8
types of martyrdom 142–5
Haft-Sīn table setting 125–6, *126*
hagiographies 35, 48, 58, 78
Halabi, Mahmoud 132
Hamas 99
Ḥamzah 9–10, 17
Ḥasan 23, 24
Hatina, Meir 11, 47
health-care workers *123*, 124–7, *125–6*
Hegghammer, Thomas 48
Henten, Jan Willem van 1, 2
Hezbollah 97–9, 101, 103–4, 109, 114–15
Hidden Imam
Hojaji, Mohsen 116–19, *117–19*
Hujjatīyeh-Mahdavīyeh 132–3
Ḥujr ibn 'Adī 23–4, 103
human-wave attacks 82, 83
Ḥusayn 24–33
impact of martyrdom 26–8, 29–30, 129, 130
Islamic revolution (1979) and 70–2
revolts after martyrdom 31–4
sayings of martyrs 30–1
in Shī'īsm 53
shrine defenders and 117
Ḥusayn ibn 'Alī ibn Ḥasan ibn Ḥasan ibn 'Alī 34–5
Hyder, Syed Akbar 110

ibn-abī-Zamānayn, Muhammad ibn 'Abdullāh 151
ibn al-Athīr, Abū al-Ḥasan 59
ibn Hāmām, 'Amir 17–18
ibn Mubārak, Abdullāh 138–41, 142–3
ibn Sulaymān, Muqātil 146–7, 148, 150
Imams
jihad 36
in Shī'īsm 54, 56–7, 60
Zayd ibn 'Alī 34
see also Hidden Imam
intercession 150–1
Iran
Islamic revolution 56, 135
Qajar dynasty wars 61–3
religious authority 50, 51
September 8 massacre (1978) 73–5
and Syria and Hezbollah 101, 104–5, 113–16
see also Islamic Republic
Iran-Iraq war (1980–8) 75–87
chants and songs 85, 86
children, recruitment of 77, 82–3
commemoration of martyrs 86
funerals 86
human-wave attacks 82, 83
Lebanon 98
love of martyrdom 78, 82
number of martyrs 83
paramilitary volunteer militia 77–8
propaganda 85–6
tours to martyrdom sites 79
wills of martyrs 84
Iraq 101–3
Islamic Republic
September 8 massacre (1978) 73–5
Shī'īsm and 51
shrine defenders 106–7
twentieth century martyrs 64–6
war with Iraq *see* Iran-Iraq war (1980–8)
Islamic revolution (1979)
martyrdom 12, 45, 55–6, 70–2
political power and 52–3, 60–1

Islamic Revolutionary Guard Corps (IRGC) 77–8, 104, 105, 117–18
Israel 98, 99, 114

Ja'far al-Sādiq 39, 57
Jafari, Mohammad 'Alī 116
Jeffery, Arthur 7
Jesus 9, 156 n42
jihad
  in Afghanistan 47–9
  defensive 58–60, 63
  Imams 36
  Qur'an 6, 7, 9, 17
  Russian Empire 61–2
  Salafism 45, 48, 49–50, 51, 64
  Sunnism and 35–6, 43, 44–5, 46, 53, 56
  see also Covid-19 pandemic; shrine defenders
John the Baptist 9
journalists 90–1
Juneau, Thomas 114
jurists
  Reza Shah 67

Kāshif al-Ghitā,' Shaykh Ja'far 61, 62
Khalīlī, 'Alī 94
Khamenei, Ayatollah 'Alī
  chants and songs 85, 93
  definitions of martyrdom 91
  nuclear martyrs 90
  Qasem Soleimani 121, 122
  shrine defenders 105, 106
  Syria 100
Khomeini, Ayatollah Ruhollah
  Basīj and 77–8
  children, recruitment of 83
  Hidden Imam 87
  Iran-Iraq war (1980–8) 75–7, 84–5
  love of 84–5
  martyrdom 66–9, 75–8, 78–9, 131
  reputation 80
  taqīya 68
  theory of *wilāyat-i faqīh* 52–3, 73
Khurāsanī, Ayatollah Wahīd 108

Lankarāni, Ayatollah Muhammad Fāḍel 99
Lebanon 97–9
liberation movements 42
love of God 31, 84

martyrdom
  previous studies 10–11
  Qur'an 6–10
  religious traditions 3–4, 5–6
  types of martyrdom 142–5
  see also Sunnism, martyrdom in
martyrs of Fakhkh 34–5
Mawdudi, Abul A'la 44
Mecca 15, 17, 34
messianism 87, 109, 115, 116
Middleton, Paul 2, 4
military martyrdom 17–18
militia 77–8
  see also Basīj
miracles 48, 54
Moses 9, 157 n44
mourning
  Ḥusayn 27–8, 31, 39, 53
  public Āshūrā rituals 28, 59, 126–7, 131
  Shī'a Muslims and 53
Mu'āwīyah 23, 24, 92
Mudarris, Sayyid Ḥasan 64–6
Muhammad
  'Ammār 15–17
Muhammad ibn 'Abdullāh ibn al-Ḥasan al-Muthanna 34
Mukhtār al-Thaqafī 32–3
Muslim Brotherhood 44, 47, 55
Muslim martyrs 15–17
Muṭahharī, Ayatollah Murteza 72

Namaki, Saeed 124–5
Naṣrallāh, Ḥasan 103–4
Navvab Safavi 55
non-violent martyrdom 90–1
Nowi-Aghdam, Rahim 105
Nowruz 125–6, *126*
nuclear martyrs 90
numbers of martyrs 83, 113
Nūrī, Shaykh Faḍlullāh 64–6, 67

Ottoman Caliphate 42, 43, 55
Ottoman Empire 42, 43, 59

Palestine 42, 46–7, 99
passive martyrdom 90–1
People's Mojahedin Organization of Iran 90
Perkins, Judith 3
political activism 68
political power 52–3
Polycarp 4
power, balance of 41–2
principles, Islamic 94
propaganda
  Iran-Iraq war (1980–8) 85–6
  shrine defenders 118, *118*, 122–3
propaganda tours 79, *80*

Qajar dynasty 61–3
quietism 56, 67, 68, 130
Qur'an
  2:143 7, 149–50, 154 n30
  2:153–4 146
  2:154 147
  2:216 9, 45, 156 n39
  3:38–9 9, 156 n41
  3:53 7, 154–5 n31
  3:134–6 8, 155 n36
  3:140–1 148–9
Qutb, Sayyid 44

Rāhīyān-i nūr (Passengers of Light) 79
religious authority 50–2, 53
revolts 31–5, 129–30
  martyrs of Fakhkh 34–5
  Muhammad ibn ʿAbdullāh 34
  Mukhtār al-Thaqafī 32–3
  penitents 31–2
  Zayd ibn ʿAlī 33–4
Reza Shah 67
Rida, Muhammad Rashid 43–4
Rubin, Jared 41–2
Russian Empire 61–3

ṣabr (patience) 151
Saddam Ḥusayn 79–80
Sādiq 38, 57
Saeidi, Shirin 116–17
Safavid dynasty 59
Sajjād 38
Salafism
  fatwa against 108
  jihadism and 45, 48, 49–50, 51, 64
  rise of 50–1
Sayyid Muhammad Mujāhid 62–3
scholar-martyrs 58
scientific martyrs 90
sectarian martyrdom 10–11, 18–24, 101–5, 113–16
sectarian sources 37–40
September 8 massacre (1978) 73–5
Services Bureau 47
shahīd/shuhadā (witness/es) 6–7, 8, 28, 37, 39, 137, 148–50
Shāʾirī, Muhammad Ḥusayn 84
Shariati, ʿAlī 70–2, 78
Shīʿa sources 37–40
  defensive jihad 58–60, 63
  introduction to 11–12, 59–60
  Khomeini 66–9
  mourning 53–4
  revival of martyrdom 56–66
  revolts 31–5, 129–30
  Russo-Persian wars 61–3
  scholar-martyrs 57–8
  Shariati 70–2
  state building 50–6
  twentieth century 64–6, 130–3
shrine defenders 99–111, 113–27
  ʿAbbās ibn ʿAlī 110–11
  Covid-19 pandemic *123*, 124–7, *125–6*
  funerals 105
  heroes *123*, 123–4
  Iraq 102–3
  Mohsen Hojaji 116–19, *117–19*
  Qasem Soleimani 117–23, *120–1*, *123*, 125, *126*
  sectarian martyrdom 113–16
  Shīʿī symbolism of 109–11
  suicide attacks 99–100
  Syria 100–1
  Zaynab 109–10, 111
Sistani, Ayatollah ʿAlī 102, 108
Soleimani, Qasem 105, 117–23, *120–1*, *123*, 125, *126*
Soviet-Afghan war 45–6, 47, 49
state building 50–6
state-sponsored martyrdom 90–1
Sufism 54

suicide attacks 98–9, 99–100, 102
suicide bombers 82, 83
Sulaymān ibn Surad Khuzā'ī 31, 32
Sumayyah 15
Sunni *tafsīrs* 146–51
Sunnism
 distribution of 51
 extremists (*takfīrīs*) 102, 103, 104, 108–9
 see also Salafism
Syria 99–101, 104–5, 113–16

Tabor, James 2
tafsīrs 146–51
takfīrīs (extremists) 102, 103, 104, 108–9
Ṭāleqānī, Ayatollah Maḥmūd 74
taqīya (cautionary dissimulation) 16, 56–7, 60, 68, 70
Tawwābūn (repenters) 31–2
Tehran, Iran 73–5
training camps 47
Turkey 43

'Umar ibn Khattab 144–5
ummah (the community of believers) 43
Uṣūlīs 62, 170 n83
'Uthman ibn Affan 92

visits to sites of martyrdom 39, 79

walī-i faqīh
 chants and songs 85, 93
 defence of shrines 107–8
 martyrdom 87
 martyrs' wills 84
Western hegemony 41–2
Western powers, resistance to 90
wilāyat-i faqīh
 Khomeini 52–3, 73
 martyrdom 92, 93
wills of martyrs 84

Yāsir 15
Yazīd
 derogatory use of name 70, 79–80
 Ḥusayn 24, 25, 26, 27
 Syria 100
Young Turks 43

Zayd ibn 'Alī 33–4
Zaynab, Sayyida 100, 104, 105, 109–10, 111
Zībākalām, Sādiq 90
zīyārat 'āshūrā 19–20, 29, 58, 133–4
Ziynuddīn, Mahdī 78

www.ingramcontent.com/pod-product-compliance
Lightning Source LLC
Chambersburg PA
CBHW062225300426
44115CB00012BA/2223
* 9 7 8 0 7 5 5 6 4 7 1 5 6 *